TRY YOUR OWN CASE

How to represent yourself in court

JORDAN MARSH

For permission requests, speaking invitations, or to know where to send gift baskets, large checks, or free Bruce Springsteen concert tickets, write to the author at info@tryyourowncase.com.

Ordering Information:
For details, contact info@tryyourowncase.com.

Print ISBN: 979-8-35096-618-3
eBook ISBN: 979-8-35096-941-2

Printed in the United States of America.

First Edition

For Stephanie, Ava, and Charlie

CONTENTS

"In all courts of the United States the parties may plead and conduct their own cases personally or by counsel as, by the rules of such courts, respectively, are permitted to manage and conduct causes therein."

28 United States Code § 1654

Introduction

Hello, and welcome to *Try Your Own Case*, the ultimate guide to representing yourself in court, also known as *"pro se"* litigation. *"Pro se"* is Latin for "on one's own behalf." In plain English, it means you're representing yourself in a legal matter rather than being represented by an attorney.

If you're reading this book, chances are:

1) you are representing yourself in a case;

2) you're thinking about representing yourself in a case; or

3) you picked this up at the bookstore and realized you've wandered away from the romance novel section.

Either way, thanks for reading!

Who should read this book?

The late Stan Lee, founder and publisher of Marvel Comics, once said, "We don't care if you buy our comic books for the staples." You can buy this book for any reason you want, including to use as a paper weight. But I wrote it for anyone who wants to learn about how the civil justice system operates. Specifically, this book will be most helpful for the following:

- Anyone currently representing himself or herself in court

- Anyone considering representing himself or herself in court

- Anyone who wants to file or defend a lawsuit and has not yet found an attorney

- Anyone who wants to understand the litigation process, including law students and new lawyers

- Anyone who wants to buy a gift for any of the people described above

Why I Wrote This Book

As an undergraduate at the University of Wisconsin-Madison (Go Badgers!), I became active in student government, and went on to law school because I thought I could make a difference in people's lives as a government lawyer. It was not until I took an Evidence class in law school that I realized I wanted to be a trial lawyer. So, after law school, I found my way to the City of Chicago Law Department, where I worked for nearly 20 years representing city employees, including Chicago police officers, in personal injury and civil rights cases. I litigated countless cases and tried dozens of jury trials in state and federal courts. I was named one of the 40 attorneys under 40 to watch by the Chicago Daily Law Bulletin. I coached a trial advocacy team, judged trial advocacy competitions, and taught trial advocacy to undergraduates and law students. I served on the faculty of the Kirkland Institute for Trial Advocacy, where I worked with young lawyers to improve their trial skills. But mostly, I tried a lot of cases and loved it.

In 2016, I went into private practice, representing individuals against the government and insurance companies. They say you can't fight City Hall, but there's a group of people who do it every day, and I'm honored to be among them. I've represented kids, moms and dads, grandparents, prisoners, police officers, teachers, and all sorts of other people. I've obtained millions of dollars in settlements for my clients and, just as importantly, provided a voice and guided them through the unfamiliar and sometimes hostile legal world.

I've been fortunate enough to have spent years representing both plaintiffs (the people who file lawsuits) and defendants (the people being sued), giving me a valuable perspective on what it takes to win a case from both sides.

But as much as I enjoy being able to help people, there are so many I can't help. Many law offices, including my own, have to turn down clients and cases every day for a variety of reasons. As a result, thousands of people are forced to go it alone if they want to assert their rights in court. The Sixth Amendment to the United States Constitution guarantees the right to an attorney for all criminal defendants, but there is no such right for people involved in civil lawsuits.

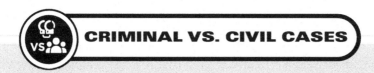

CRIMINAL VS. CIVIL CASES

Criminal cases (prosecutions) are brought by the government against defendants for violations of criminal laws, while **civil cases (lawsuits)** are brought by private citizens, corporations, and the government for non-criminal violations. This book relates only to civil cases.

It is estimated that at least 75 percent of civil cases nationally include at least one self-represented *(pro se)* litigant. (A **"litigant"** is a party to a lawsuit, usually a plaintiff or a defendant.) According to a recent study, more than 25 percent of all federal civil cases are filed by people without lawyers. That's a lot of self-represented litigants, most of whom are going up against qualified and well-paid attorneys.

It doesn't seem like a fair fight.

But isn't the point of a justice system to decide cases fairly? Yes, that's the general idea, but it rarely works out that way. The American judicial system, like the judicial systems in most countries, is adversarial. That means courts attempt to reach the best result and find the truth by two (or more) sides essentially competing against each other within the rules to convince a judge or a jury that their side should win.

The idea is that competition is the best way to get to the truth. For that to work, both sides should be evenly matched. Each party should have roughly the same level of skills, talent, and resources, or have a lawyer with those qualities. Unfortunately, most cases do not feature evenly matched parties.

The rules that govern civil litigation are supposedly neutral. But they are also complex and sometimes difficult to understand for those who do not have legal training, and even for many trained lawyers. The complexity of the web of rules and laws that govern civil litigation naturally favors the side with the best attorney who has the best training and experience to strategically use those rules to gain an advantage over the other side. The rules also favor litigants who can afford to hire the best experts and consultants.

There's another fundamental unfairness at work here. If you're a **plaintiff** (the party who files a lawsuit), more often than not, you have to find a lawyer who will represent you on **contingency**. That means the lawyer will be paid by taking a percentage of the amount the plaintiff receives in the lawsuit, whether by verdict after a trial or by settlement. But what if the case isn't worth that much in terms of **damages** (the financial value of your injuries)?

Let's say you were arrested without probable cause, spent a couple of hours in jail, and then released without being charged with a crime. You probably can't expect a large sum of money even if you win your case, so finding a good attorney willing to take that case may be difficult. Or maybe your case is tough to win. What if it's a toss-up instead of a dead-bang winner? What if you're suing a correctional officer in an area where the local prison is the largest employer and most jurors know someone who works for the prison? What if you're black and the vast majority of people in the area who will decide your case are white?

These things make it more challenging to attract a qualified attorney to take a chance on your case. Because if you lose your case, you will get nothing—and your attorney will also get nothing.

But someone with the resources to hire an attorney – such as a municipal government or a corporation – doesn't have to worry about that. A government defendant can (and will) use tax dollars to hire an attorney, no matter how bad their case is. The same applies to an insurance company or other corporation, or any person with significant financial resources. That attorney will get paid, win or lose.

How fair is that?

Fair or not, that is our system, and it's not going away anytime soon. This book is an attempt to even the playing field between litigants who are represented by attorneys and those who are not.
How? Through knowledge.

A good attorney's greatest asset is knowledge. Knowledge truly is power. This book is here to walk you through the civil justice system and provide you with the knowledge to navigate this complicated system and put up a good fight.

What To Expect From This Book

During my first year of law school, one of my professors explained his goal for the class:

"I want you to be able to go toe-to-toe with the other guy and say, '*Let's get it on.*'"

That's what I want for you. If you have to fight, you should have a fighting chance.

But I want to be clear about something: ***This book will not make you an attorney or provide the knowledge equal to that of an attorney. Not even close.*** Without an attorney, you will still be at a disadvantage. You should be at far less of a disadvantage once you've read this book, but if you can hire a qualified attorney to represent you, I highly recommend you do it. There is simply no substitute for competent counsel working on your behalf.

In fact, one of the possible outcomes of reading this book is that you will realize how complicated the process is, and you will be convinced to try to obtain an attorney.

Having said that, I understand that most self-represented litigants have tried to obtain an attorney but have been unable to do so. Additionally, many people need to file their complaint right away because of the Statute of Limitations (which you'll read about soon enough), but they can't find a lawyer in time. This book will help you get your case filed and moving until you're able to find a lawyer to represent you.

If you find yourself in court without a lawyer, for whatever reason, you should at least know what you're doing. You should have a solid understanding of how this process works. That's why this book exists.

NOTE: **In most jurisdictions, including federal court, a corporation – including an LLC – cannot represent itself. It must be represented by a licensed attorney. However, a sole proprietorship should be able to act *pro se* because it is not a separate legal entity.**

HOW TO OBTAIN AN ATTORNEY

Each state has a bar association that will try to help you find a lawyer. Most major cities also have bar associations that can try to find you an attorney. You can find these through a simple Google search. Also, the American Bar Association has a page with links to attorney referral services in each state. Just go to https://www.americanbar.org/groups/legal_services/flh-home/flh-bar-directories-and-lawyer-finders/.

There are also for-profit referral services such as Justia (justia.com) and Lawyer.com. You should not have to pay for these services – they are usually paid for by attorneys if they accept the referral.

If you have already filed a case, you can file a motion with the court to appoint an attorney. Any attorney licensed to try cases in federal court can be appointed by the court to represent a *pro se* litigant. While civil litigants are not guaranteed representation by an attorney, it certainly doesn't hurt to ask.

Also, many courts have some sort of program where the court attempts to recruit attorneys for *pro se* litigants. Check out those court websites.

Can You Do This Yourself?

One of the things you will learn in this book is just how complicated the litigation process can be. It's why lawyers spend years in law school before entering the courtroom. This is also why litigating a case without the benefit of qualified counsel is very difficult.

But is it impossible? Not at all. I have a client who defeated the defendant's summary judgment motion (you'll read about summary judgment later in the book) on his own and another client who lost a summary judgment motion in the district court but then appealed and got the court's decision reversed by the appellate court, all by himself. One of the most famous *pro se* litigators was Robert Kearns, who successfully sued Ford Motor Company and other car companies for allegedly stealing his idea for intermittent windshield wipers. Kearns spent decades in litigation with these companies, earning multiple million-dollar verdicts, all on his own.

You can do this – but it takes plenty of research, preparation, and focus. As you go through this book, you will hopefully realize that the rules governing litigation are designed to provide an even and fair playing field as much as possible. At the core of every rule, there should be a nugget of common sense. If you can see that nugget and figure out the reasoning behind the rule, you will be in good shape.

If you use this book wisely, you will be miles ahead of where you were before. You will learn valuable, practical lessons that will allow you to go toe-to-toe with your opponents, who will not expect you to know this much about litigating a case.

This book will walk you through the steps of investigating and filing your case, conducting discovery, motion practice, and trial. But reading this book will not teach you everything about the law. No lawyer or judge knows everything about the law—I sure don't. Think of the law as a vast ocean. This book will not make you familiar with every drop of water in the sea, but it should give you the tools to go for a swim without being eaten by a shark.

In federal court, the vast majority of *pro se* litigants are plaintiffs – the parties who file lawsuits. Many of the *pro se* litigants in state court are plaintiffs as well. As a result, much of this book is geared toward plaintiffs. But if you're defending a case – in state court or federal court – you can learn valuable lessons here. In fact, one of the best ways to learn how to defend a case is to look at it from the perspective of a plaintiff, and vice versa.

While this book contains some **substantive law** (which governs the rights and duties of everyday conduct), it is primarily **procedural**. In other words, the primary purpose is to guide you through the civil litigation process – introduce you to the major players, help you understand how all the pieces fit together, and guide you through the most commonly used procedures so that you go in with your eyes wide open, and understand what's coming next. Think of substantive law as the what, and procedural law as the how. For example, the law defining a false arrest is substantive, while the law governing how to file a lawsuit is procedural.

Many courts – mostly in state court systems – have specialty courts for specific circumstances. These include domestic relations, probate, landlord-tenant, drug courts, traffic court, and others. This book does not address the specifics of any of those courts. We expect to add resources to the Try Your Own Case library to assist unrepresented litigants in specific areas in the future.

LEGAL STUFF

This book does not contain legal advice, just facts and common sense tips. It does not create an attorney-client relationship between the reader and the author.

You should not try to use anything in this book as authority in court. In other words, you cannot tell the judge that this book says X or Y, so you should win the argument. The legal concepts discussed here are overviews that provide a conceptual understanding of how things work in court. This book is not intended to provide you with every specific legal element or nuance of any legal concepts. For that, you will need to do your own research.

The law is ever-changing. Statutes get amended, and cases get overturned. Remember *Roe v. Wade*? That was the law for 50 years, until one day, it wasn't. This book provides insights into relatively stable legal concepts. Most, if not all, of them are likely, *but not guaranteed*, to be valid for the foreseeable future. You should always do your own research to confirm the law before you announce to the court and the other side what it is.

LATIN IN THE LAW

It's not enough that the litigation process seems like another language. To make it more complicated, the American legal system uses an actual different language to describe many of its concepts.

Our legal system was initially developed in Europe. It was heavily influenced by Roman law because Rome dominated Europe for many years. Latin was the primary language used in Rome. As a result, our legal system today – just like our language in general – includes many Latin words and phrases.

Some of the terms are fun to say, like *"Nunc Pro Tunc"* (when a judge's decision applies retroactively) and *"ipse dixit"* (describing an assertion based only on the authority of the person who made it). Others are kind of morbid, like *"Habeas Corpus"* (literally, "Show me the body," which refers to the Constitutional protection against unlawful imprisonment). Others are closely related to our own language, like *"In Camera,"* which refers to examinations of evidence in private, usually by the judge in her chambers. For some reason, we italicize the Latin terms in the law. Don't ask me why. But italicizing Latin terms is an excellent way to make everyone else in the case think you know what you're doing. "Fake it until you make it," as the kids say.

While I have tried to use U.S. Supreme Court opinions for legal standards, the Supreme Court decisions do not cover everything. I have also used some appellate court opinions, which can differ depending on the jurisdiction. I practice primarily in the Seventh Circuit (one of 13 federal appellate circuits in the U.S. – you'll see more on that later in the book), so I have used some Seventh Circuit case law. You should always make sure to check your circuit's case law to confirm what the law is in your jurisdiction.

Federal and State Court Litigation

This book includes references to the Federal **Rules of Civil Procedure** (abbreviated as "FRCP") and federal court procedures, because there is only one set of federal rules that apply to all federal courts in the U.S., but there are 50 different state court systems, each with its own rules and procedures. But most state court procedures are similar to the federal rules, and 35 state courts have adopted some version of the federal rules. Most of the information in this book is equally applicable to state court litigation. Everything from investigating your case to filing motions (known as "motion practice") to conducting discovery to trial applies equally to state and federal litigation.

If you are involved in a state court case, you should be familiar with the rules of your jurisdiction before you file or defend your case. Check out the National Center for State Courts for links to every state court website. https://www.ncsc.org/information-and-resources/state-court-websites.

Throughout this book, you'll see references to state laws because federal courts often look to the laws of the states where they are located for specific legal standards and requirements, and as noted above, because you may be litigating in state court. But laws are often different from state to state, so it is up to you to research your state's laws on specific topics to confirm what the law is.

You should assume that almost every sentence in this book begins with "Generally speaking," even if you don't see it there. There are laws, rules, and cases that govern conduct in the courts, and they are all written in black and white. But those laws, rules, and cases are interpreted by judges, who (believe it or not) are human, and may interpret rules differently depending on the specific facts of a case. Just like your chances of success in a jury trial rely heavily on who shows up for jury duty, your chances in court often depend on which judge is assigned to your case.

Many of the rules discussed in this book will usually be interpreted the same way by most judges. Still, applying the law to your unique set of facts may result in different rulings by different judges. (This is why people say, "A good lawyer knows the facts. A better lawyer knows the law. The best lawyer knows the judge.")

I have included many practice tips along the way. These tips are based on my singular experience and are only suggestions. Obviously, I feel strongly enough about these tips that I have decided to share them with you, and I would not have included them if I did not think they would be helpful. But they are not the only way to do things; others may disagree. At the end of the day, your case is your case, and you should try it the way you think is best.

How To Use This Book

This is not a novel. You do not need to read it cover to cover. This book is divided into three specific parts and 15 chapters so you can learn about whatever aspect of litigation you need to know at any point in time.

- Part I walks you through the specific stages of a lawsuit before you get to trial.

- Part II walks you through the pretrial and trial process and includes many concepts you must know about to try your case effectively.

- Part III explains specific aspects of litigation that do not fit neatly within the chronology of a lawsuit.

- There is also a glossary with definitions for most legal terms you will encounter during the lawsuit, an index, and finally, an appendix with sample forms of various documents you may find helpful.

You can download copies of the appendix documents by going to www.tryyourowncase.com/resources

Depending on where you are in the litigation process or how you learn, you can use these sections in any way that works for you. However, certain chapters may use terms defined in previous chapters. If you come across an undefined term or acronym, refer to the index to find out where that term was introduced, or refer to the glossary for a definition.

How Do Judges Treat *Pro Se* Litigants?

In many respects, *pro se* litigants are supposed to be treated the same as lawyers. But there are some differences. In 1972, the U.S. Supreme Court held that pleadings drafted by *pro se* litigants should be held to a "less stringent standards than pleadings drafted by lawyers." Haines v. Kerner, 404 U.S. 519 (1972). That means *pro se* litigants get more leeway regarding specific pleading requirements. But different courts interpret that decision in different ways, so don't assume anything.

Many courts have specific local rules for *pro se* litigants, some of which are designed to assist *pro se* parties, but others seem punitive.

Some examples:

- The Eastern District of California requires incarcerated *pro se* parties to be provided with paper copies of all legal authority (cases, statutes, regulations) the other party is relying on in any filed pleadings.

- The Northern District of Illinois requires any party filing a summary judgment motion against a *pro se* party to provide its summary judgment papers, copies of FRCP 56, Local Rule 56.1, and a specific Notice explaining in detail what summary judgment means and what the responding party must do to respond to the motion.

- The Federal District of Hawaii specifically prohibits *pro se* litigants from using the Ninth Circuit Court Library without a court order.

- The Eastern District of Michigan does not allow *pro se* litigants to electronically file initial pleadings.

Check out those court websites!

Before setting out on your *pro se* journey, one of the first things you should do is check out the website for the court where you intend to file your lawsuit. Most, if not all, federal and state courts have a section specifically for self-represented litigants. These sections contain invaluable information regarding how that court handles *pro se* litigation, including filing requirements, forms, and other information.

You can also find specific programs for *pro se* litigants on the court websites as well as websites for nonprofit groups that provide *pro se* assistance. For a complete list of *pro se* assistance programs throughout the country, go to www.tryyourowncase.com/resources.

Court websites also contain the court's local rules and standing orders that govern many procedures you will encounter as you litigate your case. You should be familiar with these rules. Whether you win or lose your case often depends on how well you know and how effectively you can use the rules of procedure.

The Limits of Litigation

I often find myself saying to clients that civil litigation is – to put it mildly – an imperfect solution to the challenges and injuries you may have experienced that led you to file a lawsuit. Litigation has many benefits. It is a way to hold people and institutions accountable for the harm they inflict on others, by forcing them to answer questions under oath about their actions. It can help you learn the facts about something that was done to you or to someone you love. Litigation literally gives you your day in court, and that can be valuable.

But litigation can be long and grueling, and at times it can feel like the process obscures the purpose. And at the end of the day, unless you're seeking injunctive relief (in which the court orders specific things to be done or not done), the only relief you can get through the court system is money. And money, while nice, can be a poor substitute for real justice. If you take your case all the way to trial, you can force the defendant to answer questions in front of a judge and jury, but it may not be the emotional climax you were hoping for. Defendants rarely if ever break down on the witness stand and admit they were wrong and offer sincere apologies like you may have seen on TV.

Filing a lawsuit – even winning a lawsuit – cannot give you back the years of your life that you may have spent wrongly imprisoned, or erase the pain you felt when you were assaulted by a police officer, or the humiliation you felt when you were wrongfully terminated from your job. Litigation is not a magic wand you can wave to make everything right. But in an imperfect world, it is one of the most effective ways we have to hold people accountable for their actions, even if it does not provide everything we wish it could.

A Final Note: *Everyone is not against you.*

Some of the people I speak with who end up *pro se* believe everyone is against them, including not only the police, but their former attorneys and even judges. I believe a big part of this is because the legal system is so foreign to non-lawyers. It seems as if everyone in that system speaks a different language, and that they all know each other. It's like walking uninvited into a fancy club where everyone knows each other but you. It can be very alienating. The less we understand about something, the more we fear it.

But assuming everyone is against you is one of the worst things you can do for your case, and it is almost always incorrect. This doesn't mean that judges always make the right decisions, or that some judges don't get frustrated with some *pro se* individuals, and with lawyers, too.

Remember, judges are human, and have the same limited patience and the same tempers as the rest of us. But judges almost always try to do their best to decide cases fairly. And judges normally bend over backwards to accommodate *pro se* litigants, understanding the inherent disadvantage in navigating this unfamiliar environment, while still enforcing the rules equally for represented and non-represented parties, which they must do.

About a year ago, I declined to represent a potential client who believed he was the victim of a false arrest. He was a bright guy, and he went ahead and filed a lawsuit on his own. He recently contacted me to see if I would represent him now, as his lawsuit has advanced through the process. I read through the case, and saw how well he wrote, and how he seemed to grasp the basic legal concepts and tools available to him. It was very impressive.

But I also noted that he picked a fight with the judge, whom I know to be a very well-respected judge. He felt some things she said were unfair, and filed a motion to have her **recused** (meaning disqualified and removed) from the case. I don't believe the judge will hold this against him (he lost the motion), but regardless of the circumstances, it's just not a good idea to pick a fight with the person in charge of your case. You will almost surely lose that fight, and it will not help your case.

The way to be successful in court for lawyers and non-lawyers alike is to be prepared, learn the rules, and know the facts of your case inside and out. And treat everyone as you would like to be treated – with respect and courtesy. And try to assume the best about people, even when they do not always show it. This is not only the right thing to do, it is the smartest thing you can do if you want to get the best result possible in court.

So let's do this. Off we go.

PART I

The Litigation Process

Do you ever get overwhelmed with all the things you have to do in life? When you feel like you have an endless number of tasks, and they're all running around in your head, it can seem impossible to get started. Instead of doing what you have to do, you want to just curl up on the couch, eat Oreos, and watch TV.

But when you sit down and write out each task you have to accomplish, it becomes much easier to handle. Suddenly, you realize that your endless, infinite list of tasks is only a handful of things. Suddenly, it becomes manageable. It becomes *possible*.

The same idea applies to the litigation process. If you don't know what it involves, litigation can seem like a mysterious, bewildering thing, impossible to manage without years of education and experience. But, if you break it down and identify each aspect of the process, you realize it may be something you *can* do–maybe not as well as an experienced attorney, but well enough to get your day in court and make it count.

This book will help you break down the litigation process and understand what it involves so you can determine for yourself if it's something you can do on your own. Here's a quick overview of what to expect if you decide to proceed with your case. Each of these stages will be discussed in detail later in this book.

Stage 1 - Pleadings

Pleadings define the legal issues in the case.

The Pleadings stage goes like this:

First, the plaintiff files a **Complaint.** This is the initial document filed by the plaintiff to initiate a lawsuit outlining the factual and legal allegations (claims) against the defendant.

Next, the plaintiff serves a copy of the Complaint and **Summons** on the defendant. A summons is a legal document notifying the defendant of the lawsuit and explaining when and where they must file a response. Delivery of the Complaint and Summons to the defendant(s) is called **Service of Process.** You've seen likely characters on television "getting served."

The defendant files an **Answer.** An answer is the defendant's written response to the Complaint admitting or denying each specific allegation. Alternatively, they can claim they lack sufficient knowledge to admit or deny the allegation.

The Answer will probably contain **Affirmative Defenses.** Affirmative Defenses are statements by the defendant that, if true, can defeat the plaintiff's claim, even if the allegations in the Complaint are true.

The Answer may contain a **counterclaim.** The defendant may use the lawsuit to make allegations against the plaintiff arising out of the same facts as the Complaint.

The defendant may file a **Motion to Dismiss** instead of an Answer. A Motion to Dismiss is a request by the defendant to dismiss the Complaint, arguing that it does not state a valid cause of action. This is also known as "failure to state a claim upon which relief may be granted." This is the first of two points where a case may be dismissed before a trial.

Stage 2 - Discovery

Discovery is the equivalent of laying all your cards on the table. This is when the parties share information with each other related to the lawsuit.

Both sides have a duty to disclose basic information. Federal Rule of Civil Procedure (FRCP) 26 requires that each party in a lawsuit automatically disclose certain facts to the other parties regarding the party's claims or defenses without waiting for discovery requests.

These so-called **"Rule 26 initial disclosures"** must contain the names and contact information of all individuals with relevant information the disclosing party may use to support their claims or defenses. These disclosures must also contain the subject matter of the information each disclosed person has. Additionally, the disclosing party must identify all documents, materials, and other tangible things in their possession that they may use to support their claims or defenses and provide these materials to the other parties, or at least make them available for copying. In my experience, each party always provides copies of the relevant materials to the other.

After the Rule 26 initial disclosures, the parties will engage in formal discovery, which includes the following:

- **Interrogatories** - Written questions one party sends to another, requiring written answers under oath.

- **Requests for Production** - Requests by one party to another to produce specific documents, reports, records, or other evidence, like video footage.

- **Requests for Admission** - Written statements by one party to another, asking the recipient to admit or deny certain alleged facts.

- **Subpoenas** - Orders to non-parties to produce documents or records or to sit for a deposition. (A "non-party" is a person or an entity that is not a plaintiff or a defendant in the lawsuit but has information relevant to the case.)

- **Depositions** - Oral questioning of a party or witness under oath, typically transcribed by a court reporter.

Stage 3 - Summary Judgment

A **motion for summary judgment** is a request made by a party for the court to rule in its favor based on the evidence presented during the discovery phase without the need for a trial. This is the second of two points where the case can be dismissed before trial.

Stage 4 - Pretrial

The **pretrial phase**, as its name implies, includes the period right before the trial, when the parties make final preparations for the trial and submit pretrial documents to the court.

In federal court and some state courts, the parties submit a final pretrial order and related documents. The **Final Pretrial Order (FPTO)** is a document filed jointly by all parties after consulting with each other and exchanging drafts and edits. The FPTO will include proposed jury instructions, exhibit lists, and witness lists from each party. Separately, the parties will file their own pretrial motions (known as motions *in limine)* asking the court to prohibit certain evidence from being considered or discussed during the trial. The court's local rules and/ or the judge's standing orders will explain the required format and contents of the FPTO.

Next, there's a **final pretrial conference**. This is a meeting between the parties, their attorneys, and the judge to discuss trial procedures and resolve any outstanding issues.

Stage 5 - Trial

Finally, it's time for the **trial**, the climax of all the previous stages – the part of the process that most often makes its way to your TV set – the part where you get to make your case to a jury, a group of non-lawyers just like you (assuming of course it is a jury trial). This is the formal presentation of evidence and arguments to determine the outcome of the lawsuit.

The main parts of a trial include:
- jury selection
- opening statements
- plaintiff's case-in-chief, where the plaintiff presents witnesses and other evidence
- defendant's case-in-chief, where the plaintiff presents witnesses and other evidence

- plaintiff's rebuttal case, where the plaintiff may present evidence to counter, or "rebut" the defendant's evidence
- closing arguments
- jury deliberation
- verdict

Stage 6 - Post-Trial

- **Post-Trial Motions:** After a verdict, parties may file motions to alter or set aside the judgment, seeking a new trial or adjustment of the jury's decision based on claims of errors made during the trial.

- **Appeal:** If dissatisfied with the trial outcome or post-trial rulings, a party can appeal to a higher court, arguing legal errors that affected the verdict, in hopes of overturning or modifying the judgment.

- **Enforcement of Judgment:** Once a final judgment is in place, the winning party may need to take steps to enforce it, such as garnishing wages or placing liens on property, if the losing party does not voluntarily comply."

If you read all of this and you're thinking, "I'd rather not put myself through all of that," then thanks for reading—your journey ends here. But, if you're prepared to go through each of the phases on your own, then keep reading. The rest of this book will explain each of these phases of litigation and provide tips to help you get the best possible result.

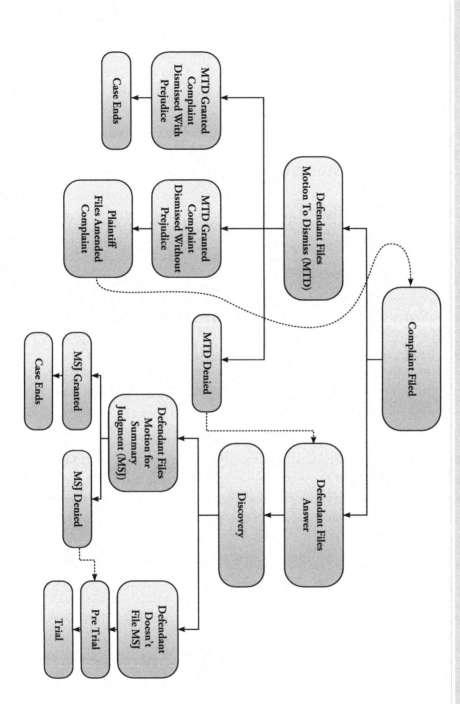

The Litigation Process

Forms Of Relief:
What Can I Get Out Of My Lawsuit?

You believe your rights were violated, and you want to sue someone.

But why?

Before you go through the hassle of a lawsuit, ask yourself what you want out of the lawsuit.

What's your goal?

Some people want their day in court–they want to be heard. Others want the defendant to be held accountable somehow for what he, she, or it did. Most want both.

However, as a legal matter, there are only two categories of relief a court can award to someone who files a lawsuit: **money damages** and **injunctive relief.**

Let's talk about them.

Money Damages

Lawsuits seeking money damages are far more common than actions seeking injunctive relief.

There are three types of money damages that can be awarded: compensatory damages, punitive damages, and nominal damages.

COMPENSATORY DAMAGES

As its name implies, **compensatory damages** are intended to compensate the plaintiff for the harm caused by the defendant if there is a finding that the defendant violated the plaintiff's rights. In federal court, the different categories of compensatory damages follow the laws of the state in which the lawsuit takes place.

Generally, compensatory damages include 1) **special damages,** which are objective and easily quantifiable damages, such as medical expenses and lost wages, and 2) **general damages**, such as pain and suffering and mental anguish. General damages are more subjective and more difficult to calculate.

PUNITIVE DAMAGES

Punitive damages, also known as exemplary damages, are not intended to compensate a plaintiff. Instead, they are designed to punish a defendant and discourage future bad acts by the defendant and others. Punitive damages are only available in certain kinds of cases and under specific conditions. For instance, in civil rights cases, punitive damages can be awarded only where the plaintiff proves the defendant's conduct involved reckless or callous indifference to the plaintiff's federally protected rights, or when the defendant's conduct was motivated by evil motive or intent.

NOMINAL DAMAGES

Sometimes, a plaintiff suffers no actual harm as a result of the defendant's violation of his rights other than the violation itself. **Nominal damages**, often as little as one dollar, are intended to demonstrate that the defendant violated the plaintiff's rights, but the plaintiff suffered no actual damages. Instead, nominal damages are intended to signify the plaintiff's vindication of his rights in court. They are only awarded in certain types of cases where the rights in question are deemed to be special, such as constitutional rights. In most state law **tort actions** (such as a personal injury case), nominal damages are not available - a plaintiff must prove he sustained actual damages in order to win the case.

Injunctive Relief

Injunctive relief, also known as equitable relief, is where a court *requires* a party to do something or *restrains* a party from doing something. Injunctive relief can only be granted by a judge, not a jury. In other words, there is no right to a jury trial when seeking injunctive or equitable relief.

Examples of injunctive relief include improving prison conditions and prohibiting the enforcement of an unconstitutional law. Injunctive relief is considered a very extreme measure, as courts do not tell people or institutions what to do and what not to do without a very good reason.

Because injunctive relief is such a coercive measure, there are a number of safeguards to protect parties from unreasonable orders.

Injunctive relief is available only when two conditions are met:

1. There is a likelihood that the plaintiff will suffer substantial and immediate "irreparable" harm, *and*

2. There exists no other remedy to adequately address this threat of harm.

In other words, failure to grant the requested relief will harm the plaintiff in ways that cannot be repaired, and money damages are insufficient to protect the plaintiff from experiencing the harm. Where money damages are intended to compensate the plaintiff for harm experienced in the past, injunctive relief is forward-looking, and intended to protect the plaintiff (and, often others in similar circumstances) from experiencing harm in the future.

The first step in obtaining injunctive relief is to seek a **preliminary injunction,** also known as a **temporary restraining order ("TRO"),** which is available only if the party seeking the relief can prove four things:

1. Irreparable injury in the absence of an order granting the injunctive relief;

2. That the threatened injury to the moving party outweighs the harm to the opposing party resulting from the order;

3. That the injunction is not adverse to public interest; and

4. That the moving party has a substantial likelihood of success on the merits.

If granted, the TRO will go into effect immediately while the lawsuit goes through the litigation process. A plaintiff can sue for injunctive relief and money damages in the same lawsuit. In that case, the judge will decide the injunctive relief issue and the jury will decide whether to award money damages, assuming at least one side has requested a trial by jury.

It is very difficult to obtain injunctive relief, even with an attorney. But it is much more difficult on your own.

Chapter Recap

When considering a lawsuit, understanding what you're signing up for and the potential outcomes and what you aim to achieve is crucial.

STAGE 1 - PLEADINGS
The litigation process begins with the plaintiff filing a Complaint to outline the allegations against the defendant, followed by the defendant's Answer, where they admit, deny, or claim insufficient knowledge of these allegations, potentially including affirmative defenses and counterclaims.

STAGE 2 - DISCOVERY
During this phase, both parties exchange information through initial disclosures required by FRCP 26 and engage in formal discovery methods such as interrogatories, document requests, requests for admissions, subpoenas, and depositions to gather evidence.

STAGE 3 - SUMMARY JUDGMENT
A party may request a summary judgment from the court, arguing that the evidence gathered during discovery clearly favors their side, thus avoiding the need for a trial.

STAGE 4 – PRETRIAL
The period right before the trial, when the parties make final preparations for the trial, and submit pretrial documents to the court.

STAGE 5 - TRIAL
The trial is the culmination of the litigation process where both parties present their evidence, examine witnesses, and make arguments before a judge or jury, followed by jury deliberation and the issuance of a verdict.

STAGE 6 - POST-TRIAL

- **Post-Trial Motions:** After a verdict, parties may file motions to alter or set aside the judgment, seeking a new trial or adjustment of the jury's decision based on claims of errors made during the trial.

- **Appeal:** If dissatisfied with the trial outcome or post-trial rulings, a party can appeal to a higher court, arguing legal errors that affected the verdict, in hopes of overturning or modifying the judgment.

- **Enforcement of Judgment:** Once a final judgment is in place, the winning party may need to take steps to enforce it, such as garnishing wages or placing liens on property, if the losing party does not voluntarily comply.

Forms Of Relief

The legal system provides different forms of relief for successful litigants, primarily categorized into two: money damages and injunctive relief.

MONEY DAMAGES

Money damages are the most common form of relief sought in lawsuits. They are intended to compensate the plaintiff for the harm caused by the defendant's actions. There are three main types of money damages:

- **Compensatory Damages** - These aim to compensate the plaintiff for actual losses, including both special damages (quantifiable losses like medical expenses and lost wages) and general damages (more subjective losses like pain and suffering).

- **Punitive Damages** - These are not compensatory but are designed to punish the defendant for particularly egregious behavior and deter similar future conduct.

- **Nominal Damages** - Awarded when the plaintiff's rights are violated but no substantial harm is suffered, nominal damages symbolize the vindication of rights rather than financial compensation.

INJUNCTIVE RELIEF

Injunctive relief, or equitable relief, involves a court order requiring a party to do or refrain from doing specific actions. It's a measure taken to prevent irreparable harm that cannot be adequately remedied by monetary compensation. Injunctive relief is sought when:

1. The plaintiff faces a substantial and immediate risk of irreparable harm.

2. No other remedy (such as money damages) can adequately prevent this harm.

Injunctive relief is forward-looking, aiming to protect the plaintiff (and sometimes others in similar situations) from future harm. Obtaining this type of relief begins with a request for a preliminary injunction or a temporary restraining order (TRO), which demands proof of:

1. **Irreparable injury** if the injunction isn't granted.

2. **Balance of harms** favors the party seeking the injunction.

3. **Public interest** is not harmed by the injunction.

4. **Likelihood of success** on the merits of the case by the party seeking the injunction.

Achieving injunctive relief is challenging and typically requires the expertise of an attorney. Those considering pursuing this path on their own should carefully evaluate the likelihood of success and the potential impact on their case. Given the complexity and challenges of obtaining injunctive relief, individuals without legal representation should consider the feasibility and potential effectiveness of their legal action.

Sources of Law

There are plenty of rules and requirements we all must live by, and it's no different for parties to a lawsuit. Some of these sources of law are **substantive**–meaning they govern how we conduct our lives–and some are **procedural**, which means they govern court proceedings. Just like there is a hierarchy of court systems, there is a hierarchy of laws, most of which you can find free online.

We'll start at the top:

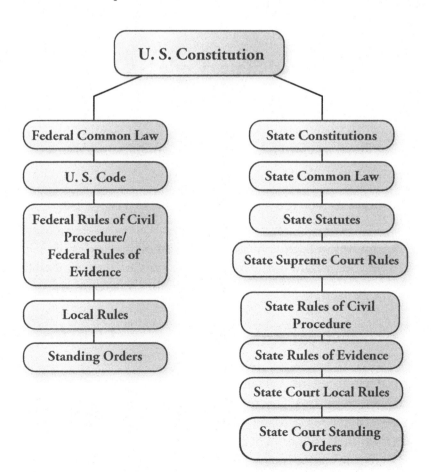

State and Federal Laws

U.S. Constitution

The Big Daddy of laws, the U.S. Constitution is the primary source of rights and responsibilities governing life in the United States. The Constitution establishes our federal government and how it works. It also contains the Bill of Rights (the first ten amendments to the Constitution), which limits the powers of government over its citizens and others in the United States.

Federal Laws

United States Code (USC)

The United States Code is a collection of federal laws passed by Congress and signed into law by the President. However, if Congress overrides the President's veto, a federal law can pass without the president's signature.

Federal Rules of Civil Procedure (FRCP)

The Federal Rules of Civil Procedure are a comprehensive set of rules that govern how we litigate in the federal court system. They are established by the U.S. Supreme Court with veto power by Congress.

Federal Rules of Evidence (FRE)

The Federal Rules of Evidence are like the Federal Rules of Civil Procedure, except they govern the admission of evidence at trial rather than procedural rules. Many states have adopted the Federal Rules of Evidence as their own rules of evidence.

Federal Common Law

The common law, also known as case law, comes from cases decided by the various federal courts that interpret federal laws as well as the U.S. Constitution and state constitutions. In other words, through the common law, judges tell us what specific Constitutional provisions and statutes mean and how they should be applied in specific circumstances.

Local Rules

Each district court has a set of specific rules that govern litigating in that district. These rules are often more detailed than the Federal Rules of Civil Procedure and fill in many gaps. For instance, local rules may govern word and page limitations in briefs, whether parties can file replies without leave of court, and the specific format of summary judgment motions. It is crucial to be aware of your district's Local Rules—failure to comply may result in your motions and other pleadings being stricken or denied. These rules can be found on each district court's website.

Standing Orders

Judges often have their own standing orders, which provide even more specific rules governing how things should be handled in their courtrooms. These orders are also contained on the courts' websites.

State Laws

State Constitutions

Each state has its own Constitution, which is the ultimate law in that state, just like the U.S. Constitution is the ultimate law of the United States. However, if there is a conflict between a state constitutional provision and a U.S. Constitutional provision, the U.S. Constitution will always prevail.

State Statutes

State statutes are laws passed by state legislatures and signed by each state's governor. (Some statutes may be passed without the governor's signature if the legislature overrides the governor's veto.) Because you can bring state law claims as well as federal claims in federal court, those claims will be governed by state statutes.

State Supreme Court Rules

State supreme court rules are similar to the Federal Rules of Civil Procedure on the state level. These are procedural rules that govern proceedings in state courts. Many state courts have adopted certain federal rules – particularly the rules of evidence – as their own.

State Rules of Evidence

Many states have adopted their own set of rules of evidence, and many have simply adopted the federal rules of evidence as their own.

State Common Law

Each state has its own court system, with trial courts and appellate courts, just like the federal system. And just like the federal courts, the state courts (including state supreme courts) have established a common law, also known as case law, in which the courts interpret state laws and state constitutions.

Local Rules and Standing Orders

Just like the federal courts, each individual state court system has its own set of local rules, and many judges have their own standing orders that govern very specific procedures in that court or in front of that judge.

Investigating Your Case

Before you file a lawsuit, you should investigate the facts and review the law to see if you have a viable (legally recognized) claim. In other words, you need to determine whether there is a legal and factual basis for the lawsuit. "Investigate before you litigate" is a phrase I just came up with, but I think it's going to catch on.

What Is Litigation?

Litigation is a step-by-step process of taking legal action. But in a larger sense, litigation is the application of the relevant facts of a case to the governing law. It's a constant interplay between facts and law. Different facts implicate different legal analysis, and different legal elements tell us whether certain facts are relevant.

To investigate whether you have a viable claim, you should take the facts as you know them and determine whether they fit into any recognized **cause of action**. A cause of action is a set of facts that the law allows you to bring as a lawsuit, such as false arrest, employment discrimination, or breach of contract.

Step 1 - Do You Have a Cause of Action?

In a moment, we'll explain the essential ingredients for a cause of action in **tort**. I thought that was an odd term when I started law school, and I still think it sounds weird. A *tort* is a wrongful act, and it should not be confused with a *torte*, which is a delightful pastry. A lawsuit that involves a claim of wrongful conduct by a defendant is a *tort claim*.

Common tort claims include allegations of personal injury, property damage, discrimination, and violation of constitutional or statutory rights, in which someone was injured because of the conduct of another. It does *not* include breach of contract claims or allegations of criminal conduct.

There are three types of tort claims:

1. **Negligence**: Unreasonable *non-intentional* conduct, such as a car accident.

2. **Intentional torts**: Unreasonable *intentional* conduct, such as a false arrest.

3. **Strict liability**: A person or company is held responsible for an injury even if it had no knowledge or intent to injure, such as products liability.

Some torts, like personal injury claims, originate in common law, which means they were created by cases decided over the years by judges. Others, like constitutional torts, are based on violations of certain constitutional rights. But these violations are only subject to lawsuit because of a federal statute known as the Civil Rights Act, 42 U.S.C. Section 1983. Claims of employment discrimination are based on other federal laws, particularly Title VII of the Civil Rights Act of 1964, the Age Discrimination in Employment Act (ADEA), and the Americans with Disabilities Act (ADA).

All of these are considered torts. To win a tort claim, you have to prove each of these things:

1. **Duty:** The defendant had a duty to the plaintiff to act or refrain from acting in a certain way.

2. **Breach:** The defendant breached (violated) her duty to the plaintiff.

3. **Causation:** The defendant's breach of her duty caused injury to the plaintiff.

4. **Damages:** The injury resulted in some form of harm to the plaintiff, such as loss of income, mental or physical pain and suffering.

Remember: Litigation is the application of facts to law.

*   The legal elements of a tort claim are the *law* part.

*   The facts of your possible lawsuit are the *fact* part.

Let's play this out:

Imagine you were arrested and forced to spend the night in jail for a crime you didn't commit. Let's consider how you might logically determine the cause of action in this situation through a conversation between fact and law.

1. ***Known Fact:*** You were arrested.

2. ***Known Law:*** An arrest is one element of a false arrest cause of action, but not the *only* element. The arrest must be *without probable cause* for you to have a cause of action for false arrest.

3. ***Question of Fact:*** Did the officer have probable cause to arrest you?

4. ***Question of Law:*** What *is* probable cause?

5. ***Probable cause defined:*** Generally, an officer has probable cause to arrest you when the officer, at the time of the arrest, is aware of facts that would cause a reasonable police officer to believe you *have* engaged in criminal activity, are *currently* engaging in criminal activity, or are *about to* engage in criminal activity.

6. ***Question of Fact:*** What facts or circumstances was the officer aware of when he arrested you?

7. ***Question of Fact:*** Would a reasonable officer believe you were engaged in criminal activity based on what this officer knew when he arrested you?

8. ***Application of Law to Facts:*** If you can answer those factual questions after learning about the applicable law, you will know whether you were arrested without probable cause. In other words, you will know whether you were the victim of a false arrest and have a legitimate false arrest claim.

Let's say you conclude that you have a cause of action (a valid legal claim). This is only the first step. If you decide to file a lawsuit, your case may also have to survive:

1) a **motion to dismiss**. Can you allege facts (not conclusions) that, if true, would mean the officer arrested you without probable cause? In other words, are the factual allegations in the complaint sufficient to state a viable cause of action?

2) a **motion for summary judgment.** Are the facts established during the discovery stage *legally sufficient* for a reasonable jury to return a verdict in your favor?

This is why you need to look carefully at the facts and the law to see if you have a reasonable opportunity to win your lawsuit before you file.

Step 2 - Know The Statute Of Limitations

Suppose you've thought about your cause of action and you think you might have a case. Before you do anything else, you have one more critically important fact and law question to consider:

Will you be able to file your claim within the Statute of Limitations?

As we discuss in detail in Chapter 10, the **Statute of Limitations** (or "SOL") is the time limit set by law that governs when a claim may be filed. You need to know the date the incident occurred (a question of fact) and the applicable Statute of Limitations (a question of law). But you also need to know the date the legal claim **accrued.** The "accrual date" is the date your case became a legally viable legal claim. In other words, it's the first date you would be allowed to file your lawsuit.

Be sure you know the facts of your case *and* the law applicable to those facts to determine whether you can or should file a lawsuit.

Statutes of Limitation dictate the strict deadlines for filing a lawsuit, and missing this deadline means you're barred from filing. Some SOLs are two years, while others may be three years or even longer. This period of time is known as the **limitations period.**

But when do you start counting the limitations period? The start of this period, known as the "accrual date," varies depending on the case type. For instance, false arrest claims accrue on the arrest date, while malicious prosecution claims do not accrue until a criminal case ends favorably for the accused (you), or a previous conviction is overturned.

In federal courts, the SOL for civil rights claims is determined by looking at state law. For example, in Illinois, the SOL for filing a personal injury lawsuit is two years from the date the cause of action accrues. Federal courts have determined that personal injury claims are most similar to federal civil rights claims. As a result, federal courts in

Illinois have adopted Illinois' two-year SOL as the applicable SOL for filing a federal civil rights lawsuit. In other words, a plaintiff has two years from the date the claim accrues to file a federal civil rights lawsuit in Illinois.

There are exceptions to SOLs. First, the SOL for minors does not begin to run until the minor's 18th birthday. So, if someone wants to file a personal injury lawsuit or a federal civil rights lawsuit for something that happened when he was 16 years old, he has until the age of 20 to file that lawsuit (the two-year SOL begins to run when he's 18). The SOL may also be extended for those who are severely disabled to the extent they cannot manage their own affairs.

But you don't have to—and you shouldn't—wait. The 16-year old in the above example should not wait until he's 18 or 19 to file. No matter what the SOL is, a plaintiff should file as soon as possible because delays can lead to lost evidence, unavailable witnesses, and fading memories. Additionally, all defendants must be named before the SOL expires. There are exceptions to this, but it is very difficult to name defendants after the SOL has passed. However, if the 16-year old wants to file before he's 18, he'll need a parent or legal guardian to file on his behalf. Minors are not allowed to file lawsuits on their own behalf.

Step 3 - Investigate The Facts

Once you determine that your cause of action is within the Statute of Limitations, it's time to investigate the facts. You may know what happened to you from *your* perspective, but there's probably a lot you don't know without access to additional information. For instance, if you want to file a claim for false arrest, you need to know what facts the arresting officer knew at the time of the arrest. You'll also need to know the officer's stated justification for the arrest, and you won't know that unless you've seen the arrest report.

Common types of materials for this step might include:

- **Court Records:** These can include pleadings, motions, transcripts, and judgments from previous or related cases, usually from the underlying criminal case.
- **Police Reports:** Arrest reports and incident or accident reports that might be relevant.

- **Police diagrams:** Sketches of the crime scene by police officers.

- **Ambulance or EMS reports:** Reports by paramedics regarding treatment of involved individuals.

- **Medical records:** Records relating to medical treatment of involved individuals.

- **Evidence Logs:** Lists of evidence collected by law enforcement in relation to a case.

- **Body Camera or Dash Camera Footage:** Video recordings from police officers' body cameras or patrol car dash cameras.

- **Surveillance Footage:** Video from privately owned or government-owned cameras in public places or on government property.

- **Cell Phone footage:** Video from individuals on the scene.

- **911 Call Transcripts:** Transcripts or recordings of emergency calls related to the incident.

- **Witness Statements:** Written accounts from witnesses collected by law enforcement.

- **Photographs:** Pictures taken by law enforcement or others at the scene of an incident or crime, or photos of recovered evidence.

- **Forensic Reports:** These can include autopsy reports, ballistic reports, fingerprint analyses, DNA test results, and other scientific analyses.

- **Property or Evidence Receipts:** Documentation of personal property taken into custody by law enforcement.

- **Jail or Prison Records:** These can include booking records, inmate logs, and records of disciplinary actions.

- **Probation or Parole Reports:** Documentation related to an individual's probation or parole status and compliance.

- **Building and Zoning Records:** Useful in property disputes or cases involving land use regulations.

- **Vital Statistics Records:** Depending on the case, a litigant might need birth certificates, marriage licenses, death certificates, property deeds, or business licenses.

- **Personnel Files:** In cases alleging misconduct by a government employee, the employee's personnel file might be relevant.

How do you get your hands on these key pieces to your litigation puzzle? Here are some of the ways you can obtain critical documents for your case.

Open Records Requests

By far, the most effective way to get records from the government is through open records laws. Each state has different open records laws. You can normally request records from police departments, sheriff's departments, prosecutors' offices, and municipalities. The federal government also has an open records law called the Freedom of Information Act (Check out FOIA.gov). To learn about each state's open records law, visit the **National Freedom of Information Coalition.**

You can find them here: https://www.nfoic.org/state-freedom-of-information-laws/

Your Criminal Defense Attorney

Suppose you were charged with a crime, and there was a criminal case. In that case, the prosecutor should have provided your attorney with **discovery,** which consists of relevant documents, records, and evidence. Your criminal defense attorney may have conducted her own investigation. If the case is over, you can request those materials from your criminal defense attorney. However, some states have specific rules about what criminal defense attorneys can provide to clients and third parties.

Internet and Social Media Search

You may (or may not) be surprised at the amount and variety of online information. Often, police shootings and other public events attract media attention, which can be found online and used to investigate your case. Many Facebook pages are set to public. If you can get your hands on evidence through any kind of social media, do it.

While we're on the topic of social media, I highly recommend that you set all your social media accounts to private so the other side doesn't have the same access to information about you if you file a lawsuit.

Obtain documents through the discovery process.

As long as you have enough information to file a lawsuit **in good faith** (meaning you have a reasonable factual and legal basis for filing), you can always amend your complaint after receiving **discovery** (where each side shows the other their evidence) from the defendants. You have much more leverage to obtain information through the discovery process than through FOIA or other mechanisms. This is why you should file as soon as you have a factual and legal basis to do so. If you need to name additional defendants, you need to name those defendants before the Statute of Limitations (SOL) expires. We'll cover this topic in depth in Chapter 10.

Before you begin to engage in the litigation process, you should check out the website for the district court where you intend to file your lawsuit, whether a federal district court or your local state court. Every district court has its own website, and most if not all state courts have their own websites. Each of these websites should have a section specifically for *pro se* litigants. These sections contain invaluable information regarding how that court handles *pro se* litigation, including filing requirements, forms, and other information.

Chapter Recap

Litigation is the application of relevant facts to governing law and highlights the constant interplay between facts and law. Here's how litigation works in three steps:

1. **Identify a Cause of Action:** Look carefully at the facts and the law to see if you have a reasonable opportunity to win your lawsuit.

2. **Understand the Statute of Limitations:** Know your accrual date, the time when a legal claim becomes viable, and the strict deadline for filing your lawsuit, as missing this deadline means you're barred from filing.

3. **Investigate the Facts:** Gather comprehensive information through various sources, such as court records, police reports, witness statements, body camera footage, 911 call transcripts, and forensic reports using open records requests, collaboration with a criminal defense attorney, online searches, and the discovery process.

Defendants

Who or what should you sue?

Deciding who to name as a defendant is a crucial part of the litigation process.

Generally speaking, you should sue everyone who you *reasonably believe* was involved in violating your rights. You should identify the people involved through your pre-suit investigation. Even if you can't identify everyone involved, you can file against at least one individual and then try to discover other defendants' identities through the discovery process. Allow me to reiterate here the importance of filing well before the SOL expires—you may need that extra time to discover more defendants.

While you should sue everyone you reasonably believe violated your rights, that does *not* mean you should sue everyone under the sun. Doing so would be a mistake, and it makes everything more difficult for you and the court. Often, there will only be a few people who are *actually* responsible for violating your rights.

Here's an example: You sue Officer Bob and Officer Roger for falsely arresting you. Okay, fine. But what about Officer Joe, who processed you? He took your prints and your mugshot. Do you sue him?

Ask yourself: *"What did Officer Joe do to violate my rights? Did he know there was no probable cause to arrest me? Did he have any idea about the facts of my arrest?"*

If all he did was process an arrest executed by other officers, you probably don't want to sue Joe, even though he was technically involved in your arrest. On the other hand, if you know he *was* involved in your arrest but don't know exactly what role he played, you may want to name him as a defendant until you can obtain additional information through discovery. You can always voluntarily dismiss him later if you find he had no significant involvement in violating your rights.

WHAT IS "REASONABLE BELIEF?"

One of the concepts you'll run across often during your litigation journey is the concept of *reasonableness.* Whether something is reasonable in court is not that different from whether it is reasonable outside of court. It is often a common-sense analysis.

You do not need a specific amount of proof or admissible evidence to establish reasonable belief (also known as a "good-faith basis to believe") that a particular defendant violated your rights.

Your belief should be based on facts rather than speculation or a hunch. You should be able to rationally explain your decision to include someone as a defendant. But you do not want to compromise your case by failing to name a certain defendant within the Statute of Limitations.

Can I Sue the Police Department?

Generally, you can sue individual police *officers* and municipalities (such as cities, towns, and villages), but you cannot sue police *departments.*

Federal courts look to state law to determine who or what can be named as a defendant in a lawsuit (FRCP 17(b)). For instance, to be sued in Illinois, a defendant must have an independent legal existence. This should be true in most states, but you should check your state laws on this. Police *departments* are generally considered internal departments operating as part of the municipalities rather than stand-alone entities with a legal existence separate from those municipalities. So, police departments typically cannot be defendants in civil lawsuits. If you think you want to sue a police department, then you should sue the city or town that operates the department, not the department itself. As always, you should research the law to confirm this is true in your state.

Can I Sue the Sheriff's Department?

Unlike police departments, county sheriff's departments in many states *can* be sued because a county sheriff is an independently elected constitutional officer. Therefore, the Sheriff's office has a legal existence separate from the county and the state, and can be a proper defendant in a lawsuit. Again, you should check your state laws to determine how your state defines Sheriff's departments. You should also check federal case law in your district to see how this issue has been handled in previous cases.

Respondeat Superior: Suing the Employer

Under state law, you can sue municipalities and companies for the acts of their employees under a doctrine known as *respondeat superior* (Latin for "the master must answer") as long as the employee is acting within the scope of his employment.

Example: If you get into an accident with someone who happens to be a gas company employee, but he is in his personal vehicle and on his way to the grocery store to buy food for his family, *respondeat superior* will not apply because he's not acting within the scope of his employment as a gas company employee at the time of the accident.

But if he's in a gas company vehicle on his way to check someone's gas meter, he is in the scope of his employment, so you can sue the gas company for his actions in a lawsuit filed under state law. This is the general concept of *respondeat superior*. Carefully research the specific elements of *respondeat superior* in your state before you file any pleadings on the issue.

Under federal civil rights law, you cannot sue the employer for the acts of the employee—you have to sue the employee individually. The only way you can sue a municipality under federal civil rights law is by filing a so-called policy and practice claim (also known as a *Monell* claim because it is based on a U.S. Supreme Court decision called *Monell v. Department of Soc. Svcs.*, 436 U.S. 658 (1978)). Under a policy and practice claim, a plaintiff must allege (and ultimately prove) that the policies or practices of a municipality caused or contributed to the violation of the plaintiff's constitutional rights.

Legal Immunities

You may have heard the term "diplomatic immunity," especially if you've seen *Lethal Weapon 2*. Think of an immunity as a shield. Just like some people have immunity to certain diseases, certain types of defendants have different immunites to being sued. Some immunities are partial (usually referred to as *qualified immunity)* and some are complete or absolute. Under **qualified immunity**, the immunity applies depending on the specific facts of the case. But an **absolute immunity** applies no matter the facts, as long as the defendant performed a specific function, as discussed below.

Absolute Prosecutorial Immunity

Prosecutors are protected by something called **absolute prosecutorial immunity**. Under this immunity, a prosecutor (known in some states as an Assistant State's Attorney and known in other states as an Assistant District Attorney) cannot be held liable in a civil lawsuit for any conduct "associated with the **judicial phase of the criminal process.**" *Imbler v. Pachtman,* 424 U.S. 409, 430 (1976).

WHAT IS THE "JUDICIAL PHASE OF THE CRIMINAL PROCESS"?

The judicial phase of the criminal process is any conduct by a prosecutor while engaging in her prosecutorial function, i.e., advocating for the prosecution of a criminal defendant. This includes witness preparation, in-court activities, drafting a complaint or an application for an arrest warrant, and other prosecutorial functions.

Prosecutorial immunity is a *huge* immunity. It protects a massive amount of wrongful conduct by prosecutors. This immunity applies even if the prosecutor:

- presents false evidence
- willfully suppresses exculpatory evidence (**exculpatory evidence** is evidence that is favorable to the criminal defendant)

- prosecutes maliciously
- acts without probable cause
- coerces witnesses to lie
- hides evidence of innocence
- fabricates evidence of guilt—even when the prosecutor intentionally violates the Constitution or causes a wrongful conviction

Why on earth does this immunity exist, you ask? Good question. It is not in the Constitution. It is not in a federal statute. Like qualified immunity, it was created by judges. The purpose is to allow prosecutors to do their jobs without second-guessing themselves for fear of harassing lawsuits.

Of course, the same logic would apply to everyone, including police officers. But the rest of us do not get such broad immunity. Police officers are entitled to *qualified* immunity, which is more limited, but also protects unconstitutional conduct. We'll get to qualified immunity in a minute.

WHEN CAN I SUE A PROSECUTOR?

Like it or not, you cannot sue a prosecutor for anything he does while prosecuting a case. However, you *can* sue a prosecutor for any activity outside the judicial phase of the criminal process. For instance, prosecutors often act as investigators and occasionally offer advice to police officers regarding whether they have probable cause to make an arrest. These activities are not protected by absolute immunity, but will generally be protected by qualified immunity.

If a prosecutor questions a witness or a suspect before there is probable cause to make an arrest, she is acting as an investigator, not a prosecutor, as there is no prosecution yet. Under those circumstances, there is no absolute immunity. *Whitlock v. Brueggemann,* 682 F.3d 567, 580 (7th Cir. 2012).

If a prosecutor signs an application for a search warrant, an arrest warrant, or a criminal complaint *as a complaining witness* (verifying the facts alleged in the document), there is no absolute immunity. *Van de Kamp v. Goldstein,* 555 U.S. 335, 343 (2009). However, absolute immunity applies if the prosecutor merely prepares the application or signs it as the drafting prosecutor. *Kalina v. Fletcher*, 522 U.S. 118, 129 (1997).

WHAT ABOUT JUDGES? CAN I SUE THEM?

Like prosecutors, judges are entitled to absolute immunity for their actions during the judicial phase of the case. By definition, judges are almost always involved only in the judicial phase of the case. Judges rarely investigate or provide advice, as judges decide legal matters in court. There is virtually no circumstance where a judge will act outside the judicial phase of the case. A judge who signs a search warrant or an arrest warrant is protected by judicial immunity. So, unless a judge acted in a non-judicial capacity (which is extremely rare), she is not a proper defendant in a lawsuit.

A recent case, *Gibson v. Goldston,* decided by the Fourth Circuit Court of Appeals, involves a judge who searched a litigant's home in a divorce proceeding. This judge actually *drove to the litigant's home and searched it herself.* Because her activity was investigative rather than judicial, she was not entitled to immunity. *Gibson v. Goldston,* No. 22-1757 (4th Cir. Oct. 30, 2023). This is very rare.

Qualified Immunity

All government employees, including police officers, correctional officers, sheriff's deputies, and prosecutors, are protected by **qualified immunity,** which shields them from civil liability even if they violate someone's constitutional rights, as long as the right allegedly violated was not "clearly established" at the time of the alleged violation. Qualified immunity is very fact-specific, as opposed to absolute (i.e. prosecutorial or judicial) immunity, which applies to any set of facts as long as the defendant was acting as a prosecutor or a judge. Even if a prosecutor is determined to be acting outside the judicial process, and thus not entitled to absolute immunity, they may be entitled to qualified immunity based on the facts of the case. Like other forms of immunity, qualified immunity is not contained in the Constitution or any statute. It was created by judges through case law. Because prosecutorial and judicial immunity are absolute, you would not name prosecutors or judges as defendants except under very specific circumstances, as discussed in this chapter. However, because qualified immunity is *qualified,* and very fact-specific, you would still sue the officers or others who you believe violated your rights, and let the court sort out whether the defendant is entitled to qualified immunity.

Sovereign Immunity: The King Can Do No Wrong

"Sovereign immunity" protects states and the federal government from being sued. It came from a British common law doctrine based on the idea that the King could do no wrong.

CAN I SUE THE UNITED STATES?

The federal government gave up its sovereign immunity when Congress passed the Federal Tort Claims Act ("FTCA"), 28 U.S.C. 171. Under certain limited circumstances, the FTCA authorizes private tort actions (lawsuits) against the United States, for the actions of its employees. The FTCA contains specific rules for making claims and filing lawsuits against the federal government.

CAN I SUE FEDERAL OFFICIALS?

The answer to that question is usually no. In a case called *Bivens v. Six Unknown Fed. Narcotics Agents,* 403 U.S. 388 (1971), the U.S. Supreme Court held that people had a right to file civil lawsuits against federal government officials who violated the Fourth Amendment (which prohibits unreasonable searches and seizures) because a constitutional protection would not be meaningful if there were no way to seek a remedy for a constitutional violation. However, since the *Bivens* case was announced in 1971, the U.S. Supreme Court has whittled it down to very little, asserting that Congress is in the best position to determine the extent of federal officials' liability.

CAN I SUE A STATE?

In 1793, the U.S. Supreme Court held that a citizen of one state could sue another state, but the Eleventh Amendment to the U.S. Constitution,which was ratified two years later, changed that. As a result, you cannot sue any state. However, you can sue state employees, who are typically indemnified by state governments, assuming the action by the state employee was taken within the scope of their employment by the state.

Just like the federal government has the FTCA, many states have something called a **Court of Claims,** in which you can file an action against the state itself. But this is different from filing a regular lawsuit and has different rules.

If a defendant is **indemnified,** it means the employer will pay any civil judgment against an employee for actions taken within the scope of that person's employment. As with most things, however, each state has its own indemnification statute, which spells out the specific circumstances under which indemnification applies. You have to do your own research to find out how your state handles indemnification.

Chapter Recap

When it comes to the question of who to sue, you should sue everyone you reasonably believe to be involved in violating your rights. If you don't know all the possible defendants, you can file suit against the ones you know and try to identify others through the discovery process. You can always drop your claim against individuals named in your suit if it turns out they were not involved. You should file well before the **Statute of Limitations (SOL)** expires to allow time to discover additional defendants and add them to the lawsuit.

- **Exercise Caution in Naming Defendants:** While you should sue everyone you believe violated your rights, you should not sue everyone related to the incident. That makes everyone's jobs more difficult–including yours.

- **Reasonable Belief Standard:** "Reasonable belief" does not require a specific amount of proof, but it should be based on facts rather than speculation or a hunch.

- **Suing police departments:** In most states, individuals can sue police officers and municipalities but not police *departments,* which are usually internal departments and not separate legal entities.

- **Suing County Sheriff's Departments:** Unlike municipal police departments, county sheriff's departments can often be sued because sheriffs are independently elected, so their departments are considered separate entities from the counties in which they operate.

- *Respondeat Superior* **Doctrine:** A doctrine allowing plaintiffs to sue employers for the actions of their employees if they are acting within the scope of employment. Still, it does not apply in federal civil rights cases.

- **Legal Immunities:** Limitations on suing certain categories of defendants under particular facts. Some immunities are absolute and some are qualified.

    - **Prosecutorial and Judicial Immunity:** Prosecutors and judges have absolute immunity from civil lawsuits for actions taken while performing their duties as prosecutors and judges. Prosecutors are not entitled to this immunity if they are acting as investigators or engaging in some other non-prosecutorial function.

- **Qualified Immunity:** This immunity protects public officials if the constitutional right they are alleged to have violated was not "clearly established" at the time of the incident.

- **Sovereign Immunity:** The immunity of states and the federal government from being sued. The federal government allows certain actions against it pursuant to the Federal Tort Claims Act. Under very limited circumstances, you can see a federal official for violating your constitutional rights.

- **State Sovereign Immunity:** States are generally immune from lawsuits, but state employees can be sued for actions within the scope of their employment and are often indemnified, meaning the state will pay a judgment against the employee under certain circumstances.

- Many states have a **Court of Claims** that handles actions against the state itself.

Federal Court vs. State Court: Where Should You File?

- U.S. Const., Art. III: Judicial Branch

- 28 USC § 1367: Supplemental Jurisdiction

- 28 USC § 1332(a): Diversity of Citizenship

- 28 USC § § 1441 and 1446: Removal of Civil Actions

One of the most important questions you'll ask yourself as you prepare for litigation as a plaintiff is whether you should file your lawsuit in federal court or state court. Is one court more advantageous than the other? Is there a reason you might prefer federal court over state court, or vice versa?

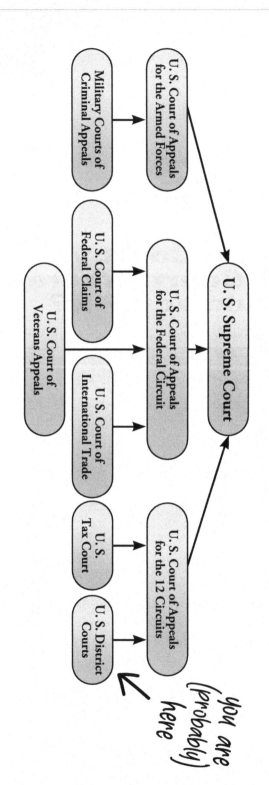

Federal Courts

The federal court system starts with **district courts**. There are other courts at the district court level, such as the Court of International Trade, but you don't see many *pro se* litigants there. Every state has a certain number of federal district courts, depending on that state's population, and there are currently 94 federal district courts in the United States. These are the trial courts where lawsuits are filed and where they are tried. These courts also hear federal criminal cases.

A state may have anywhere from one to four districts, depending on the size of the state. For example, Illinois has three federal judicial districts, North Dakota has one district, and New York has four districts.

Each of these districts has different divisions, which hear cases from specific counties within that district. You can find the jurisdictional maps of each state's federal district courts on the district court's website.

Federal district courts hear all sorts of cases, including criminal prosecutions and civil lawsuits. There are some exceptions, such as patent and bankruptcy cases, which require very specialized knowledge, and which are heard by specific federal courts.

KNOW YOUR JUDGES

Federal district judges, also known as **Article III judges**, are the primary judges in the district courts. These judges have all been nominated by the President of the United States and confirmed by Congress. Once appointed, they serve for life.

There are also **magistrate judges** who assist the district judges. Magistrate judges can hear cases just like district judges if all the parties to a lawsuit agree. Magistrate judges supervise discovery, decide discovery disputes, and conduct settlement conferences. Magistrate judges work closely with the parties to try to settle cases or move them along.

State court judges are either elected or appointed. They can be appointed by the governor, other judges, or some other official or panel. Most states elect their judges, though many states also have some appointed judges. Unlike federal judges, state court judges do not serve for life. They must either be reappointed or re-elected after their terms.

The next level above the district courts is the **appellate courts**. This is where you go when you want to appeal a district court's decision. The federal appellate court system is divided into 13 **circuits**. Twelve of those circuits are geographic. This includes 11 numbered circuits plus the District of Columbia Circuit, which only decides cases from Washington, D.C. The 13th circuit is called the Federal Circuit, which decides specific types of cases, including patents, trademarks, and government contracts, from all over the country.

Geographic Boundaries of the 13 Federal Appellate Circuits

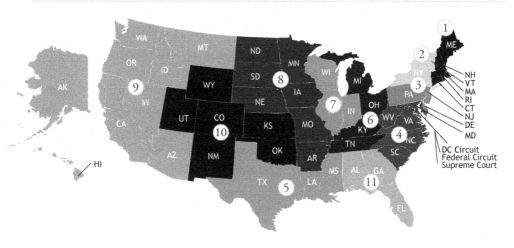

Puerto Rico   U.S. Virgin Island

First Circuit	Second Circuit	Third Circuit	Fourth Circuit	Fifth Circuit
Maine	Connecticut	Delaware	Maryland	Louisiana
Massachusetts	New York	New Jersey	North Carolina	Mississippi
New Hampshire	Vermont	Pennsylvania	South Carolina	Texas
Puerto Rico		Virgin Islands	Virginia	
Rhode Island			West Virginia	

Sixth Circuit	Seventh Circuit	Third Circuit	Eighth Circuit	Ninth Circuit
Kentucky	Illinois	Delaware	Arkansas	Alaska
Michigan	Indiana	New Jersey	Iowa	California
Ohio	Wisconsin	Pennsylvania	Minnesota	Hawaii
Tennessee		Virgin Islands	Missouri	Idaho
			Nebraska	Montana
			North Dakota	Nevada
			South Dakota	Oregon
				Washington

Tenth Circuit	Seventh Circuit	District of Columbia Circuit
Colorado	Illinois	
Kansas	Indiana	
New Mexico	Wisconsin	
Oklahoma		
Utah		
Wyoming		

The next level up from the federal appellate courts is the **U.S. Supreme Court,** which hears cases from federal appellate courts and from the highest court in any state (often known as that state's supreme court). The U.S. Supreme Court hears only a small fraction of the cases heard in the lower courts, and accepts only 100 to150 of the thousands of cases it is asked to review each year. The Supreme Court has original jurisdiction over certain cases, such as disputes between two or more states. **Original jurisdiction** means the Supreme Court is the only court that hears these cases. Most Supreme Court cases involve **appellate jurisdiction**, in which it decides cases on appeal from lower courts. **Jurisdiction** refers to the legal authority of a court to try cases and rule on legal matters within a particular geographic area and/or over a certain type of legal case.

How Do You Get Your Case Into Federal Court?

There are two main ways to get into federal court: **Federal Question jurisdiction** and **Diversity jurisdiction.**

Federal Question jurisdiction means the lawsuit is based on an alleged violation of a federal law, including the U.S. Constitution, a federal statute, or a federal regulation. Civil rights and employment discrimination claims may be brought in federal court because they are based on federal statutes. As discussed later in this chapter, federal courts can also hear state law claims as long as there is at least one active federal claim, and as long as the state law claims arise from the same facts as the federal claim. 28 USC § 1367. These are called **supplemental state law claims**, but you may also hear the term "pendant" claims.

Diversity jurisdiction in the context of federal jurisdiction means the parties are from different states. 28 USC § 1332(a). Claims based on diversity jurisdiction are often based entirely on state law. For instance, a state law personal injury case can be tried in federal court if there is diversity of the parties.

Diversity cases must involve amounts greater than $75,000, and *complete diversity* of the parties is required. In other words, none of the opposing parties can be from the same state. If three plaintiffs are suing three defendants, and one of the plaintiffs and one of the defendants are both from Ohio, there is not complete diversity, and there is no diversity jurisdiction. However, if two of the plaintiffs or two of the defendants are from the same state, that will not defeat diversity jurisdiction.

State Courts

Each state has its own court system, with trial courts, appellate courts, and the state's highest court, known in almost every state as the state supreme court.

The state court systems are organized by county. Each county has its own court system, but all the county court systems operate under statewide procedural rules, just like federal district courts operate under federal procedural rules. Like federal courts, each county court system has its own local rules, and its judges may have their own standing orders for very specific procedures. There are two exceptions to this: Louisiana has parishes, which operate like counties, and Alaska has boroughs and census areas.

You can file federal claims based on federal law in state court. However, if your case includes at least one federal claim, any defendant in your lawsuit may file a motion to **"remove"** (i.e., transfer) the lawsuit to federal court–if they seek removal within 30 days of service of the complaint.

Plaintiffs who file in federal court often do so because federal judges are more familiar with federal laws and may be better prepared to deal with federal issues. But if you want to file in your local state court, you may be able to find state law claims that are similar to your federal claims. For instance, many states have their own false arrest or wrongful imprisonment claim. A federal claim of excessive force under the Fourth Amendment to the U.S. Constitution can be filed as a **battery claim** under state law. A "battery" is generally defined as a harmful or offensive contact by one person against another without the consent of that person.

The same applies to employment discrimination claims. Most if not all states have their own set of employment laws that mirror federal employment laws, although some state laws may be broader than federal law.

So, if you want to be in state court, you can file only state law claims. Or you can file federal and state law claims, and if the defendant tries to remove the case to federal court, you could dismiss your federal claims and stay in state court, or try your case in federal court.

Differences Between Federal Court & State Court

Jurors

From a tactical perspective, one of the biggest differences between federal and state courts is the jury pool. Jurors are crucial – they are the ones who will be deciding your case, unless both sides opt for a trial by judge (known as a "bench trial"), which is extremely rare.

A federal court will draw jurors from the entire division within its district, or the entire district if it does not have separate divisions. As an example, the Northern District of Illinois Eastern Division contains eight counties. But federal districts and divisions in more rural areas will include many more counties than that. For instance, the Western District of Wisconsin contains 44 counties, because the counties are less populated.

State court systems, on the other hand, are divided into separate counties. Each county will have its own court system and will draw jurors only from that county. A county is a much smaller area than a federal judicial district— while there are only **94 federal judicial districts** in the U.S., there are **3,143 counties**. A plaintiff who files a case in state court will file in the specific county where the incident took place, or where one or more of the parties are located, just like a plaintiff who files in federal court will file in the specific federal district court that is appropriate for that case.

If your incident occurred in Atlanta, your state court system would be the Superior Court of Fulton County. If you file in state court, all of your jurors–the people who would decide your case–would be from Fulton County, which is a much smaller and more specific area than a federal judicial district.

But if you filed in federal court–in this case, the Northern District of Georgia, Atlanta Division–your jurors would be drawn from *ten counties,* including Fulton and nine other counties. Before you file, you will want to consider the demographics of each jurisdiction. Fulton County, for instance, is far more liberal and racially diverse than the ten-county area your jurors would be drawn from if you filed in federal court, so you are far more likely to get racial minorities and liberal jurors on a Fulton County jury than a federal jury.

On the other hand, if the incident occurred in Georgia's Cherokee County, which is 86% white, you may want to file in federal court, which is certainly more diverse than Cherokee County.

Judges

As noted above, federal district court judges are appointed by the President and serve for life, while state court judges are either elected or appointed and serve for specific terms after which they have to be reappointed or re-elected.

So what does this mean for you? What difference does it make for your lawsuit? That's a complicated question. One thing to remember is that the federal Civil Rights Act was originally passed in 1871 because state courts, with elected judges, were often seen as hostile to civil rights. So Congress provided federal jurisdiction for civil rights claims. Things have changed since then, but you should look closely at your state and federal court and consider what kind of jury and what kind of judge you may want for your case.

I prefer to file in federal court because I am more comfortable and familiar with the federal rules. Federal court is far less chaotic than state court, which handles far more cases. Also, because there are fewer cases in federal court, the judges are more familiar with each individual case and, in my experience, are better at enforcing discovery deadlines than state court judges. Federal civil rights claims also include a fee-shifting statute, which means if the plaintiff wins at trial, the attorney can file a petition for reasonable costs and attorneys' fees to be paid by the losing defendant. Obviously, this does not apply to *pro se* litigants.

Federal civil rights claims include the possibility of punitive damages. It can be far more challenging to seek punitive damages in state court. Also, while you can file federal claims in state court, the case may be removed to federal court anyway, so if you want to maintain claims under the U.S. Constitution, you might want to just file in federal court and save the hassle.

Look carefully at what it would mean to file in your local state court as compared to filing in your local federal court, as there is no simple answer.

Supplemental Jurisdiction

As discussed earlier, if you file a federal claim in state court, even if you file it along with state law claims, the defendant can remove the case to federal court. But it does not work the other way—you can file state law claims in federal court as long as you also have at least one federal claim, and they cannot be removed to state court by the defendant. These state law claims are called **supplemental** or **pendant claims**. The defendant cannot remove a federal case to state court, so you can stay in federal court as long as the case is active and at least one of your claims involves a federal question. A plaintiff can file supplemental state law claims in federal court as long as at least one claim is based on federal law.

Chapter Recap

Be strategic about whether you file your case in federal court or state court. One of the major differences between state court and federal court is the jury pools. State courts draw their jurors from one county only, while federal courts draw jurors from multiple counties. It is generally easier to seek punitive damages under federal law than under state law.

Federal Courts

- The key players in federal district courts are federal district judges and magistrate judges. Federal judges are appointed for life.

- There are two ways to get your case into federal court:

  - **Federal Question Jurisdiction**, which applies to cases based on alleged violations of federal law

  - **Diversity Jurisdiction** for cases involving parties from different states

State Courts

- Most state courts are organized by county.

- Each county has its own court system, but they are all part of the larger court system operated by the state.

- A plaintiff can file federal claims in state court, but those claims may be removed (i.e. transferred) to federal court by the defendant.

- State court judges may be appointed or elected, but they do not serve for life.

- Laws, rules, and procedures differ from state to state, so make sure you check the state court website and rules for your own state.

Pleadings

KEY SOURCES OF LAW

- FRCP 3: Commencing an Action

- FRCP 4: Summons

- FRCP 7: Pleadings Allowed; Form of Motions and Other Papers

- FRCP 8: General Rules of Pleading

- FRCP 11: Signing Pleadings, Motions, and Other Papers; Representations to the Court; Sanctions

- FRCP 12: Defenses and Objections

- FRCP 38: Right to a Jury Trial; Demand

- *Bell Atlantic Corporation v. Twombly*, 550 U.S. 544 (2007)

- *Ashcroft v. Iqbal*, 556 U.S. 662 (2009

DO YOUR HOMEWORK

This chapter relies primarily on federal rules for lawsuits in federal court. State laws and rules are often similar to the federal rules, but of course they will differ to some degree. The basic principles outlined in this chapter should be the same in every state, but make sure you check your state's laws and rules for specifics if you want to file in state court.

The term "pleadings" is used to describe court papers generally. Pleadings documents might include **motions** (formal requests made to a judge or court), **briefs** (legal documents submitted to court that present legal arguments), **complaints** (a formal legal document that initiates a lawsuit)**,** and **answers** (a formal written response filed by the defendant in a civil lawsuit in which they admit or deny the allegations made against them).

In the context of litigation, the "pleadings" stage refers to the period of time beginning with the filing of the complaint, all the way through the filing of the answer or other responsive document, such as a motion to dismiss.

Let's start with the complaint, which is the document that initiates a lawsuit:

SPECIAL RULES FOR EMPLOYMENT CASES

There are very specific rules for filing employment discrimination cases. See Chapter 15.

Drafting The Complaint

The key rule governing complaints and answers is FRCP 8. Here's what that means to you:

The complaint, as its name suggests, is a series of statements (known as "allegations") complaining about the wrongful acts committed by the defendant(s) against the plaintiff. The purpose of a complaint is to inform the defendants what the plaintiff claims they did wrong, how their actions violated the plaintiff's rights, or otherwise violated a legal standard, how these actions harmed the plaintiff, and what the plaintiff wants out of the lawsuit (known as a prayer for relief). The complaint is organized by numbered paragraphs.

Know The Legal Requirements Of A Complaint.

Under FRCP 8, a complaint must contain three things:

1. A short and plain statement of the grounds for the court's jurisdiction, unless the court already has jurisdiction and the claim needs no new jurisdictional support;

2. A short and plain statement of the claim showing that the pleader is entitled to relief;

3. A demand for the relief sought, which may include relief in the alternative or different types of relief

In other words, a complaint has to answer three questions:

1. Why is the lawsuit here in federal court (jurisdiction), and why is it in this federal district (venue)?

2. What did the defendants do wrong? (Legal and factual allegations)

3. What do you want out of this lawsuit? (Prayer for relief)

And that's it! That's the whole enchilada.

DEMAND A JURY

The Seventh Amendment guarantees a trial by jury in civil cases. To get your jury, you have to include a jury demand in your complaint, or within 14 days of serving the last pleading. FRCP 38. You can always withdraw a jury demand, but as long as one party properly demands a jury, it will be a jury trial. That being said, there are certain rare cases where a jury trial might be denied, such as a claim for injunctive relief. All you have to do is say "The Plaintiff demands trial by jury", or anything to that effect somewhere in your complaint, ideally at the end.

Two U.S. Supreme Court cases, *Bell Atlantic Corporation v. Twombly*, and *Ashcroft v. Iqbal*, tell us how specific a federal complaint needs to be. Under these cases, a complaint must contain facts that, if true, would plausibly entitle the plaintiff to relief.

As an example, a complaint alleging false arrest might say:

- **Officer Smith arrested Plaintiff Bob on January 12, 2022 for burglary without probable cause to believe Bob had committed a burglary.**

The fact that Officer Smith arrested Plaintiff Bob on January 12, 2022, is a fact. But the assertion that the arrest was without probable cause is a legal conclusion. It's fine to say that, but Bob still needs to assert facts establishing the lack of probable cause. Simply stating the arrest was without probable cause is not enough.

Here's an example of a factual allegation:

- **Officer Smith arrested Plaintiff Bob on January 12, 2022 for burglary despite knowing that the victim's description of the burglar did not match Bob.**

This is a completely factual allegation. The plaintiff here is stating facts which, if proven true, would entitle him to relief. Remember, it's okay to plead conclusions. We do it all the time to state the legal requirements of a particular cause of action. But a plaintiff must also plead facts establishing those conclusions. So you can say that "Defendant Smith arrested Bob without probable cause," but you must also include facts in your complaint establishing that there was no probable cause. These facts do not need to be particularly detailed, but they must be factual rather than conclusory.

The complaint does not have to be a masterpiece, and it should not be excessively long. It does not need to contain legal mumbo-jumbo. The less mumbo, the better. In fact, complaints do not even have to be typed. They can be handwritten, although I would not recommend that unless you have no other choice. If your handwriting is like mine, you will want to spend money on a word processor.

There is no magic format for a complaint. Some complaints tend to be very simple and short, while others are more structured.

You could divide your complaints into sections, including:

- **INTRODUCTION**

  A broad explanation of the allegations. I would only include this if the case is particularly complex.

- **JURISDICTION AND VENUE**

  Explanation of why the court has jurisdiction to hear the case. This can be done in a sentence or two.

  Here's a sample statement explaining federal jurisdiction:

  This case arises under the Fourth Amendment to the United States Constitution and is expressly authorized by 42 U.S.C. § 1983 as a civil action to redress the deprivation of rights under color of state law. Accordingly, this Court has jurisdiction over this case pursuant to 28 U.S.C. §§1331 and 1343.

  Here's a sample statement explaining venue – why the case is in the appropriate federal district court:

  "Venue is proper in the United States District Court for the District of South Carolina under Title 28 of the United States Code, § 1391(b)(2), as the events complained of occurred within this district."

- **PARTIES**

  Introduction to the plaintiff and the defendant(s) with relevant information.

Example:

1. At all times relevant, Plaintiff BOB JONES (hereinafter "Bob") was a resident of the County of Beaufort, State of South Carolina.

2. Defendant, HILTON HEAD ISLAND is a government entity operating within the State of South Carolina. The CITY OF HILTON HEAD ISLAND is responsible for the actions of its employees while acting within the scope of their employment. At all times relevant to this action, CITY OF HILTON HEAD ISLAND was the employer of Defendant SMITH.

3. Defendant SMITH is sued in his individual capacity and was at all times relevant, a police detective employed by Defendant CITY OF HILTON HEAD ISLAND, and was acting within the scope of his agency, service and/or employment with the CITY OF HILTON HEAD ISLAND, and was acting under color of the statutes, ordinances, regulations, customs, and usages of the State of South Carolina

- **FACTS**

This is where you tell the story of the case, fact by fact. Each factual paragraph should consist of a single, simple fact. Remember, the defendant has to admit or deny each statement, or state he lacks knowledge. You want to force the defendant to admit any fact that must be admitted. This can be particularly effective when you have video, or when you have a good fact in a police report. I prefer more detailed facts. It helps me frame the case in my mind, and as noted above, it can be helpful in getting admissions right out of the gate if the facts are stated in simple, declarative statements. But other attorneys – including very well-respected attorneys – prefer to make their complaints much simpler and more basic.

Remember, the jury will never see your complaint. It is simply a legal document intended for a specific purpose.

- **LEGAL CLAIMS (divided into specific counts)**

  I like to separate out the specific allegations, such as excessive force, false arrest, and malicious prosecution. If you do this, it's important to include a statement at the beginning of each count that all preceding allegations are incorporated by reference. You also need to make sure you include the legal elements required by that cause of action. As you'll see below, articulating specific legal counts is not legally required, but it can help to frame the issues in a case.

- **PRAYER FOR RELIEF**

  This is where you articulate what you want out of the case.

  "For the foregoing reasons, the Plaintiff prays for judgment against Defendants, in a fair and reasonable amount, including compensatory damages, punitive damages and costs, and for any additional relief this Court deems just and proper."

Other complaints are much more brief. Many complaints do not contain specific counts for legal claims. The legal claims are contained in one or two simple paragraphs:

"As a result of the foregoing, all of the defendants caused plaintiffs to be deprived of rights secured by the Fourth and Fourteenth Amendments."

Examples of both types of complaints are included in the appendix.

Bottom line: the format of the complaint is up to you. Just make sure the facts sufficiently place the defendants on notice as to what you allege they did wrong.

Don't Plead Yourself Out Of Court

Factual assertions in a filed pleading, including a complaint, are treated as judicial admissions of the party filing the pleading. That means they are not disputed issues in the case, and will be considered as true, unless the plaintiff properly seeks to withdraw the assertion under FRCP 15.

If a plaintiff makes a factual assertion in a complaint that has the effect of defeating his legal claim, he has effectively "pleaded himself out of court." For instance, if a plaintiff asserts in his complaint that the incident occurred on a date that is more than two years before the complaint was filed, he may be demonstrating that that the complaint was filed too late, depending on the Statute of Limitations. So, you need to think carefully about the facts you're going to assert before filing the complaint. If you realize that a certain fact defeats your claim, then you need to think about whether you have a valid claim in the first place.

Rule 11: Keep It Real

Federal Rule of Civil Procedure 11 is the law's way of saying that your pleadings must be based on evidence and valid arguments. Rule 11 says that if you sign a pleading (including any legal document you file), you'd better know what you're talking about, both legally and factually. Under Rule 11, "every pleading, written motion, and other paper must be signed by at least one attorney of record in the attorney's name—*or by a party personally if the party is unrepresented.*" By signing these documents, you represent to the court that:

1) the pleading is not being presented for any improper purpose.

2) the legal arguments in the pleading are supported by existing law or by a valid argument for changing the law.

3) the facts in the pleading are supported by evidence, and

4) denials of another party's factual allegations are supported by evidence.

Most if not all states have similar rules. For instance, Ohio Civil Rule 11 states that "[t]he signature of an attorney or *pro se* party constitutes a certificate by the attorney or party that the attorney or party has read the document; that to the best of the attorney's or party's knowledge, information, and belief there is good ground to support it; and that it is not interposed for delay." If this rule is violated, the document may be stricken as if it had never been filed, and the offending party may be sanctioned if the violation is willful.

Bottom line: Don't make things up. Don't make frivolous arguments. Even as an unrepresented party, you could get into serious judicial hot water if you litigate dishonestly. If you violate Rule 11, or your state court's equivalent, you could be sanctioned, meaning you may be ordered to pay a financial penalty to the court, or pay reasonable attorney's fees to the other side, or the court may enter an order making it more difficult to win your case.

Be As Specific As You Can

If defendants think your complaint is too vague, they might move to dismiss it, claiming it fails to put them on notice as to what you are claiming each of them did. If you file against a number of defendants, but are not able to specify exactly what each of them did and what role each of them had in violating your rights, the defendants may move to dismiss your complaint, arguing that you engaged in something called **group pleading**, which means suing a group of defendants without telling them what each of them did.

This argument has some merit. A lawsuit against multiple defendants is essentially multiple individual lawsuits that are part of the same case because they all arose from the same set of facts. Case law requires that each defendant in a civil rights lawsuit have personal involvement in the alleged misconduct. So you have to do the best you can to be as specific as possible in identifying the misconduct of each defendant.

But sometimes you don't have that much information. Ironically, the defendants, who know exactly what they did, will complain that the plaintiff, who doesn't have the same access to information, is not being specific enough about what the defendants did.

Fortunately, the courts understand this problem.

Here's a great quote from a case decided by the Seventh Circuit Court of Appeals:

> **"We do not think that the children's game of pin the tail on the donkey is a proper model for constitutional tort law. If a prisoner makes allegations that if true indicate a significant likelihood that someone employed by the prison system has inflicted cruel and unusual punishment on him, and if the circumstances are such**

as to make it infeasible for the prisoner to identify that someone before filing his complaint, his suit should not be dismissed as frivolous. The principle is not limited to prisoner cases. It applies to any case in which, usually because the plaintiff has been injured as the consequence of the actions of an unknown member of a collective body, identification of the responsible party may be impossible without pretrial discovery…"

Rodriguez v. Plymouth Ambulance Service, 577 F.3d 816, 821 (7th Cir. 2009).

In the paragraph above, the appellate court acknowledges the limitations plaintiffs often have in knowing exactly who did what. Plaintiffs should not be forced to guess blindly which officials committed which act. But you should still be as specific as possible in identifying the correct defendants and explaining what they did wrong.

After Drafting The Complaint

File Your Civil Cover Sheet.

The **civil cover sheet** is a very busy document you'll find on the court's website. You must fill it out and file it to tell the clerk's office what kind of case you're filing. This is how the Clerk's office knows how to categorize your case. The civil cover sheet contains all the basic information about the case being filed.

As a self-represented party, the Clerk's office may help you complete this form, or they may do it themselves. Some courts will allow *pro se* litigants to skip the civil cover sheet. Check out the court's website for specific rules for *pro se* litigants. It's never a bad idea to contact the Clerk's office for the district court you'll be filing in. I've dealt with many different Clerks' offices, and they have always been extremely helpful and friendly.

Submit Your Summons…

A **summons** is a two-page notice to each defendant informing the defendant of the lawsuit and explaining when and where the defendant needs to appear and file an answer or other responsive document. The summons must be **issued** (approved and stamped) by the Clerk's Office. Each Clerk's office does it a bit differently.

Normally, once you've drafted the summons, you email it to the Clerk's office for the specific court you're filing in. The Clerk's office reviews your summons and either lets you know what's incorrect and needs to be changed, or simply sends back the summons with their stamp and seal. Sometimes they will also file the summons for you. Check with the Clerk's office in your jurisdiction to find out how they handle this.

...Or Use A Waiver

A **waiver of service of summons** can be used instead of a summons, if the defendant agrees to accept it. You can mail a waiver to the defendant, and if the defendant does not respond within 30 days, you will serve the summons and you can ask the court to make the defendant pay the costs of service. If a defendant agrees to accept the waiver, they will have 60 days from the date the waiver was sent to respond instead of 21 days with service of the summons. Most defendants will often agree to accept a waiver because it gives them more time to respond.

File Your Complaint

In the federal system, litigants are required to file all documents using the PACER/CM/ECF system. "**PACER**" stands for Public Access to Court Electronic Records. **CM/ECF** means Case Management/ Electronic Court Files. This used to be two different systems. You would use PACER to view filed documents, and you would use CM/ ECF to file documents. Now they are combined and simply referred to as PACER.

PACER is extremely useful. You can always jump on PACER and view or download all filings in the case, including filings by the parties as well as order from the court. You can see all the parties and attorneys and their contact information, and you can file documents. If you are a registered PACER user with an **Appearance** filed in a particular case, you will receive an email every time anything is filed in that case, including pleadings and court orders. The email has a link to the document that was filed.

You will be charged a certain amount of money for certain things, like pulling up a docket report and opening/downloading a document. Typically, you can download a document you get from a link on an email for free, but downloading directly from the PACER website will cost you. However, some courts may waive your costs if you cannot afford it. Call your local Clerk's office to confirm.

To create an account,go to https://pacer.uscourts.gov/. If you have any questions, you can call (800) 676-6856, unless you're in San Antonio, where you call (210) 301-6440. I'm not sure why San Antonio is so special, but apparently the PACER people think it is. PACER offers training, and may even require that you be trained in order to register.

Your first step should be to check out the court's website and look for a link for *pro se* or unrepresented litigants. Some courts have specific rules for filing as a *pro se* litigant that make it easier for you to file. On the other hand, some courts prohibit electronic filing by *pro se* litigants, at least initially.

State courts all have their own filing systems. Most if not all state courts offer some form of e-filing, although it may not be as robust as PACER, which is strictly for federal court.

Pay Your Filing Fees If You Can

Filing fees in federal court are around $400. If you cannot afford this, you can apply to file *"in forma pauperis"*, which means "In the manner of a pauper".

Under U.S. Law (28 USC § 1915), a court may (but is not required to) allow a person to proceed without paying filing fees. This is discretionary with the court, meaning it is the judge's decision. If you want to proceed *in forma pauperis*, you must fill out a form and an **affidavit** (examples in the appendix) stating all of your assets to show that you cannot afford to pay the filing fee. If you are allowed to proceed *in forma pauperis*, there are specific procedures to follow, and service of process may be different. You should check your court's website and local rules for specific information on how to proceed *in forma pauperis*.

Prisoners are not eligible to file *in forma pauperis*. Under the Prison Litigation Reform Act ("**PLRA**") (discussed more thoroughly in Chapter 13), prisoners must pay filing fees, even if they cannot afford them. The court is required by law to deduct certain amounts from the prisoner's account until the fee is fully paid. However, a prisoner can still file an action before all the fees are paid.

Remember that the PLRA applies only if the plaintiff is incarcerated in a jail or prison *at the time he files his case.* So if you are going to be released shortly, and you still have time left before your SOL runs, you may want to wait to file until after your release. For purposes of the PLRA, being on parole or probation does not count as being incarcerated, so you will not be subject to the PLRA if you file while out on parole, while you are on probation, or even if you are on electronic monitoring.

Service Of Process

Service of process is the formal delivery of the summons and complaint to the defendant. The summons provides notice to the defendant of the lawsuit and informs the defendant of his or her legal obligations to respond to the complaint. In the federal system, service of process is governed by FRCP 4(c). Once the defendant is properly served, the defendant is now under the court's jurisdiction and must respond to the lawsuit within a certain amount of time, usually 21 days from the date he or she is served with the lawsuit.

If you are a prisoner, the judge assigned to your case will usually direct the U.S. Marshal to serve your summons and complaint for you.

Who Should Serve Process?

First, let's clarify who should *not* serve process: you. A party is usually not permitted to serve process.

So who *can* serve process? Normally, any adult who is not a party can serve process. There is an entire industry of people who do this for a fee, known as process servers. Most process servers are also licensed private investigators. It shouldn't cost more than $50 - $100 for a process server to serve a summons and complaint (or a subpoena), but prices can vary depending on the circumstances.

To find a process server near you, check out the website for the National Association of Professional Process Servers, where you can put in an address or zip code and find nearby process servers: https://napps.org/.

In state court, the requirements for service of process may be different, depending on the state. For instance, in Illinois, you normally have to use (and pay) the sheriff to serve process, although you can have a special process server do it instead. In Cook County (Illinois' largest county), if you don't use the sheriff, you have to file a motion to appoint a special process server, which means a licensed private investigator. In other counties, you can use a special process server without filing a motion. Check your state laws for specifics.

Don't Delay Service Of Process

In federal court, a defendant must be served within 90 days after the complaint is filed, or the case may be dismissed without prejudice. FRCP 4(m). State courts have different rules for when you have to serve the defendant, but whether you're in federal or state court, you should get your service completed as soon as you can after you file the complaint. There's no reason to delay.

Answer Or Otherwise Plead

A defendant normally has 21 days to **answer or otherwise plead**. This means the defendant has 21 days to file an answer to the complaint ("answer") or file a motion to dismiss part or all of the complaint ("otherwise plead"). An answer is usually a point-by-point response to the allegations in your complaint. A motion to dismiss is a request by the defendant to dismiss the complaint, in which the defendant argues the allegations in the complaint are not sufficient to state a valid claim under the law.

Answer

In an Answer, a defendant is allowed to 1) Admit, 2) Deny, or 3) Claim lack of knowledge to each and every allegation. This is governed by FRCP 8.

Rule 8 also allows a defendant to issue a general denial instead of responding to each allegation. In my experience, it is rare for a defendant to issue a general denial. You're more likely to see a general denial if you file a lot of allegations against a lot of defendants.

If a defendant issues a general denial, or any answer you feel is not legally sufficient, you can file a motion to strike the answer, explaining why it is deficient, and requesting the answer be stricken and the allegations be deemed (i.e. considered) admitted. If the judge agrees with you, he or she will likely strike certain parts of the answer, and allow the defendant to file amended answers by a certain date. But you're not going to win the case on this. Think about whether filing such a motion will truly benefit you, or whether it's just busywork.

A defendant can also issue a general denial along with admissions of only certain allegations.

Legal Effect Of An Answer

If a defendant admits an allegation in an Answer, that is known as a *binding judicial admission,* meaning it is no longer a disputed issue in the case, and will be considered as true, unless the defendant properly seeks to withdraw the admission under FRCP 15.

If the party that made the admission ever tries to contradict an answer in a deposition, answers to interrogatories, or at trial, you can move to strike the response.

Forms of Answers

Most defendants will include the allegations as part of the answer, like this:

> **14. Defendant Officer Jones used excessive force against Plaintiff.**

> <u>ANSWER:</u> **Defendants deny the allegations contained in this paragraph.**

Other defendants will simply provide a list of responses by paragraph number without including the original allegations, so the plaintiff must figure out which allegation each response relates to, like this:

> 14. Defendants deny the allegations contained in Paragraph 14 of the Complaint.

> 15. Defendants deny the allegations contained in Paragraph 15 of the Complaint.

> 16. Defendants admit the allegations in Paragraph 16 of the Complaint.

It's annoying, and bad practice in my opinion. But it is allowed, so you have to deal with it.

PRACTICE TIP

When a defendant answers without including the original allegations, I highlight each paragraph of the filed Complaint based on the specific answer to each allegation. Green is **Admit**, Red is **Deny**, Yellow is **lack sufficient knowledge**, and Gray is **OTHER**. Of course, you can use any code you want. That way you can easily reference how the defendant responded to a particular allegation without looking at two separate documents.

Affirmative Defenses

An **Affirmative Defense** is a factual and/or legal assertion by a defendant that the defendant asserts defeats the plaintiff's claim, even if the plaintiff's facts are true. The defendant will have the burden of proving his Affirmative Defenses just like the plaintiff will have the burden of proving his allegations. Affirmative defenses are normally filed in the same document as the answer to the complaint.

So what does it mean to *"otherwise plead"?*

When people in the law say a defendant may "answer or otherwise plead", they mean the defendant can file an answer or file a motion, usually a motion to dismiss the complaint.

Motion To Dismiss

A **motion to dismiss** in federal court is normally filed under FRCP 12(b)(6), which allows a defendant to argue that the complaint *fails to state a claim upon which relief can be granted,* which means that even if the factual allegations in the complaint are accepted as true, the plaintiff cannot win under the law.

In a motion to dismiss, the court can only accept "well-pleaded facts" as true. As discussed earlier in this chapter, a "well-pleaded fact" means a truly factual statement, rather than a conclusion, although the facts do not need to be particularly detailed. What is the difference between a factual allegation and a conclusory allegation? That often depends on what your judge thinks, so try to be as factual as possible.

When a motion to dismiss is granted, the court will usually dismiss the complaint *without prejudice,* meaning the plaintiff can amend the complaint and file it again if she is able to fix the problems that caused the court to dismiss the complaint.

LEGAL STANDARD FOR A MOTION TO DISMISS UNDER FRCP 12(b)(6)

The **legal standard** is the portion of a legal brief that informs the court of the primary legal principles governing that particular type of motion. Here is a good summary of the legal standard for a motion to dismiss from a recent case in the Northern District of Illinois:

> A Rule 12(b)(6) motion challenges the "sufficiency of the complaint." *Gunn v. Cont'l Cas. Co.*, 968 F.3d 802, 806 (7th Cir. 2020). A complaint must provide "a short and plain statement of the claim showing that the pleader is entitled to relief," Fed.R.Civ.P. 8(a)(2), sufficient to provide defendant with "fair notice" of the claim and the basis for it. *Bell Atl. Corp. v. Twombly*, 550 U.S. 544, 555 (2007). This standard "demands more than an unadorned, the-defendant-unlawfully-harmed-me accusation." *Ashcroft v. Iqbal*, 556 U.S. 662, 678 (2009). While "detailed factual allegations" are not required, "labels and conclusions, and a formulaic recitation of the elements of a cause of action will not do." *Twombly*, 550 U.S. at 555.
>
> The complaint must "contain sufficient factual matter, accepted as true, to 'state a claim to relief that is plausible on its face.'" *Iqbal*, 556 U.S. at 678 (quoting *Twombly*, 550 U.S. at 570). "Facial plausibility exists 'when the plaintiff pleads factual content that allows the court to draw the reasonable inference that the defendant is liable for the misconduct alleged.'" *Thomas v. Neenah Joint Sch. Dist.*, 74 F.4th 521, 523 (7th Cir. 2023) (quoting *Iqbal*, 556 U.S. at 678). In applying this standard, the Court accepts all well-pleaded facts as true and draws all reasonable inferences in favor of the non-moving party. *See Hernandez v. Ill. Inst. of Tech.*, 63 F.4th 661, 666 (7th Cir. 2023).

Klauber Bros. v. The P'ships & Unincorporated Ass'ns identified in Schedule "A", 23 C 10407, at *12-13 (N.D. Ill. Jan. 17, 2024).

Chapter Recap

Legal Requirements Of A Complaint

Under FRCP 8, a complaint must answer three questions:

1. Why is the lawsuit here in federal court (jurisdiction), and why is it in this federal district (venue)?
2. What did the defendants do wrong?
3. What do you want out of this lawsuit?

Plead Facts

Under Supreme Court case law, a complaint must contain facts that if true, would plausibly entitle the plaintiff to relief. Legal conclusions are not sufficient to state a claim. You need to plead facts to establish a legal cause of action.

Format Of A Complaint

There's no magic format to a complaint. Some are very short and simple. Others are more structured, with an introduction, sections explaining jurisdiction, identification of parties, factual allegations, specific legal claims, and a prayer for relief.

Rule 11 – Keep It Real

FRCP 11 requires that all lawyers and self-represented parties sign all pleadings, which represents to the Court that:

1. the pleading is not being presented for any improper purpose;
2. the legal arguments in the pleading are supported by existing law or by a valid argument for changing the law;
3. the facts in the pleading are supported by evidence; and
4. denials of another party's factual allegations are supported by evidence.

Violation of Rule 11 can result in severe penalties, including financial sanctions.

Avoid Group Pleading

Group pleading means that a complaint is not specific enough about what each individual defendant did to violate the plaintiff's rights. But courts understand that plaintiffs often do not have enough information before they engage in discovery.

Filing Your Complaint

Once your Complaint is drafted, you will need to take the following steps:

File your Civil Cover Sheet.

This form, available on the court's website, categorizes your case for the Clerk's office. Complete it and file it with the Clerk's office. Some courts may allow *pro se* litigants to skip this step.

Submit your Summons or use a waiver.

Draft a summons to inform defendants about the lawsuit and when to respond. Email it to the Clerk's office, which reviews and stamps it. Alternatively, use a waiver of service if the defendant agrees.

File Your Complaint via PACER.

Use the PACER system to file all documents electronically. PACER allows you to view, download, and file documents related to your case. Register on the PACER website, pay associated fees, and follow court-specific rules. If possible, pay the filing fees, which are around $400 in federal court. Alternatively, apply to file *"in forma pauperis"* if you cannot afford the fees.

Serve the Defendants with Process

Serve the summons and complaint to the defendant formally. The defendant must respond within a certain timeframe, usually 21 days from service. Choose an adult who is not a party to serve the process. Alternatively, hire a licensed process server. Each state may have specific requirements for service of process. Serve the defendant within the required timeframe to prevent dismissal of the case.

Defendant's Response

Defendants have 21 days to "answer or otherwise plead", unless the plaintiff uses a waiver of service of summons, in which case a defendant has 60 days to answer or otherwise plead. The defendant can file an answer admitting, denying, or claiming lack of knowledge to the allegations, or file a motion to dismiss. Defendants may assert affirmative defenses, which are factual or legal assertions that defeat the plaintiff's claim. Defendants may also file a motion to dismiss under FRCP 12(b)(6), arguing that the complaint fails to state a valid claim. If granted, the court may dismiss the complaint without prejudice, allowing the plaintiff to amend and refile it.

NOTE: Defendants will often ask the plaintiff for additional time to answer the complaint, because 21 days is not much time for the lawyers to receive the complaint and conduct a sufficient investigation to be able to answer each allegation. You should grant reasonable requests for extensions, for reasons we will discuss later in the book.

Discovery

KEY SOURCES OF LAW

- FRCP 16: Pretrial Conferences; Scheduling; Management

- FRCP 26: Duty to Disclose; General Provisions Governing Discovery

- FRCP 30: Depositions by Oral Examination

- FRCP 31: Depositions by Written Questions

- FRCP 33: Interrogatories to Parties

- FRCP 34: Production of Documents and Other Materials

- FRCP 35: Physical and Mental Examinations

- FRCP 36: Requests for Admission

- FRCP 37: Failure to Make Disclosures or to Cooperate in Discovery; Sanctions

- FRCP 45: Subpoenas

What Is Discovery?

Discovery is how the parties find out information and obtain materials from other parties as we as **non-parties** - people and organizations who are not part of the lawsuit but who possess relevant information. Discovery is the meat of the case. This is how you create the **evidentiary record** for the case. The evidentiary record is the collection of all the evidence related to a case, including deposition testimony, other sworn testimony, affidavits, declarations, answers to interrogatories and requests for admission, documents, video and audio footage, and other tangible materials related to the case. The evidence obtained in discovery is what the parties will use to support or defend a summary judgment motion, and to support their claims or defenses during the trial.

The different methods of discovery fall into three buckets:

1.   Written discovery

- **Rule 26 initial disclosures** (FRCP 26(a)(1)) are disclosures each party makes in writing by a certain date specified in the Court's scheduling order or discovery plan, usually within a few weeks of the entry of the scheduling order/ discovery plan.

- **Interrogatories** (FRCP 33) are written questions by each party to other parties that must be answered under oath, in writing. A sample set of interrogatories and interrogatory responses is included in the appendix. Each party is limited to 25 interrogatories to each other party without **leave of court** (without the court's permission).

- **Requests for production** (FRCP 34) This is how each party requests specific documents and other materials (video, audio, emails, text messages, etc.) from the other parties. There is no limit to the number of production requests a party can make.

- **Requests for Admission** (FRCP 36) is how parties request other parties to either admit or deny specific facts. This can be an extremely powerful tool, and a big money-saver!

2.   Subpoenas

A subpoena (FRCP 45) is the discovery tool parties use to obtain information from people and entities that are not associated with the lawsuit (a.k.a. "non-parties"). A subpoena is essentially a court order, except that it is issued by a party or a party's attorney. A subpoena can be issued to request documents or other materials such as video footage (called a "**subpoena** *duces tecum*", because "**document subpoena**" would make too much sense), or to request the deposition of someone (called a "deposition subpoena" because they couldn't figure out how to say it in Latin). Both of these subpoena types are contained in the Appendix.

3. Oral discovery

- **Depositions** (FRCP 30) are essentially question-and-answer sessions, similar to interviews. These occur between a lawyer or a self-represented party and a witness. Depositions normally take place in conference rooms or remotely through services like Zoom, away from the courthouse, and without a judge. The witness in a deposition gives answers under oath.

When Do We Start Conducting Discovery?

Discovery normally begins after the pleadings stage, although there can be some overlap. The pleadings stage includes filing and serving the complaint, answering the complaint, and filing and responding to motions to dismiss. If a defendant files a motion to dismiss, discovery may not begin until after the court rules on the motion. However, if the motion to dismiss is only addressed to certain claims, the judge may allow discovery on the other claims.

Parties may not engage in discovery (meaning they cannot send out discovery requests or subpoenas or take depositions) until the **Rule 16 conference**, which will be scheduled by the judge. The Rule 16 conference (named for FRCP 16) is a meeting between the judge and the attorneys or unrepresented parties to discuss the **scheduling order**, which contains deadlines to complete discovery, amend the complaint, and name additional parties. The Rule 16 conference is usually scheduled a month or two after the complaint is filed.

The scheduling order (sometimes referred to as a **discovery plan** or a **joint status report**) is the court's way of making sure the case moves along. It governs the litigation going forward. If you need to extend the dates in the scheduling order, you must file a motion to extend the dates *before the deadline to do what you want more time to do*. If you file the motion after that date, it may be denied. The parties often agree to file a joint motion to extend the time to complete discovery, because everyone is busy, and discovery usually takes longer than first anticipated.

The judge will likely require that a proposed scheduling order be filed a few days before the Rule 16 conference. The proposed scheduling order is filed after the parties get together and try to agree on the deadlines they want for the case. Then, one of the parties will file the proposed scheduling order with the court. Once it is filed, the judge will often **vacate (cancel)** the actual conference and adopt the dates agreed to by the parties in the scheduling order. Different judges do it differently. Make sure you check your judge's **standing order** or the Court's **Local Rules** (on the court's website) to see how your assigned judge – or your district court – prefers to do this. Often, the standing order will contain a sample of how the judge wants the scheduling order to look.

Scheduling Orders Will Contain The Following Information:

- Identification of all parties and attorneys

- Status of service (have all parties been served and have they all appeared?)

- Basic description of the case, including major legal and factual disputes

- Basis for jurisdiction of the court to hear the case

- What motions have been filed

- Proposed discovery schedule

- Status of settlement discussions

- Whether the parties all agree to use a magistrate judge instead of the assigned district judge for the entire case. In that case, all parties must agree to use a magistrate judge. If all parties do not agree, the district judge will handle the case, although the district judge may refer some aspects of the case – such as managing discovery – to the magistrate judge.)

As noted above, different courts and different judges do it differently. Some judges do not require all of this information. Again, check the Court's website for applicable local rules and/or your assigned judge's standing orders.

STATE COURT: Different state courts will have varying procedures for scheduling discovery, but most courts should have some sort of case management order filed at the beginning of the case to set deadlines for different parts of the case. Check your state court rules, local rules, and standing orders for specifics.

Written Discovery

Rule 26 Initial Disclosures

Rule 26 is the overarching discovery rule. You should read it carefully. Rule 26 tells us what is and what is not discoverable. It governs the isclosure of facts, opinions, and witnesses.

Under Rule 26, a party must disclose:

- The name, address and telephone number of any individual who may have discoverable information, who the disclosing party may call to support its claims or defenses. Any witness not disclosed under Rule 26 may be barred from testifying.

- Copies of all documents, electronically stored information (such as e-mails and other electronic communications and computerized records), and tangible things that the disclosing party has in its possession, custody, or control and may use to support its claims or defenses. Instead of providing copies of these items, a party may simply provide a description of them by category and location. In practice, parties normally provide these items to the other parties.

- A computation of each category of damages claimed by the disclosing party, as well as any documents or other items the party may use to support her claim of damages. In other words, a party claiming damages (usually the plaintiff) must disclose the specific categories of damages she is claiming, and explain how they calculate those damages. For example, if you are claiming lost wages, you should explain how much you are claiming in lost wages, and how you arrived at that figure. The same applies for medical or other bills. Additionally, you need to provide any documents relevant to your claim of damages.

• For defendants, any insurance policies that may be used to pay any judgment.

This rule does not require parties to disclose anyone who may have information, only witnesses favorable to their case. This is why, in your interrogatories, you will want to request the names of anyone who may have information, regardless of whether the responding party intends to use that witness to help their case.

The disclosure requirements do not include witnesses or materials you may use to impeach the credibility of any of the other party's witnesses. However, the best practice is simply to disclose everyone and everything you believe supports your case. You don't want to take a chance that your witness or evidence might be barred because you did not disclose it.

The Rule 26 disclosures must be made by each party without a request by the other party, in contrast to the other written discovery devices, which begin by one party sending specific discovery requests to another party.

Interrogatories

Interrogatories are written questions each party gets to ask each other party, which must be answered in writing and under oath. That means the party must sign the interrogatories with verification language. Interrogatories are intended for specific factual information rather than long narratives answers.

HOW CAN I EFFECTIVELY USE INTERROGATORIES?

Interrogatories are valuable for a number of different reasons. In addition to very case-specific information, interrogatories can provide the following types of information:

• Identification of witnesses

• Identification of possible defendants

- Specific activities of each defendant or potential defendant regarding the incident in question
- Identification of individuals who did certain things, such as:
  — drafted a report
  — approved a report
  Made the final employment decision
  — made specific decisions related to your case
  — provided specific information to the police or other decision-maker
- Factual basis of legal contentions, such as denials of a plaintiff's allegations or affirmative defenses
- Location of evidence, such as video footage
- What happened to specific evidence, i.e. whether certain evidence was recycled or destroyed, by whom and when it was recycled or destroyed
- Identification of specific internal rules and regulations governing the conduct at issue.
- "Contention" interrogatories, in which you can ask an opposing party its position on specific issues (for example, "at what point do you contend you had probable cause to arrest the plaintiff?")

For example, the defendant might send an interrogatory that says something like this:

- *"Identify each and every fact supporting your contention in Paragraph 14 of the Complaint that you were fired without due cause."*

Or the plaintiff might send an interrogatory that says:

- *"Identify each and every fact supporting the defendant's denial of the allegation in Paragraph 14."*

Police officers and other bureaucrats love to speak in the passive tense. For instance, instead of saying, "Officer Jones placed the subject in handcuffs", a report will say "the subject was handcuffed". Or a disciplinary allegation may say, "You were found to have engaged in misconduct at work" or something like that. Not only are these examples of bad writing, they are unhelpful if you need to know who was involved in violating your rights.

If you need to know who handcuffed you, or who determined that you committed misconduct, you can just ask in interrogatories.

Remember: do not waste your interrogatories on useless attempts to get the other side to admit what you know they will not admit, unless you have drop-dead proof, and you can lock them into impossible positions.

HOW MANY INTERROGATORIES AM I ALLOWED TO SERVE ON ANOTHER PARTY?

Most jurisdictions allow each party to serve 25 to 30 interrogatories on each other party. The Federal Rules allow a party to *"serve on any other party no more than 25 written interrogatories, including all discrete subparts." (FRCP 33(a)(1).)* Any more interrogatories requires leave of court. In other words, you'll have to file a motion for permission to serve more than 25 interrogatories to one party.

Let's break this down piece by piece, because there's a lot to unpack here.

First, remember that *each party* is allowed to serve 25 interrogatories on *each other party*. So for example if there are three plaintiffs and three defendants, each plaintiff will be able to serve 25 interrogatories to each defendant, for a total of 150 interrogatories (25 interrogatories x 6 parties = 150 interrogatories). If you sue the municipality under state law, you can serve one set of interrogatories on the municipality, and another set of *different* interrogatories on the individual officer defendant.

Try not to use all of your available interrogatories during your first set of interrogatories. It is always good to have some interrogatories available to use in case you think of something else down the road.

If you believe you really need to serve more than 25 interrogatories on another party, you can file a motion asking the court for leave to file additional interrogatories. However, judges rarely grant such motions, as you rarely truly need more than 25 interrogatories.

Always think strategically about how you use your interrogatories. If you have two sets of defendants (let's say local police officers and also county sheriff's deputies) represented by two different sets of attorneys, you may be able to get them to point the finger at each other. Under those circumstances, you might want to think about asking the same question to both sets of defendants.

I like to include a couple sections in my written discovery requests before the actual requests. The first section is called **Definitions**, and the second section is called **Rules of Construction.** You can see them in the samples in the Appendix.

WHAT DOES "INCLUDING ALL DISCRETE SUBPARTS" MEAN?

Generally speaking, if a subpart is intimately related to the main question, it will not be counted as a separate interrogatory.

For example:

Please identify each and every communication you had regarding the plaintiff's arrest, and for each such communication, please state the following:

> *a Date of communication;*
>
> *b Manner of communication (in person, by phone, by email, etc.);*
>
> *c. Summary of communication;*
>
> *d. Identify all parties to the communication.*

These subparts are all related to the main question, and will normally be counted as one interrogatory, although judges have a lot of discretion to make these determinations, so there is really no hard and fast rule.

HOW DO I USE OBJECTIONS IN RESPONDING TO INTERROGATORIES?

When deciding whether to object to an interrogatory, remember that the scope of discovery is extremely broad.

Rule 26 says:

"Parties may obtain discovery regarding any nonprivileged matter that is relevant to any party's claim or defense and proportional to the needs of the case, considering the importance of the issues at stake in the action, the amount in controversy, the parties' relative access to relevant information, the parties' resources, the importance of the discovery in resolving the issues, and whether the burden or expense of the proposed discovery outweighs its likely benefit. Information within this scope of discovery need not be admissible in evidence to be discoverable."

Fed. R. Civ. P. 26(b)(1)

That's another way of saying the scope of discovery is broad, and while the requested information must be **relevant,** it does not have to be **admissible at trial.** Generally, if the requested information *could lead to admissible evidence,* that is enough.

Often, parties will respond to a discovery request by stating a number of objections, and then provide the discovery anyway. They'll say something like, "subject to and notwithstanding said objection…" and then answer the interrogatory or provide the requested information. Lawyers never want to **waive** anything. Waiving something means you give it up because you did not raise the argument or objection at the right time. It is the legal way of saying "You snooze, you lose".

WHAT ARE BOILERPLATE OBJECTIONS?

Parties will also issue so-called **"boilerplate" objections.** That means they just throw in the same objections regardless of the request. Judges really don't like boilerplate objections.

Having said that, most discovery disputes should never get to a judge in the first place. Parties are required to try to work out any discovery disputes among themselves before asking a judge to intervene.

Requests For Production (FRCP 34)

Requests for Production of Documents is a bit misleading. "Documents" means more than just pieces of paper. It means any tangible item. You can seek any type of "thing" in a production request, including:
- Reports
- Records
- Investigative files
- Employment files
- Personnel files
- Disciplinary files
- Witness statements
- Correspondence
- Memoranda
- Photographs
- Video footage
- Audio footage
- Diagrams
- Graphs
- Charts

- Social media posts and communications
- text messages
- Emails
- Internal communications
- Phone records
- Policies, guidelines, rules and regulations

This does not mean you'll receive all of these things. The defendant may object to a request for production and withhold certain materials based on privilege, relevance, or another stated reason. So you may have to ask the court to compel production of certain requested items if they're important enough.

You can also request a site visit to a relevant location, such as a police station, a prison, or your former place of employment for employment cases.

When serving production requests, try not to be redundant. Try to organize the materials you want to request into specific categories. Here are some examples:
- Communications
- Video and audio footage
- Photos and images
- Blueprints and floor plans
- Policies, guidelines, procedures
- Training materials
- Disciplinary materials
- Personnel files

Do not assume disciplinary records will be maintained as part of someone's personnel files. These should be separate requests.

The *Monell* Advantage In Discovery

Monell claims are also known as policy and practice claims. **Monell** claims are named for the U.S. Supreme Court's decision in *Monell v. New York City Department of Social Services*, 436 U.S. 658 (1978), which holds that government entities cannot be liable under Sec. 1983 (the Civil Rights Act) unless the plaintiff can prove the municipal defendant's policies, customs, or practices caused the plaintiff's constitutional rights to be violated. A *Monell* claim alleges that the municipal defendant caused the plaintiff's rights to be violated because of a written or unwritten policy, custom or practice.

If you have a *Monell* claim, your discovery requests can be much broader. This is because *Monell* claims by definition encompass far more than just a single incident involving you—they involve other similar incidents as well.

Requests For Admission (FRCP 36)

Requests for Admission (RFAs) can be extremely useful, especially for a plaintiff. Although they are considered part of the discovery process, RFAs are not used to discover new information like the other discovery tools. The purpose of requests for admission under Rule 36 is to narrow the issues to be resolved at trial by effectively identifying and eliminating those matters on which the parties agree.

RFAs are used to obtain admissions from another party as to specific facts relevant to the case. The purpose of RFAs is to streamline litigation and avoid having to establish facts that are essentially undisputed.

Some categories of information useful for RFAs include:

- **Establishing facts contained in documents, or in video and audio footage.**

For instance:

"Admit that at 3:47 of the body camera video, Officer Johnson tells the plaintiff she is under arrest."

Once this fact is admitted, you do not need to play the video for the judge or the jury to establish that fact. You may still choose to play the video to the jury because you may decide it is more effective that way, but now you have the option of just publishing the admission. Perhaps more importantly, admissions like this can be used in a motion or a response to a motion for the judge, so you do not have to attach a copy of the video with your motion or response. Also, judges do not want to search through video footage to decide a motion.

- **Establishing the absence of facts in documents, or in video or audio footage.**

Let's say you have video of a 30-minute interaction between an officer and the plaintiff. Nowhere in that 30 minutes does the officer ever read the plaintiff her Miranda rights. Do you want to have to play the entire 30-minute video to the jury to establish that the officer never read the plaintiff her rights? No! That would be an insane waste of time, and the jury would hate you.

Don't make the jury hate you.

It would also be impractical to cross-examine the officer on that issue, because the officer could say, "I would have to see the video to be sure." Instead, establish that fact in an RFA early in the case, well before trial, and it's all done.

"Admit that Officer Bob never reads Plaintiff's Miranda rights to her on the bodycamera footage."

Then you read the admission to the jury whenever you want, and boom, you're all set. This also works for police reports and other evidentiary materials.

- **Establishing the authenticity of documents.**

"Admit that Exhibit A to this request is a true and accurate copy of the arrest report of the plaintiff's arrest."

- **Establishing facts about internal policies:**

"Admit that General Order 36-3 requires officers to include all relevant facts in the arrest report."

- **Establishing that certain facts or names are or are not contained in documents.**

"Admit that the plaintiff's name was never mentioned in the general offense case report."

"Admit that the arrest report does not contain any claim that the plaintiff resisted arrest."

One of the best ways to use an RFA is to put the other side in a difficult or impossible position. Let's say the arrest report does not contain any claim that the plaintiff resisted arrest, but the officers now claim he resisted arrest.

Do this:

"Admit the arrest report contained all relevant information regarding the plaintiff's arrest."

If the defendant admits the request, it is very difficult for him to claim the plaintiff resisted arrest. If the defendant denies the request, he is admitting that he failed to write a complete report, as required by General Order 36-3, as noted above. In other words, he is admitting he violated a police order. There is simply no good answer to this request for the defendant. This is valuable material for cross-examination, and for that reason, it increases the value of the plaintiff's case. All of this adds more power to the plaintiff's argument that 1) he did not resist arrest, and 2) the defendants are lying.

There are limitless reasons for propounding an RFA, depending on the facts of your case, and your creativity.

Tips For Requests For Admission

Tip #1 - Do not ask the other side to admit facts they are not going to admit and have no reason to admit, unless you have the other side in an impossible position. For instance, "Admit that you arrested the plaintiff without probable cause" is probably not going to help you.

Tip #2 - The other side will look for any excuse to deny the request, so make sure your request is airtight, and impossible to interpret more than one way. Think very carefully about how to phrase each request to make sure there is no way out.

Tip #3 - Make sure each request involves a single fact. If the request involves multiple facts (in legal terms, if it is a "compound" request), the other side may object and not answer the request.

For instance: *"Admit the light was red when the defendant's vehicle entered the intersection at a high rate of speed"* will probably draw a couple objections: First, it is compound, meaning it includes multiple facts. The request involves two separate facts: the color of the light and the speed of the defendant's vehicle. It also contains a conclusion: "a high rate of speed" can mean different things to different people.

So try this:

> **Request No. 1:** Admit the light was red as the defendant entered the intersection.

> **Request No. 2:** Admit the defendant's vehicle was exceeding the speed limit as it entered the intersection.

Now you've solved both problems.

Tip #4 - Do not include a conclusion in a request, only a fact. A fact is information about a circumstance or an event. A conclusion is a judgment (similar to an opinion) about a fact or set of facts. You may recall this from our earlier discussion about pleading requirements for Complaints.

Conclusion: Bob drove too fast.

Fact: Bob exceeded the speed limit.

Tip #5 - Be strategic. Only ask for admissions on issues that will be helpful in proving your case. Rule 36 contains no limitation on the number of requests a party can serve, but an RFA can be stricken if a court determines it contains an excessive number of requests. For instance, 300 requests is obviously excessive. Twenty requests is probably not excessive. Like any other discovery tool, think carefully about how best to use it, and do not overuse it.

Tip #6 - Do not use RFAs as a substitute for testimony. If you get a good admission in an RFA, and you get the same admission in a deposition, it is much better to elicit the admission from the witness directly at trial than by publishing the admission from the RFA. Live testimony from a witness is much more compelling than simply publishing a written admission. When I say "publishing", I mean reading something aloud to the jury or the judge. Of course, if that witness says something different at trial, you can **impeach** (contradict) him with his deposition testimony and the RFA admission. Think of the RFA admission as something to have in your back pocket in case you need it.

Subpoenas (FRCP 45)

A **subpoena** is a document (technically a court order) requiring an individual, or an entity such as a company, an institution, or a municipality, to produce documents or other items, to testify in a deposition (or at trial), or allow an inspection of a certain place, like an office or a jail.

The difference between a subpoena and other forms of written discovery is that while the other forms of written discovery apply to parties to a lawsuit (plaintiffs and defendants), a subpoena applies to non-parties. A subpoena is how you get information from someone or something that is not involved in the lawsuit.

There are two general types of subpoenas: **document subpoenas** (also known as subpoenas *duces tecum*, which is Latin for "you shall bring with you"), and **deposition subpoenas**.

- **A document subpoena** is just like a request for production of documents and other materials, except it is for non-parties instead of parties.

- **A deposition subpoena** requires the witness to appear for his, her, or its deposition. We'll discuss depositions in the next section.

NOTE 1: Even though subpoenas serve the same purpose for non-parties as discovery requests do for parties, they do not look the same. There are very specific court-approved forms for subpoenas. You can find these forms on the Court's website, and we also have examples in the Appendix.

NOTE 2: You cannot issue written interrogatories by subpoena. You can only seek testimony and materials.

HOW DO YOU KNOW WHETHER A PERSON OR AN ENTITY IS A PARTY TO THE LAWSUIT?

This is a surprisingly complicated question. For instance, if you sue the City of Chicago, is the Chicago Police Department a party? The answer is yes and no.

When you sue a municipality (a town, city, or village), the entire municipality is a defendant, including all departments operated by that municipality. Generally, a city's police department is part of the city government. So if the City of Chicago is a defendant, you would not use a subpoena for anything from the Chicago Police Department–you would request all police documents from the municipal defendant, the City of Chicago. It is their job to go to the appropriate City department and obtain the requested documents for you.

By that logic, you don't have to subpoena the Chicago Park District, because it's part of the City. Right?

Wrong.

The Chicago Park District is a municipality all its own, separate from the City of Chicago. So is the Chicago Housing Authority. *And* the Chicago Transit Authority! *And* the Chicago Board of Education. Also, Cook County is a different entity from the Cook County Sheriff's Office.

But that is not necessarily the case with other municipalities, especially smaller ones.

Confused yet?

If you have a question about whether a certain agency or entity is part of the municipal defendant, you have to figure out the answer before you serve discovery. First try asking the attorney for the municipal defendant, ideally in writing, so you have a record of the answer. The attorney should respond, but if they do not, a last resort is issuing discovery on the municipal defendant to ask whether a particular entity is part of the municipality.

Having said that, if you only sued individual defendants, and you did not sue the municipality, then you will need to use a subpoena to obtain documents from that municipality. Also, if you are suing prison officials employed by the state or the state's department of corrections, remember that you cannot sue the state or any department of the state, because most such suits are barred under the Eleventh Amendment to the U.S. Constitution.

However, while you cannot generally sue a state or any of its departments, you *can* sue a state employee who you claim violated your rights under the U.S. Constitution. So, for example, you can sue a correctional officer who works for the Illinois Department of Corrections ("IDOC") for violating your constitutional rights, but you cannot sue the State of Illinois or IDOC, except through the Court of Claims, which is a whole other topic.

In a lawsuit against a correctional officer, you should ask the attorney for the defendant officer if you need to subpoena the department of corrections for relevant documents or if you can request them from the officer using a Request for Production. Often, you will need a subpoena to obtain records from the department of corrections.

WHAT IS THE DIFFERENCE BETWEEN A SUBPOENA AND A DISCOVERY REQUEST?

A discovery request to another party is slightly less complicated than a subpoena. To serve a discovery request, you would send it to the attorney for the other party. This can easily be done by U.S. Mail, fax, email, or personal service.

For a subpoena, you have to figure out how the person or entity accepts service. Although Rule 45 requires personal service, many agencies will accept service by email, U.S. mail, or fax. You should contact the agency in question and ask how they accept service of subpoenas. Many agencies will have a general counsel (which is like the head lawyer) or legal department that will handle these issues.

Service of a subpoena on individuals is different. Normally, you have to use *personal service,* which means you have to have the person served by hand. The subpoena cannot be served on someone else in the house, which is known as *substitute service.* Also, for individuals, you need to include a witness fee if the subpoena requires the person's attendance. That is also true for non-individuals, but they rarely require a fee.

Witness fees are governed by the federal statute 28 United States Code § 1821, which requires witnesses to be paid attendance fees of $40 per day, plus mileage.

What is a rider?

A rider is a document you attach to a subpoena that explains exactly what you want because subpoenas contain very little room to write.

Time To Respond

The responding party has 30 days to respond to written discovery, including interrogatories, requests for production, and requests for admission. However, this is not an inflexible deadline like the statute of limitations. Often, the receiving party will reach out to the party who served the discovery and request an extension of time to answer. Almost always, the party serving the discovery will (and should) grant a reasonable extension.

Extensions Of Time

There are plenty of occasions when the other side will request an extension of time to do something: file a motion, answer or otherwise plead to the complaint, or answer discovery, for instance. Some of these require a court order, like filing an answer or a motion. Essentially, any deadline established by a court order, such as a briefing schedule, requires court approval for an extension. Responding to discovery is a bit less formal.

Any request for an extension of time to file something or respond to discovery should routinely be allowed, as long as it is reasonable and is not abusive.

For instance, a request for a 30-day extension of time to answer the complaint or to answer discovery is reasonable (although it is on the longer end of reasonable, in my opinion). I will almost always agree to a 30-day request for an extension of time. On the other hand, a six-month extension is not reasonable. I would never agree to such an extension. Multiple extensions for no articulated reason are not reasonable. In nearly every case, I will receive requests for extensions, and I almost never object. One reason is that the request, assuming it is reasonable, will almost always be granted by a judge, so why fight it? The only thing you can do by objecting to a motion that will be granted is to alienate the judge and the other side. So, why not look like the good guy or gal?

Another reason is that what comes around goes around, and you will likely need to request an extension at some point during the case. So try to abide by the golden rule – treat others as you would like them to treat you.

Finally, and perhaps most importantly, where at all possible, I try to make life easier for my opposing counsel and get along. Litigation is hard and adversarial enough without being difficult. You spend enough time fighting over things that matter. Don't spend time fighting over the other stuff. Pick your battles. Know what is important and what is not. If you can make someone else's life easier and it doesn't cost you anything, why not do it? This may sound a bit naive, especially in the competitive and adversarial world of litigation, but I believe being kind wherever possible is important *because* litigation can be so competitive and adversarial.

Oral Discovery

Depositions (FRCP 30)

Depositions, otherwise known as **oral discovery**, are essentially oral versions of interrogatories in Question and Answer format. Depositions are often the backbone of a case. Think of a deposition as an interview in which the questions and answers are recorded.

Like interrogatory responses, deposition answers are given under oath—the same oath used at any trial. Unlike interrogatories, however, depositions involve many questions and answers. In a deposition, you are not limited to a certain number of questions, but you are limited in time. In federal lawsuits, a deposition may take up to seven hours, not including breaks. In Illinois, by contrast, state court depositions are limited to three hours. These time limits can be extended by the court in response to a motion, or by agreement of the parties. But seven hours is a lot of time, and very few depositions need more than seven hours to complete.

You can take depositions of parties and non-party witnesses. In order to take the deposition of a party, you need to send a **Notice of Deposition ("NOD")** (also referred to as a "Dep Notice" in lawyer shorthand) to the other attorney or party. The Notice of Deposition includes:

- the case caption

- the name of the deponent (the person to be deposed)

- the location

- date and time of the deposition

- the method of recording

The last item is important. You have to let the other side know how the deposition will be recorded. If you plan to record the deposition by video, you have to put that in the notice. If the deposition will be audio-recorded, you have to include that as well.

Depositions may be recorded by audio, audiovisual, or stenographic means. The "stenographic" method is a certain way trained court reporters record what is said during a legal proceeding. Years ago, court reporters took shorthand notes on a pad of paper. Since then, the process has become more sophisticated. Court reporters now use machines, software, and laptops to record proceedings. They almost always audio-record the proceedings just to have a backup to refer to in case there is any question regarding what was said. Under the rule, any party may arrange to transcribe the deposition.

Traditionally, a deposition would take place in the office of the attorney who was taking the deposition. The attorney would hire a court reporter, who would be present at the deposition and take down every word that was said on the record—all of the questions, answers, objections, and arguments. From there, assuming one or more parties orders it, a **transcript** would be prepared, or a word for word record of everything that was said on the record in the deposition. Attorneys and parties can choose to go "off the record" when discussing mundane matters such as scheduling or logistics that do not need to be recorded. Those "off the record" discussions do not end up in the transcript. But all parties must agree to go off the record, so if you think you might want the conversation to be "on the record", just say you do not agree to go off the record.

Things have changed a bit since those pre-pandemic days. Many depositions–like many court appearances—are now conducted over Zoom, which makes things much easier and more convenient, especially when the parties and the witness may be in different states.

WHOSE RESPONSIBILITY IS IT TO RECORD THE DEPOSITION?

The party who initiates the deposition is required to record it (by court reporter or other method discussed below), unless the parties come to an agreement otherwise.

DO I HAVE TO HIRE A COURT REPORTER?

While I highly recommend hiring a court reporter for depositions, a court reporter is not required under Rule 30. You just need someone authorized to administer oaths, such as a notary public, and some way of recording the deposition, like a tape recorder or a video camera.

Some court reporting firms will record the deposition by video and send someone who is authorized to administer oaths and can work the video recorder, but who is not a court reporter. If someone requests a copy of the transcript, the firm has the transcript written by a certified court reporter who produces the transcript based on the video. These firms can travel to the location of the deposition (assuming it is not too far from their offices), or set it up by Zoom or some other video-conferencing system.

The bottom line is that depositions can cost money–potentially lots of money. This is one of the reasons why the civil justice system does not operate the same for wealthy litigants as it does for those with less money. Wealthy litigants can hire court reporters and videographers and order transcripts, while everyone else has to be a lot more strategic about where they put their limited dollars.

Under the rules, you can simply hire a notary public to administer the oath to the witness and record the video using a reliable recording device. That would save a lot of money. That way you would have a recording of the deposition to refer to, and any party could order a transcript of the recording later by hiring a court reporting service to transcribe the audio recording. That will cost several hundred dollars or more, depending on the length of the deposition. Remember that in order to use the transcript in court, you will have to have it produced by a certified court reporter.

Also, if you do not plan to hire a court reporter, the other side may choose to bring one. If you self-record the deposition, you must provide a copy of the video or audio to all other parties after the deposition.

Under FRCP 30, you need the court's permission (also known as "leave of court") to take more than 10 depositions. You obtain this permission by filing a motion seeking leave to take in excess of 10 depositions, explaining why the case requires additional depositions.

30(b)(6) Depositions

FRCP 30(b)(6) is an amazing tool. It allows you to take the deposition of an entity rather than an individual. That entity may be a municipality, a company, a police department (or any department of a government agency), or an institution. You can take a 30(b)(6) deposition of a municipal defendant or a non-party, including institutions such as a state department of corrections. If you want to take a 30(b)(6) deposition of a non-party entity, you have to serve a subpoena just like you would if you were requesting documents.

The beauty of a 30(b)(6) deposition is that you don't have to figure out on your own whose deposition to take if you're looking for specific information. You serve a 30(b)(6) deposition notice on the agency or institution, and you specify what topics you want to ask about. It is that entity's responsibility to identify people who will testify about the topics you listed. Obviously, the topics must be related to the specific entity you're serving. Also, the entity may name more than one person to testify about different topics.

If you're taking the deposition of a party, you would send the other parties a Notice of Deposition, just like you would for any deposition. Remember that you need to send notices (and subpoenas) to all parties in the case, regardless of which party (or non-party) you want to depose.

A **Notice of Deposition** for a 30(b)(6) deposition must contain a list of topics you want to cover in the deposition. If you are taking the deposition of a non-party entity, you would attach a rider to your subpoena, which will contain the topics you want to cover. Sample 30(b)(6) NODs and subpoenas with riders are in the appendix.

Once it receives a 30(b)(6) Deposition Notice or subpoena, the entity is required to designate one or more witnesses to testify about the topics you've listed. Those designated witnesses will be testifying as official representatives of the entity that designated them. It is as if the entity itself is testifying. However, the attorneys for the receiving entity may want to discuss the topics you've listed, and clarify or narrow them. Parties are required to meet and confer to resolve any disputes they may have before taking the matter to a judge.

Tips For Taking A Good Deposition

1. Have a plan. Think about your theory of the case. What facts do you need to prove, and which witnesses do you need to prove those facts? That way you will know what facts you need from each witness you depose. How will you get those facts? What questions do you need to ask to get that information? Create a deposition outline, but try not to make it too detailed. You want to put the witness at ease so they feel comfortable and talkative. Also, you want to be able to ask follow-up questions if the witness says something unexpected and helpful.

2. Know your case. Review all available documents, reports, written discovery responses, and other relevant documentation.

3. Make sure the witness is sworn. Make sure the witness swears the oath to tell the truth. This may seem routine, but if everyone forgets, you will have wasted a lot of time and money.

4. Make sure you ask whether the witness is being represented by one of the attorneys for the parties. Any attorney in a deposition may object to a question, but only the witness's attorney can direct the witness not to answer a question based on a privilege.

5. Figure out what exhibits you will want to use, and get them ready. You may want to use certain records, reports, discovery responses, etc., and have the witness testify about them. You may also want to use photos, video, and audio. Google Maps diagrams and street images are great to use as exhibits. For an in-person deposition, you probably want several copies of each exhibit. Court reporters usually have exhibit stickers to mark the exhibits. For a Zoom deposition, you probably want to learn how to screen-share.

6. Use the "funnel" system. Start with broad, open-ended questions to gather as much information as possible about a topic. Then, break down the answer step by step, and confirm each fact in single statements. This is called **locking the witness into her answer.**

Example:

Q. Please describe all of your job duties as a foreman.

A. Blah blah blah (goes through a long list of duties).

Q. Let me break that down a little bit. One of your job duties as foreman is to supervise laborers?

A. Yes.

Q. One of your job duties as foreman is to investigate complaints against company employees?

A. Yes.

Q. One of your job duties as foreman is to approve or deny vacation requests?

A. Yes.

Then, you lock him in on the list to make sure you got everything.

Q. So your job duties include supervising laborers, investigating complaints against company employees, and approving or denying vacation requests?

A. That's correct.

Q. Do you have any other job duties besides those I mentioned?

A. No.

Boom.

Now you have the witness locked in. If he tries to add to his list of job duties at trial, you can impeach him with his deposition testimony.

7. Do what we tell our kids to do: *Listen.* If you're too focused on asking the next question in your outline, you may miss the amazing admission coming out of the witness's mouth. I cannot tell you how many times I have been surprised by a completely unexpected answer by a deposition witness. And be prepared to follow up on unexpected answers.

8. Understand the difference between advocating for your position and being a jerk. In other words, disagree without being disagreeable. This applies to all aspects of litigation, but it is tested most often during depositions, when everyone is engaged with each other–sometimes in the same room–in real time. This does not mean you lay down and let yourself be intimidated. Learn to stand up for yourself respectfully. Don't raise your voice.

9. Take a break. Think about taking a break once every hour or two, just to clear your mind and stretch your legs, and look at your outline and your notes. Remember, federal depositions can take up to seven hours. It is especially important to take a break when you think you're finished, just to make sure you didn't miss anything.

10. Control the tempo and pace of the deposition. By that, I mean primarily that you should make sure you and the witness are not talking over each other–make sure you are asking questions in a deliberate, slow-paced manner, and direct the witness to wait a beat after you complete your question before beginning the answer.

Likewise, make sure you allow the witness to finish answering the question before you begin your next question. Be careful not to slip into "conversation mode." A deposition should be more like an interview than a conversation. At the same time, you do not want to be too formal or stiff. You want the witness to feel comfortable sharing information. The pace of the questions and answers should be even, deliberate, and unhurried.

11. Except in very rare circumstances, do not interrupt the witness, even if the answer is long and not responsive to your question. The solution to non-responsive answers is to wait until the witness has completed the answer, and then, for the record, move to strike the answer as nonresponsive. If the witness is taking up the deposition time with repeated long, nonresponsive answers, and you run out of time, the solution is to file a motion afterwards and seek additional time to complete the deposition, unless the other party agrees.

12. Always treat the witness with respect. For that matter, be respectful toward all individuals involved in the case: the opposing party and attorneys, court reporters, clerks, and of course judges. This is not only the right thing to do, it will be better for your case.

13. Understand how objections work in depositions. See FRCP 30(c)(2). There is no judge present in a deposition (with very few exceptions). Attorneys and *pro se* litigants make objections "for the record." That means the objections are preserved in the transcript, but the rare occasion when an objection is ruled upon by a judge, it will not be until later, probably right before the trial.

While federal deposition testimony is technically trial testimony, the fact that a question was asked at a deposition does not mean it is going to be allowed at trial. Parties can file pretrial motions, known as motions *in limine,* seeking to prohibit the admission of certain facts and/or testimony. So any deposition objections will be ruled on right before trial, if they are ruled on at all.

Even if there is an objection, the witness will answer the question, unless the witness's attorney directs the witness not to answer the question, which happens very rarely.

WHAT IS IMPEACHMENT?

To impeach a witness in court is to attack the witness' credibility (i.e. believability or truthfulness) by introducing evidence contradicting her testimony in court. That evidence may be testimony from another witness, a document, a video or audio recording, or from a previous statement by the same witness. Often, witnesses are impeached by their deposition testimony. This is why you want to be very careful about crafting your "lock-in" questions. You want to ask simple, clear questions, with one fact per question.

Deposition Objections

Only certain objections are allowed in depositions. These are known as "legal objections". The most common legal objections include the following:

a) **Objection to form.** That means the person objecting believes there is something defective about the way the question is phrased. Maybe it is confusing, or compound,meaning more than one question is being asked in a single question. Maybe it is a leading question. which is not necessarily improper.

b) **Objection to foundation, or "calls for speculation."** A foundation objection is the legal way of saying, "How would she know that?" It suggests the witness has no knowledge to answer the question. Remember, however, that even though a federal deposition is **evidentiary,** meaning it may be read in court as trial testimony, you can still ask questions you would not ask in court. So the witness does not need to answer based only on personal knowledge. She can testify to what others told her, even if her testimony would not be admissible in court because it is based on hearsay.

c) **Question assumes facts not in evidence.** This objection suggests that the question is misleading or is based on a premise that has not been established.

d) **Relevance.** This is self-explanatory. It suggests the question is not relevant to any matter in the lawsuit.

The following types of objections are improper and not allowed (and may result in sanctions if it gets that far).

- **Speaking objections.** A speaking objection is an objection that suggests to the witness how the attorney or party would like them to answer. This is also known as "coaching the witness." Objections must be concise (short) and state the legal basis, period.

- **Directions not to answer the question** based on anything other than privilege or otherwise prohibited testimony, such as testimony that may compromise national security or reveal trade secrets.

WHO CAN OBJECT DURING A DEPOSITION?

Any attorney or unrepresented party can make objections to any deposition questions, but only the witness' attorney may direct the witness not to answer a question.

CAN A NON-PARTY WITNESS HAVE AN ATTORNEY AT THE DEPOSITION?

A non-party witness is allowed, but not required, to be represented by an attorney at their deposition. The witness's attorney can make objections and direct the witness not to answer, if legally appropriate, just as a party's attorney can for their clients.

WHO CAN ATTEND A DEPOSITION?

Any party is entitled to attend any deposition. In other words, any plaintiff or defendant can attend any deposition regardless of whether that plaintiff or defendant is represented by counsel.

Plaintiffs attend depositions on occasion. I sometimes find it helpful for my client to be present. For instance, if a treating doctor is testifying, the doctor may remember her patient's face even if she does not otherwise recall the treatment based only on the records. But of course as a *pro se* litigant, you would always attend all depositions.

Only parties and their attorneys may attend a deposition, unless the parties all agree that someone else may be present during a deposition.

SIGNATURE

A witness can choose to **waive** or **reserve** her signature after the deposition. This means that a witness may reserve the right to review the deposition transcript once it is written, or they may choose to waive their right to review the transcript. A witness who reserves her signature cannot change the transcript, but may fill out a form (known as an errata sheet) explaining what she thinks was incorrect. In my experience, this is not a particularly important issue. I would say 50 percent of deponents waive, and 50 percent reserve. I have never seen it come up later in a case.

Tips For Testifying at a Deposition

BEFORE THE DEPOSITION

1. Get a good night's sleep.

2. Eat a healthy breakfast – not too heavy.

3. Dress comfortably but appropriately. No jeans, shorts, t-shirts, tank tops, etc.

4. Prepare by reviewing relevant documents, videos, photos, etc. before the deposition.

DURING THE DEPOSITION

1. Be truthful and reasonable.

These are the two most important elements of your deposition and trial testimony. At the end of the day, if you've testified truthfully and reasonably, you can count your testimony as a success. This doesn't necessarily mean you'll win your case, but if you *don't* testify truthfully and reasonably, you're far more likely to lose.

The legal system functions on the assumption that people tell the truth while testifying. That's why we take an oath to tell the truth in depositions and at trial. That's why knowingly false testimony can subject you to prosecution for perjury.

Strategically, once you start fudging the facts, you get into trouble. You can be impeached, which means that an attorney can confront you with a prior statement different from the one you're making now. Once you stray from the truth, it can be hard to find your way back. And juries hate being lied to more than they hate almost anything else. So make it easy on yourself: honor your oath and tell the truth.

At the same time, you need to testify *reasonably*. A trial is a battle for the hearts and minds of the jury or the judge. Frankly, it's more heart than mind. One of the quickest ways to succeed in front of a jury or a judge is to be sincere and reasonable–make them see the case through your eyes.

Here's an extreme example of what I mean when I talk about testifying reasonably:

> You're asked how old you are. You can say you're 15,768,000 minutes old, or you can say you're 30 years old.
>
> Both are true.
>
> One is reasonable. One is clearly not.

Here's a real-life example of a deposition witness who thought she was being clever:

Q. How many clients did you have at XXX as of September 2015?

A. Well, I don't know how many clients I had [in September of 2015].

Q. Can you approximate?

A. I don't know the number.

Q. More or fewer than 30?

A. I don't know. I don't feel comfortable answering that because I'm not sure.

Q. More or fewer than 500?

A. I'm not comfortable answering. I'm not sure of the number.

Q. More or fewer than 10,000?

A. I'm not sure. I don't know. I'm not comfortable to answer.

So this witness could not say if she had more or fewer than *30* clients, and could not say if she had more or fewer than *10,000* clients. This, of course, is ridiculous, and no jury would believe anything she says after this answer. She may have thought she was being smart, but in reality, she was undermining her own case and destroying her own credibility.

So it is crucial to be truthful and *reasonable* during your testimony.

2. Listen carefully to each question.

Just as you want to remain truthful during the deposition or trial, you want to make sure you understand the question being asked of you.

Carefully listen to the question before answering, and let the attorney finish asking the question before speaking.

In fact, wait until you are sure the question has been completed, then wait a beat before answering. This not only helps you think about the question and make sure you understand it, but it prevents a quick back-and-forth that drives court reporters crazy and also may lead to split-second answers you regret later. It also helps you control the pace of the deposition.

3. Make sure you understand the question, and don't be afraid to ask that the question be repeated or rephrased.

If a question is unclear or confusing, ask for clarification. Do not attempt to answer a question that you do not know how to answer. This applies if it is the questioner's fault (a confusing question) or if it's your own fault (thinking about the Bears game instead of listening to the question). Ask that the question be repeated if necessary.

4. If you don't agree with the premise of a question, say so.

If a question implies something that you do not believe is true, say so.

The classic example is, "When did you stop beating your mother?" If you didn't beat your mother, you would respond by stating you cannot answer the question, because you never beat your mother. Or just say, "I never beat my mother." A less provocative example: "What time did you arrive at the roller rink that day?" If you were never at the roller rink on the day in question, you can't answer that question. So just say: "I was never at the rink that day."

5. Answer only the question asked.

Attorneys are only allowed to ask one question at a time. Do not assume a follow up question is coming. Only answer the question that is asked of you.

6. Don't try to tell your story or plead your case with every answer.

Your answers should be as succinct and clear as possible. You will have the opportunity to elaborate later if necessary.

7. Don't try to out-think or outlawyer the lawyers.

Remember: just because you are acting as your own attorney, does not mean you went to law school. Lawyers are trained to try and elicit the answers they want for their case. They are also trained to look for dishonest or evasive answers. If they sense you are making something up or are otherwise being dishonest, they will make you pay for it.

Simply put, it's not worth the risk to stretch the truth or outmaneuver an opposing attorney. It will almost always end up backfiring. Just answer as straight as you can.

8. Answer confidently.

By telling the truth, you can answer with confidence, even if you believe the answer may paint you in a bad light. If you answer confidently, you convey that you're not afraid of the answer. Let's say you struck someone in self-defense. You're asked, "You punched my client, right?" If you *did* punch the client, you answer confidently and without shame: "Yes, I did." This conveys to the jury or the judge that you're not afraid of the truth, and they can rely on you to play it straight. This is a huge advantage. It also shows the jury or judge that you don't believe you did anything wrong, that your actions were fully justified.

Here's a real-life example: My client was punched numerous times by police officers. I asked one of the officers if he punched my client. He responded that he "administered a closed fist strike." We spent the next 5 minutes discussing the fact that there is no difference between a closed fist strike and a punch. At the end of the exchange, the officer admitted he punched my client.

This had three consequences:

1) The officer's credibility (his believability) took a hit;

2) The officer's reluctance to admit he punched my client made it easier to argue the officer used excessive force, and;

3) We spent far more time talking about the officers punching my client than we would have if he had just said, at the beginning, "Yes, I punched him."

9. Don't overcommit–qualify answers as appropriate.

If you cannot answer something 100%, but you believe it's true, just say that.

Q. My client suffered a broken clavicle as a result of this incident, correct? (Assuming this is not a contested issue in the case.)

Wrong answer: "How should I know? I'm not a doctor."

Better answer: *"That's my understanding."*

This accomplishes two things:

1) The witness retains credibility by not disputing or evading an obvious fact, but;

2) does not overcommit her knowledge by personally vouching for what is essentially a medical opinion.

10. Be careful of estimating time, distance, and speed.

We all have different ideas of time, distance, and speed. When you don't have a stopwatch or tape measure with you at the moment something happens, your perception of how long it took, how far away something was, or how fast your vehicle or another vehicle were moving, can be all over the map. So when you answer questions about time, distance, and speed, make sure to qualify your answer appropriately by saying—if true—"I'm not great at estimating.." Also, give a range rather than a specific figure. But again, be reasonable. The fact that you don't know exactly how far away something was does not justify refusing to answer the question, which makes you look evasive and dishonest.

The same principle applies to any type of numerical estimate. Remember the example I gave earlier of the witness who could not say if she had more or fewer than 30 clients or 10,000 clients.

As a witness, you're not expected to know exact figures, but you are expected to provide a reasonable estimate or range. So qualify your answers. Don't overcommit your knowledge or memory, but answer the question reasonably.

11. A deposition is not a memory test.

If you don't remember a particular fact, just say you don't remember. Don't worry about what people would think about you not remembering. People forget stuff all the time. So, if you genuinely don't recall something, don't try to make it up. If you fudge one thing and you get caught, it will be very difficult for anyone to believe anything you say. Obviously, you should recall the big important facts, like whether your traffic light was green or red when you entered the intersection.

12. Be nice.

Your demeanor on the witness stand, or in the witness chair, should be consistently sincere and respectful, regardless of whether the questioning attorney is on your side or the other side, even if the attorney is being disrespectful or confrontational. You want to convey that you're grateful to be able to tell your story, even if it is actually the last thing you want to be doing at that point.

Bottom line:

- Your deposition is one of the most important parts of your case. You will probably not win your case at your deposition, but you can definitely lose your case at your deposition.

- One of the primary goals of your testimony is to have the jury or the judge see the case through your eyes. You want them to believe you're answering questions the way they would answer those questions. You do this primarily by being truthful and reasonable.

- The best deposition witnesses are truthful, reasonable, sincere, respectful, confident, and careful.

- The worst witnesses are evasive, confrontational, untruthful, and unreasonable. They exaggerate, they overcommit, and they fudge things or outright lie.

The Duty To Meet & Confer About Discovery Disputes (FRCP 37)

Your ability to obtain the information and materials you are entitled to depends not only on your ability to craft effective, strategic, and comprehensive discovery requests, but also on your ability and commitment to follow up and demand full compliance with your requests.

The Dirty Little Secret about discovery is that parties will often provide minimal responses to discovery requests, and wait for the other side to call them on it. *Pro se* litigants are probably more likely than others to encounter this It is then up to the side that served the discovery to contact the other party to discuss their inadequate responses–ideally in writing–and then file a **motion to compel** if the attempts to resolve their differences are not successful. This is generally done under FRCP 37, which governs failure to make disclosures or to cooperate in discovery, as well as sanctions. Many courts have local rules with additional requirements related to Rule 37. For instance, the Northern District of Illinois has Local Rule 37.2, which requires the party filing a motion to compel to consult with the other side and make a good faith effort to resolve the discovery dispute.

MOTION TO COMPEL

A **motion to compel** is a written motion asking the court to require another party to do something, like answering discovery within a certain amount of time or allowing a site visit. You can find a sample motion to compel in the appendix.

As discussed in this chapter, most if not all courts require parties to meet and confer before filing a motion to compel. Judges don't love having to referee discovery disputes, just like parents don't love having to referee fights between their children.

However, a number of courts allow parties to skip the "meet and confer" step and immediately file a motion to compel if one of the parties in the litigation is *pro se*. That means you can immediately file a motion to compel if there is any dispute about discovery. Check the local rules of your court to see what rules apply to unrepresented litigants.

My recommendation is to write a letter to the other side setting out in detail what you believe is inadequate about each response. A letter is not required–you can do this by phone or in person (if you're not incarcerated)–but writing down your issues is helpful for many reasons:

First, it forces you to articulate everything you believe is insufficient about the discovery responses, which helps to focus your mind and your strategy.

Second, it gives you a distinct advantage if and when the matter gets to a judge, if you ultimately end up filing a motion to compel.

Third, it establishes to the other side that you know what you're doing, that you're serious about demanding full compliance, and that you've read this amazing book.

Your letter should contain bullet points referring to each specific insufficiently answered request, and explain why the response was insufficient. At the end of this detailed letter, you should ask for dates and times the other side is available to discuss.

During your discussion, take specific notes about the representation of the other side with respect to what they will agree to do to improve their responses, and also what they refuse to do. Then, you send a detailed follow-up letter documenting all of the agreements and disagreements from your discussion, and at the end of this follow-up letter, you direct them to let you know if they disagree with any of the characterizations in your letter.

Or if you can't discuss it, because you're, you know, in prison or something, then the letter will have to do.

Don't fight for the sake of fighting. Let's say when you are preparing your opening letter, you realize that even though the other side has not sufficiently answered a particular discovery request, you now realize you don't really care about the answer – maybe because you've learned more about the case, or you see things a bit more clearly now. If you don't really *need* the answer to that request, leave it alone. Save the time and the hassle.

Chapter Recap

Discovery is a crucial phase in legal proceedings, in which parties gather information and materials from each other, as well as non-parties. There are three main methods of discovery:

1. Written Discovery

- Rule 26 Initial Disclosures (FRCP 26(a)(1)): Parties make written disclosures by a specified date, including the names, addresses, and contact information of individuals with discoverable information that supports their case, documents, electronically stored information, tangible items, computations of damages, and relevant insurance policies.

- Interrogatories (FRCP 33): Written questions posed by one party to another, answered under oath and in writing. Parties are limited to 25 interrogatories, including subparts, without court permission.

- Requests for Production (FRCP 34): Parties request specific documents and materials from each other, such as video, audio, emails, text messages, etc. No limit on the number of production requests.

- Requests for Admission (FRCP 36): Parties request other parties to admit or deny specific facts.

2. Subpoenas

- Parties obtain information from non-parties by issuing subpoenas, which are essentially court orders issued by attorneys. Subpoenas can request documents, materials, or depositions.

3. Oral Discovery

- Depositions: A party can question a witness (deponent) under oath, and a court reporter records the testimony.

Initiation of Discovery

- Discovery typically begins after the pleadings stage.

- Discovery cannot begin until the Rule 16 conference, scheduled by the judge, where parties discuss the scheduling order containing deadlines for discovery.

Scheduling Order:

- The scheduling order, also called a discovery plan, is the court's way of ensuring the case progresses. It includes information on parties, service status, case description, basis of jurisdiction, filed motions, proposed discovery schedule, settlement discussions, and the choice of using a magistrate judge.

Tips For Taking A Deposition

1. Have a plan.

2. Know your case.

3. Make sure the witness is sworn

4. Ask whether the witness is being represented by one of the attorneys for the parties.

5. Figure out what exhibits you will want to use, and get them ready.

6. Use the "funnel" system

7. Listen.

8. Disagree without being disagreeable.

9. Take a break.

10. Control the tempo and pace of the deposition.

11. Do not interrupt the witness.

12. Treat the witness with respect

13. Understand how objections work in depositions.

Tips For Testifying In A Deposition

1. Be truthful and reasonable.

2. Listen carefully to each question.

3. Make sure you understand the question, and don't be afraid to ask that the question be repeated or rephrased.

4. If you don't agree with the premise of a question, say so.

5. Answer only the question asked.

6. Don't try to tell your story or plead your case with every answer.

7. Don't try to out-think or outlawyer the lawyers.

8. Answer confidently.

9. Don't overcommit – qualify answers as appropriate.

10. Be careful of estimating time, distance, and speed.

11. A deposition is not a memory test.

12. Be nice.

Summary Judgment

KEY SOURCES OF LAW

- FRCP 56: Summary Judgment

- *Anderson v. Liberty Lobby, Inc.,* 477 U.S. 242 (1986)

- *Celotex Corp. v. Catrett,* 477 U.S. 317 (1986)

What is Summary Judgment?

A party that files a **motion for summary judgment** (some jurisdictions call it "summary disposition") argues that the party filing the motion, known as "the movant," is entitled to judgment as a matter of law based on the evidence in the record. In other words, they should win the case without going to trial. The "evidence in the record" is the evidence that has come out through the discovery process.

While any party may file a summary judgment motion, it is more often filed by defendants. In a typical case, the defendant will file a motion for summary judgment after discovery has been completed, arguing that even if the court views the evidence in a light most favorable to the plaintiff, the plaintiff cannot win, and the defendant is entitled to judgment as a matter of law.

If a summary judgment motion is granted as to a specific claim, that means the trier of fact,usually the jury, will not be deciding that claim. The judge has already decided it. This is because the judge has determined there are no material facts to be decided.

A fact is *material* if it would change the outcome of the case under the law. If the judge grants a defendant's summary judgment motion as to a specific claim, judgment is entered in favor of the defendant on that claim, and the trier of fact will not be deciding that claim. If the judge grants the defendant's summary judgment motion as to all the claims, the case is over, and the only thing left to do for the plaintiff is to file a motion for reconsideration or an appeal.

In other words, summary judgment is a *big freaking deal.*

Example 1

Plaintiff Bob files a lawsuit against police officer Smith, accusing Smith of falsely arresting him for a purse-snatching that he did not commit.

Bob can win his case if he proves that Officer Smith arrested him without probable cause. Under the Fourth Amendment to the U.S. Constitution, an officer has probable cause to make an arrest if a reasonable officer, knowing what the arresting officer knows at the time of the arrest, would believe the person to be arrested:

- had committed a crime;
- was currently committing a crime; or
- was about to commit a crime.

Probable cause requires more than a hunch and must be based on specific facts, but it is less than the amount of evidence needed to convict a defendant in court, which is beyond a reasonable doubt. Essentially, an officer only needs to have a reasonable belief that the suspect committed a crime in order to arrest him.

During discovery, Officer Smith testifies that a woman stopped him on the street and pointed to Bob, telling him that Bob took her purse. So the officer arrested Bob for stealing the purse. Officer Smith argues that he had probable cause to arrest Bob because of the statement of the woman that Bob stole her purse.

In this example, it turns out Bob was innocent, and that the purse-snatching victim—let's say her name is Mary—mistakenly thought he was the one who stole her purse. But that does not come out until Bob's criminal trial, when Mary testifies that she made a mistake, and Bob did not steal her purse. Because of Mary's testimony, Bob is found Not

Guilty. In other words, he is acquitted.

Under these facts, even though Bob was found Not Guilty at trial, Officer Smith will probably win his motion for summary judgment in Bob's lawsuit against him because at the time of the arrest, a reasonable officer would have believed Mary's statement that Bob had stolen her purse. The fact that the officer may have *later learned* that Mary was mistaken does not change the equation, because under the law, the question is what Officer Smith knew *at the time of the arrest.*

Assuming all these facts are undisputed, Officer Smith would probably be entitled to summary judgment because under the law, as applied to the undisputed facts of the case, Officer Smith had probable cause to make the arrest. As a result, Officer Smith cannot be held liable on the false arrest claim, and the judge would enter judgment in favor of Officer Smith without going to trial. Another way of saying this is that under the law as applied to this case, no reasonable jury could return a verdict for Bob.

Example 2

But let's say Mary testifies in a deposition that *she never told Officer Smith that Bob had stolen her purse.* She told the officer her purse was stolen by someone named Ray, and she gave the officer a description of Ray that did not match Bob's appearance. Under these facts, summary judgment should be denied, because there is *a question of material fact for a jury to decide.*

If the jury believes Officer Smith's story that Mary told him Bob stole her purse, and described Bob accurately, Officer Smith would probably win the case, because the jury would believe he had probable cause to make the arrest.

On the other hand, if the jury believes Mary's story that she told Officer Smith that *Ray* stole her purse, and her description of Ray did not match Bob's appearance, then *Bob* would likely win the case, because under those facts, the officer did *not* have probable cause to make the arrest. No reasonable officer would believe that Bob committed the crime if the name and description of the purse-snatcher did not match Bob. But the bottom line is that the case would go to trial because there was a dispute about what the victim told the officer.

Example 3

As noted above, a disputed fact must be **material** in order to defeat summary judgment and go to trial. A *material fact* is a fact that would change the outcome of the case under the law.

For instance, let's say the purse-snatching victim, Mary, testifies in her deposition that she told the officer the purse-snatcher's name was *Robert* instead of Bob, but the physical description of the purse-snatcher still matched Bob. So Officer Smith says Mary told him the perpetrator's name was Bob, but Mary says she told the officer his name was Robert. There is now a disputed question of fact—but that fact is not *material*. In other words, it would not change the outcome of the case. The officer still had probable cause to believe that Bob was the purse-snatcher.

So, Officer Smith should be entitled to summary judgment and that claim would not proceed to trial, even though there was a factual dispute. Because the dispute was not material (significant), it would not defeat Officer Smith's summary judgment motion.

Example 3a

Let's say that *both Officer Smith and Mary* testify in their depositions that Mary told the officer it was Ray who stole her purse and gave a description that did not match Bob—and no one disputed this fact. In that case, *Bob* could file a summary judgment motion, arguing that as a matter of law as applied to the facts of the case, Officer Smith did *not* have probable cause to arrest Bob. In that case, the judge would enter summary judgment in Bob's favor, and he would not have to prove the false arrest claim at trial. The only question at trial would be how much Bob should be awarded in damages.

Example 3b

Let's say Mary tells Officer Smith that Bob stole her purse, and points to Bob. But Mary also tells the officer that she is being eaten alive by a zombie and that Bob snatched her purse while they were both vacationing on Mars. And when the officer looks at Bob, he does not have a purse, and he is not on Mars.

Under those facts, even though Mary accurately identified Bob, it would not have been reasonable to rely on her accusation based on the **totality**

of the circumstances known to the officer at the time of the arrest. The "totality of the facts" means all of the information the officer had. In that case, Officer Smith likely did not have probable cause to arrest Bob because Mary was not credible (because of the whole zombie-Mars thing), and Officer Smith would likely lose his motion for summary judgment, and the case would go to trial. If Mary's report about Bob and the zombies is the only evidence of probable cause, Bob may file (and likely win) his own summary judgment motion, arguing that no reasonable jury would find Mary's statement credible.

Police officers and other government employees in civil rights cases have an extra layer of protection from liability, which shows up often in summary judgment motions. It's called **qualified immunity**. Qualified immunity is a way for police officers to avoid liability even when they violate a person's constitutional rights.

Under the doctrine of qualified immunity, an officer can violate your constitutional rights without having to pay money damages—or even go to trial—if the court finds that the constitutional right in question was not "clearly established" at the time of the incident.

Qualified immunity—like the absolute immunity discussed earlier in this book—is not part of the Constitution, and it is not a law passed by Congress. It was created by judges (through case law), who continue to enforce it. It is an extremely controversial doctrine because it has denied many plaintiffs access to the courts for unconstitutional police conduct that often seems outrageous.

Legal Standard For Summary Judgment

As we discussed in Chapter 5, the legal standard is the portion of a legal brief that informs the court of the primary legal principles governing that particular type of motion. Below is a typical legal standard section for a summary judgment motion with case law from the Seventh Circuit, which covers Illinois, Indiana, and Wisconsin. Of course, you should use the case law in your circuit when you cite case law.

Summary judgment is appropriate where the movant, the party who files the motion, shows, through "materials in the record, including depositions, documents, electronically stored information, affidavits or declarations, stipulations ... admissions, interrogatory answers, or other materials" that "there is no genuine dispute as to any material fact and the movant is entitled to judgment as a matter of law." Fed.R.Civ.P. 56. In resolving a motion for summary judgment, "[t]he court has one task and one task only: to decide, based on the evidence of record, whether there is any material dispute of fact that requires a trial." *Waldridge v. Am. Hoechst Corp.*, 24 F.3d 918, 920 (7th Cir. 1994).

For a dispute to be genuine, the evidence must be such that a "reasonable jury could not return a verdict for the non-moving party." *Anderson v. Liberty Lobby, Inc.*, 477 U.S. 242, 248 (1986). For the fact to be material, it must relate to a disputed matter that "might affect the outcome of the suit." Id. "Summary judgment is not appropriate 'if the evidence is such that a reasonable jury could return a verdict for the nonmoving party.'" *Payne v. Pauley*, 337 F.3d 767, 770 (7th Cir. 2003). "On summary judgment [a court] must view the facts and make all reasonable inferences that favor them in the light most favorable to the party opposing summary judgment." *Johnson v. Advocate Health and Hospitals Corporation*, 892 F.3d 887, 893 (7th Cir. 2018). "On summary judgment a court may not make credibility determinations, weigh the evidence, or decide which inferences to draw from the facts; those jobs are for a fact finder. Rather, '[t]he court has one task and one task only: to decide, based on the evidence of record, whether there is any material dispute of fact that requires a trial.'" *Payne*, 337 F.3d at 770 (internal citations omitted). Where the material facts specifically asserted by one party contradict the facts asserted by a party moving for summary judgment, the motion must be denied. *Id.* at 773.

SUMMARY JUDGMENT IN EMPLOYMENT CASES

Summary judgment in employment cases is very specific.

There are two ways for a plaintiff to survive summary judgment in an employment case:

1. Point to direct evidence of intentional discrimination. If you can do this, you should survive summary judgment and get to a trial. But it is extremely rare to have direct evidence of discrimination. Such evidence would be a so-called "smoking gun", like an email by the employer stating that he terminated you because of your race. This almost never happens, but if you have this evidence, even if it is not substantial, you should be able to get to trial.

2. Establish circumstantial (indirect) evidence of discrimination. The most common way to do this is to use something known as the "*McDonnell-Douglas* burden-shifting framework", named for the U.S. Supreme Court's decision in *McDonnell Douglas Corp. v. Green*, 411 U.S. 792 (1973). In this framework, the plaintiff must meet her initial (known as "*prima facie*") burden of showing evidence that

   a. she is a member of a protected class;

   b. she was meeting the defendant employer's legitimate expectations,

   c. she suffered an adverse employment action such not being hired, being terminated, being demoted, or having her pay reduced, and

   d. similarly situated employees who were not members of her protected class were treated more favorably.

The plaintiff does not have to prove these things – that would be for trial – she only needs to point to evidence of them.

If the plaintiff meets her burden, the burden then shifts to the defendant employer to articulate a legitimate, nondiscriminatory reason for the adverse employment action.

If the employer is able to articulate a nondiscriminatory reason for the adverse employment action, the burden shifts back to the plaintiff to point to evidence that the allegedly nondiscriminatory reason was pretext, that is, that it was not the real reason the plaintiff suffered the adverse employment action.

Format Of Summary Judgment Motions

Almost as important as the *content* of a summary judgment motion is the *format* of the motion. Many courts have their own local rules regarding how a motion for summary judgment should be formatted. It is the responsibility of the parties to be aware of the court's local rules regarding motions generally and motions for summary judgment in particular. The individual judge might also have specific standing orders regarding these topics. If your motion, response, or reply does not comply with the rules, the court may strike it and allow the other party to win by default. This applies not just to motions but to all aspects of litigation. *You need to know the rules.*

For instance, many courts require that the parties file a **statement of material fact (SMF)**. A statement of material facts is a list of facts that the party asserts are undisputed that support the party's position on the summary judgment motion. All material facts must be supported by specific references to the evidentiary record, such as deposition testimony, exhibits, or affidavits. Each proposed material fact must be supported by either sworn testimony (like deposition testimony or sworn affidavits), or authenticated exhibits, like documents or video or audio footage.

Here are some common sources of evidentiary facts, part of what we call the **evidentiary record,** used to support or oppose summary judgment:

- Deposition testimony

- Other sworn testimony, such as testimony from a previous trial or hearing

- Sworn affidavit or declaration

- Answer to Request for Admission of Facts

- Verified answers to interrogatories

- Authenticated documents

- Video or audio footage

In courts requiring a statement of material facts, a summary judgment argument will not refer directly to the evidentiary record. It will refer to the statement of material facts, which will refer to the evidentiary record. Courts do this presumably to avoid having to dig through multiple documents, transcripts, exhibits and video or audio footage–instead, they only have to look at one document.

The party opposing the motion for summary judgment will be required to respond to each item in the moving party's statement of material facts, by stating whether each item in the statement of material facts is disputed or undisputed. If the non-moving party claims the item is disputed, it has to cite to the portion of the evidentiary record supporting its claim that the item is disputed. For instance, if the proposed material fact is "The light was green for westbound traffic," the other party could respond by citing testimony of a witness who said the light was red for westbound traffic.

In addition to filing a response to each item in the statement of material facts, the responding party must also file his own statement of material facts, usually referred to as a statement of additional material facts. In its reply brief, the moving party will respond to each item in the opposing party's statement of additional material facts.

MOTION FOR SUMMARY JUDGMENT VS. MOTION TO DISMISS

Remember when we talked about motions to dismiss in Chapter 5? As a refresher, a motion to dismiss is usually filed before discovery begins, and addresses the sufficiency of the *allegations* in the complaint. A motion for summary judgment, on the other hand, is usually filed after discovery has closed, near the end of the case, and addresses the sufficiency of the *evidence* that came out during the discovery process.

When a motion to dismiss is granted, it usually results in the dismissal of the complaint. But such a dismissal is normally without prejudice, meaning the plaintiff can file an amended complaint to try to fix the problems identified in the judge's dismissal order.

But a motion for summary judgment–if granted–will usually end the case, at least as to the specific claim or claims at issue. There is no amended complaint that can be filed after a court grants summary judgment in favor of a defendant, because you're no longer talking about allegations. Summary judgment addresses the evidence that would come out at trial.

Chapter Recap

What Is Summary Judgment?

- A motion filed by a party arguing it is entitled to judgment as a matter of law based on the evidence, meaning the moving party wins that claim or that case without going to trial.

- Typically filed after discovery closes.

- Summary judgment motions are most often filed by defendants, who assert that even viewing evidence favorably to the plaintiff, the plaintiff cannot win, and the defendant is entitled to judgment.

Outcome of Summary Judgment

If a defendant's summary judgment motion is granted as to certain claims or certain defendants, those claims or defendants will be dismissed and not go to trial. If summary judgment is granted as to all claims and all defendants, the case is over, and the plaintiff my file a motion for reconsideration or appeal.

Qualified Immunity

Extra layer of protection for government employees, like police officers, in civil rights cases.

Allows officers to avoid liability if the violated right wasn't "clearly established" at the time.

Summary Judgment in Employment Cases

A plaintiff can survive summary judgment in an employment case either by pointing to direct evidence of discrimination, or by pointing to circumstantial evidence of discrimination, most commonly achieved by using the *McDonell-Douglas* burden-shifting method.

Legal Standard For Summary Judgment

Movant must show no genuine dispute of material facts, and the moving party is entitled to judgment as a matter of law.

Format of Summary Judgment Motions

- Courts may have local rules on formatting.

- Parties must comply; non-compliance may lead to striking motions.

- Statement of Material Fact (SMF) lists undisputed facts supported by references to the evidentiary record.

Motion for Summary Judgment vs. Motion to Dismiss

- Motion to dismiss addresses complaint sufficiency before discovery.

- Motion for summary judgment addresses evidence sufficiency after discovery.

- Entry of summary judgment in favor of the defendant is usually final for the specific claims.

PART II

Pretrial

KEY SOURCES OF LAW

- FRCP 16: Pretrial Conferences; Scheduling; Management

At some point during the litigation, the judge will set dates for the trial and **final pretrial conference,** and for submission of the **final pretrial order**. These dates may change from time to time if the judge grants extensions of time to complete discovery, which pushes back other deadlines.

The Final Pretrial Order

The final pretrial order is typically prepared collaboratively by the parties, sometimes with input from the court. Often, the plaintiff will put together the first draft and send it to the defendants for their review and edits. However, if the plaintiff is *pro se,* the defendants will probably prepare the first draft. Once finalized and approved by the judge, the final pretrial order will serve as a roadmap for the upcoming trial, outlining essential details about the case, such as the evidence that will be presented and the legal issues to be decided by the court. The final pretrial order is an important part of the trial preparation process and helps ensure that the trial proceeds smoothly.

The specific requirements of a final pretrial order will normally be set out in the court's local rules and/or the judge's standing orders. You're probably super sick of reading this by now, but *make sure you are familiar with those rules and orders.*

The final pretrial order may contain information or orders related to trial procedure, such as the use of technology, time limits for opening statements and closing arguments, or other special considerations.

The format for pretrial orders differs from court to court, and sometimes from judge to judge. Some courts will require the pretrial order to contain the statement of the case, the stipulations, and the legal and factual issues to be contained in the body of the proposed PTO. Courts may also require the jury instructions, witness list, and exhibit list to be attached to the proposed pretrial order as exhibits. Motions *in limine* are often filed separately from the proposed pretrial order, because the parties will be allowed to file responses and sometimes replies, so the judge will often set a briefing schedule for motions *in limine*.

Key Documents In The Pretrial Process

The items listed below are filed as part of the pretrial process. Sometimes they are filed as part of the final pretrial order, sometimes they are filed as exhibits to the final pretrial order, and sometimes they are filed separately from the pretrial order, depending on the court and the judge. *Here it comes…* **Check your court's local rules and your judge's standing orders for specific requirements.**

• Statement Of The Case

A **statement of the case** is a short summary of the case, including a description of the dispute, the claims being made, and the legal issues to be resolved. This should be no more than a few sentences, and should be written as neutrally as possible. The statement of the case should contain the date and location of the incident, the general nature of the incident, the names of the parties, and their claims and defenses.

Here's a fictional example:

On February 25, 2020, after fleeing from the police, Plaintiff John Smith was arrested in the backyard of a house at 334 West 115th Street, in Chicago, Illinois, by Chicago police officers Alex Jones and Jack Moore, who are defendants in this case. The plaintiff claims the defendant officers used excessive force against him during the arrest, causing him to sustain serious injuries. The defendants deny they used excessive force in arresting the plaintiff, and deny the plaintiff suffered injuries to the extent claimed.

The purpose of the statement of the case is to inform the potential jurors of the basic facts and allegations of the case, before the judge (and perhaps the attorneys or parties) question the potential jurors. A potential juror may be personally familiar with the address of the incident, or may know one of the parties, which will probably disqualify the potential juror from serving in that case.

• Stipulations

A stipulation is a factual or legal statement agreed to by all parties. This can help streamline the trial process by avoiding unnecessary disputes. These stipulations may or may not be read to the jury, but they can be helpful to the judge, who will decide objections and other issues as they arise during the trial. Stipulations can be read to the jury, if the parties agree.

• Legal Issues

Identification of the legal questions or issues to be decided by the court, which helps the judge focus on the critical aspects of the case.

• Lists of Witnesses

Each party typically provides a list of witnesses they intend to call during the trial, along with a brief description of the witness's expected testimony. The judge will normally read the witness list to the jury pool right after she reads them the Statement of the Case, to make sure none of the potential jurors is personally familiar with any of the witnesses. Identifying witnesses a party intends to call ahead of time makes it easier for the judge and the parties to prepare for trial. For instance, let's say a party disclosed a particular witness earlier in the case, but decided they will not be calling that witness at trial. Once the other party sees the witness is not on the witness list, they know they won't have to prepare to cross-examine that witness.

• Exhibit List

A list of documents, photographs, records, or other evidence the parties plan to introduce during the trial. Parties are required to submit exhibit lists so there will be no surprises during the trial, and everyone can prepare for the trial knowing what the exhibits will be.

• Motions *in Limine*

Also known as pretrial motions, **motions *in limine*** are requests by the parties to exclude certain evidence or arguments during the trial based on specific legal grounds. "*In limine*" is Latin for "at the threshold".

• Jury Instructions

If the trial will be decided by a jury, the parties will propose jury instructions outlining the legal principles the jury should apply in reaching its verdict. The bulk of the jury instructions are contained in a set of pattern instructions published by each federal appellate circuit (and each state for state court cases) because they are based on applicable case law in each circuit or state. The jury instructions are super important, as they will serve as the road map for the jury to analyze the evidence and make its decision.

• Final Pretrial Tips

#1 - Pretrial Order

Although it may seem like a boring, technical exercise, the pretrial order is an important document and you should review it carefully. It is a roadmap for the trial, containing all the basic elements of the trial: legal and factual issues, witnesses, exhibits, and stipulations. Think about how each section will be used at trial and play it out in your mind.

#2 - Motions *in limine* and Jury Instructions

Motions *in limine* and jury instructions are–to use a complicated legal term–super-important. They will go a long way to determine who will win the trial. Motions *in limine* dictate what the jury will hear (and what they won't hear), and jury instructions will tell the jury how to decide the case. Pay close attention to these two aspects of the trial.

#3 - Witnesses & Exhibit Lists

Make sure every witness you might want to call is on that witness list. If you forget a witness, you may not be able to call him or her. Make sure every document or other item you might want to use (including video or audio footage) is listed as an exhibit. Just like witnesses, if an exhibit is not listed on the exhibit list, you may not be able to use it at trial.

Final Pretrial Conference

The final pretrial conference is normally the last meeting between the parties, attorneys, and the judge. This is where the judge will go over her procedures, how she selects a jury, what time each trial day will start and end, who to talk to about courtroom technology, and where the witness-attorney conference rooms are located, among other things. The judge will often rule on motions *in limine* at the final pretrial conference, although some motions may require additional briefing or consideration and may be ruled on closer to trial. Often, the judge will reserve ruling on specific motions *in limine* depending on how the evidence comes in at trial.

Trial Preparation

If you are the plaintiff, you are the party with the burden of proof. As a result, you are the one who determines how the trial will proceed. Play out the trial in your head, or on paper. What evidence do you need to prove your case? Where will that evidence come from? Witnesses and exhibits, right? Let's start with witnesses.

Witnesses

Start by identifying which witnesses you will need to prove your case. You should do this two to three months before the trial to make sure the witnesses are available. If you have to subpoena witnesses, you will need to make sure you get the subpoena drafted and serve the witness at least a week before trial, but probably sooner than that—ideally 3-4 weeks.

- Do you want to call the other parties as adverse witnesses in your case?

- What will the order of witnesses be?

- Are there specific non-party witnesses controlled by the other side who you want to call in your case? If so, you need to let the other side know ASAP so they can make sure the witnesses are available. These witnesses might include police officers or employees of the corporate or municipal defendant.

- Will you need to lay the foundation to admit specific exhibits? **Laying the foundation** means providing enough evidence to admit the exhibit in court. What witnesses will you need to do that? We'll discuss that in detail in Chapter 9.

Exhibits And Courtroom Technology

What exhibits will you need and how do you plan to show them to the jury? Think about using maps, diagrams, photos, and video and audio footage. We used to go to Kinko's and get our exhibits blown up and put on foam board, but that was crazy expensive, and it's completely unnecessary now, although if you're old school or allergic to technology, it may make sense for you, as long as there are not too many images to blow up. You can probably get an image on foam board blown up to 18 x 24 without paying too much.

Most federal courtrooms have been updated with new display technology. Now, you can plug a laptop into a cord at your table and it will connect to a projector that displays images, video, and audio. If you don't have a laptop, or you're not comfortable with technology, most federal courtrooms have a document camera, more commonly known as an ELMO.

The ELMO you'll find in courtrooms is NOT a red puppet from Sesame Street. It is a document projector, similar to one you may have used in school. You put your document on the ELMO and it shows up on the screen for everyone to see. If you have technology questions or you want to see how everything works, make sure you contact the court's technology person before trial. The judge or the judge's deputy should give you that information during the final pretrial conference.

If you're in state court, do not assume anything about technology. Check it out. Many state courts do not even have an ELMO.

Whether you're in federal court or state court, make sure you check with the judge's staff and check out the courtroom to see what kind of technology they have so you know what you may need to bring to court.

Chapter Recap

After the initial pretrial conference, the judge typically sets the trial date along with dates for the final pretrial conference and submission of the Final Pretrial Order.

Final Pretrial Order

This is a document prepared collaboratively by the parties, outlining essential details for the upcoming trial. It serves as a roadmap, detailing case information, evidence, legal issues, and more. Requirements for the final pretrial order are often outlined in the court's local rules and the judge's standing orders. Be sure to review the listing of witnesses and exhibits thoroughly to avoid omissions during trial.

KEY ITEMS IN THE PRETRIAL PROCESS

- **Statement of the Case:** A neutral summary of the case's facts, claims, and legal issues.

- **Stipulations:** Agreements between parties on factual or legal issues.

- **Legal Issues:** Identification of legal questions for the court to decide.

- **Lists of Witnesses:** Each party provides a witness list with brief descriptions of expected testimony.

- **Exhibit List:** A list of evidence to be introduced during the trial.

- **Motions in Limine:** Requests to exclude certain evidence or arguments.

- **Jury Instructions:** Proposed instructions outlining legal principles for the jury.

- **Other Procedural Details:** Information on trial procedures, technology use, time limits, etc.

FINAL PRETRIAL ORDER FORMAT

This varies between courts and judges, but typically includes the statement of the case, stipulations, legal and factual issues, and exhibits. Motions in limine may be filed separately. The preparation of a final pretrial order is often a collaborative effort between parties, with the plaintiff usually initiating the first draft. Once approved by the judge, it becomes a binding document governing trial conduct.

FINAL PRETRIAL CONFERENCE

This is the last meeting between parties, attorneys, and the judge before the trial. It addresses trial procedures, jury selection, timing, courtroom technology, etc. The judge may decide some motions *in limine* during the FPTC.

Trial Preparation

Think carefully about the upcoming trial: what evidence will you need? What witnesses and exhibits will you have to coordinate?

TECHNOLOGY CONSIDERATIONS

- Use of technology in courtrooms, including laptops and document cameras.

- Contact the court's technology person before trial for technical assistance.

Trial

- FRCP 45: Subpoenas
- FRCP 48: Number of Jurors; Verdict; Polling
- FRCP 50: Judgment as a Matter of Law
- FRCP 59: New Trial; Altering or Amending Judgment
- FRE 401, 402: Relevance
- FRE 403: Excluding Relevant Evidence for Prejudice, etc.
- FRE 609: Impeachment by Evidence of a Criminal Conviction
- FRE 801-807: Hearsay

This is it—the big event! The trial. You've survived (or avoided) a motion to dismiss, you've survived (or avoided) summary judgment, you've conducted discovery, and now here you are at 8:30 or 9:00 a.m. on the first day of trial. This is my favorite part of the process because finally, after all of the procedural stuff you've gone through, after investigating what happened, filing your complaint, responding to motions, filing motions, engaging in written discovery and depositions, filing and responding to more motions, scheduling, waiting, waiting some more, *and then waiting even more,* you are *finally* ready to tell a jury why you filed this case and went through all those hoops in the first place.

This is when you present your case to a group of citizens who are required by law to sit and listen while you put on your case.

First, let's go over the order of events in a trial.

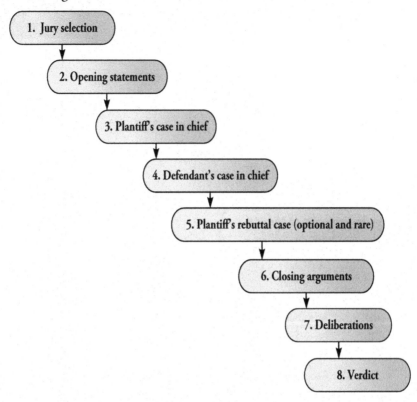

There have been books written about each of these stages that would fill entire libraries. You have probably not read any of them. Lucky for you, most trial lawyers have not read them either. But you have a secret advantage, because those lawyers have probably not read *this* book (although after the trial, you are free to recommend they buy it!).

Jury Selection

"In suits at common law, where the value in controversy shall exceed twenty dollars, the right of trial by jury shall be preserved..."

-Seventh Amendment to the United States Constitution

The Constitution guarantees a jury trial in civil cases. The U.S. is one of very few countries that guarantee this right. So, let's talk about the jury.

In federal court, a **civil jury** must contain at least six people, and no more than 12 people. A **jury verdict** must be unanimous unless the parties agree otherwise. There must be at least six jurors to return a proper verdict (FRCP 48.) Judges are allowed to select up to 12 jurors, but many judges will select around eight jurors, which allows for the possibility that one or two of those jurors does not complete the trial for some reason. If all eight jurors remain on the jury for the entire trial, they will all deliberate and return a verdict.

This is different than in state court, where judges will often choose **alternate jurors,** who will not be told they are alternates until the end of the case. They will listen to the evidence with the rest of the jury, but they will only **deliberate** (discuss and decide the case with the other jurors), if the jury loses members throughout the trial. If the alternates are not necessary at the end of the trial, the alternate jurors will be excused, and do not get to deliberate with the others. Alternate jurors in federal civil cases were abolished in 1991, because the drafters of the federal rules felt it was unfair for an alternate juror to have to listen to all the evidence, but not be allowed to participate in deliberations.

So there are no alternate jurors in federal trials. Instead, the judge will often select at least two more jurors than the minimum required number of six. This provides some insurance in case the jury loses a member or two during trial.

Jury Selection, A.K.A. "Voir Dire" (Latin For "To Speak The Truth")

During the first day of trial, the judge will call in a certain number of potential jurors, known as **the venire,** or **the jury pool.** They will file into the courtroom and sit on the spectator benches and in the jury box. The judge will determine which potential jurors will sit in the **jury box** to be questioned first. The jury box is simply a collection of 12 seats where the jury will sit when it is selected.

Each of the parties will be given a set of questionnaires the venire completed before coming into the courtroom. This questionnaire will provide each potential juror's address, age, and occupation, and provide some information about their family. This is all you will know about each of these people until they start to answer questions.

In federal court, the judge will question the potential jurors. Before a trial begins, most judges will provide a list of their usual questions to the parties and allow the parties to submit additional questions they feel would be important to determine if a potential juror will be fair and impartial. The judge will then decide whether to ask any or all of those additional questions to the venire.

In state court, judges normally allow the attorneys and unrepresented parties to ask their own questions. This is a nice way for the attorneys and parties to establish a rapport with potential jury members and obtain more information than if the judge did all the questioning. But it is probably better for unrepresented litigants that the judge asks all the questions. Attorneys have an advantage because they have experience questioning potential jurors. Questioning the people who will decide your case can be nerve-wracking if you haven't done it. I enjoy this process, but many lawyers do not.

Jury selection is a crucial part of the trial. Of course, many aspects of litigation are super important. But picking a good jury for your case is right up there, because these are the judges of the facts. These are the people who will decide if the plaintiff has proven his case, and if so, how much money to award the plaintiff in damages. How often do you get to be involved in picking the judges who will decide your case?

Pretty cool, right? Let's hear it for the Seventh Amendment!

Jury selection involves a lot of luck and randomness. For the most part, you will be stuck with the group of people who happen to be called to jury duty that day, and who happen to be selected to come to your courtroom that morning. And you will have maybe 5 minutes to listen to each potential juror to learn about who they are and what makes them tick, and to try to figure out how they will react to your case. We spend our entire lives trying to understand our own friends and family. So, how are you supposed to know how a total stranger is going to look at your case?

The more you know about this process, and the more skills you learn, the more you can add some *purpose* to that mix of luck and randomness so you can pick the best jury.

Picking a jury is a lot like life. There is so much randomness, so much in life we cannot control. Some people get cancer, some don't. Some people get hit by cars, some don't. Many people are born into poverty or have abusive parents, and some are born luckier. A million things can happen that are simply out of our control.

But even though much of life is beyond our control, we can always do things that give us a better shot at living a good, long, healthy life. We can eat healthy, exercise, get enough sleep, choose good people as friends and mentors, study hard, work hard, and treat others the way we want to be treated. We can do the things that can remove some of the randomness of life and put ourselves in the best position to succeed.

If you're a *pro se* litigant and you've made it to trial, chances are you've done it with hard work and diligence. You know about these things. And the more you know about jury selection, the better prepared you will be to use that hard work and hard-won knowledge and make it work for you, to put yourself in the best position to pick a great jury—or at least a not-so-bad jury.

De-Selecting The Jury

The first thing you need to understand is that when you select a jury, ***your goal is not to select jurors.*** (Wait, what?) If you do it right, you are not *selecting* jurors. Rather, your goal is to *de-select* jurors. In other words, you are not out there looking for the best jurors for your case. Your goal is to figure out which are the *worst* jurors for your case, and make sure they don't get on that jury. If you can do that, you will be left with the best possible jury for your case.

A jury is selected by each party issuing **challenges** (also known as "strikes") to the potential jurors they don't want on the jury. Remember: parties do not tell the judge who they *want* on the jury. They tell the judge who they *don't want* on the jury.

Challenges

Jury selection is a process of elimination. Each side attempts to knock off the people they do not want on the jury by issuing **challenges** to those members of the jury pool.

There are two kinds of challenges in the jury selection process: **peremptory challenges** and **for-cause challenges.**

PEREMPTORY CHALLENGES

Peremptory challenges allow a party to excuse or dismiss a potential juror for almost any reason they want, and they don't have to explain the reasoning, except in certain situations. Each side in a case will have a certain number of peremptory challenges, usually 3 or 5, depending on the judge's preference. Judges often allow fewer peremptory challenges because the more challenges the parties have, the longer it takes to select the jury.

FOR-CAUSE CHALLENGES

A party will always have the right to challenge a potential juror on the basis that *the potential juror will be unable to be a fair and impartial juror in the case.* In a **for-cause challenge,** the challenging party must convince the judge that a potential juror would not be fair and impartial.

For instance, the potential juror may state in response to questioning that she believes police officers are more **credible** or believable than civilians, or that it is immoral to sue the government. This is often explained by referring to a starting line in a race. If both sides are not equally positioned at the same starting line, and one party is starting ahead of the other in the mind of the potential juror, that party may be excused for cause.

Another reason to excuse someone for cause may be that the potential juror disagrees with the civil justice system and is unwilling or unable to deliberate in good faith with her fellow jurors if she is selected. In that situation, it may be unclear which party will be hurt by the juror, but it is clear the potential juror will not be fair and impartial.

A third reason may be that the potential juror cannot speak the English language well enough to understand the testimony or to deliberate with her fellow jurors. Or perhaps the potential juror is related to or close friends with one of the parties or one of the attorneys. There are any number of reasons why a potential juror may be disqualified from sitting on a jury.

While peremptory challenges are limited in number, there is no limit to the number of for-cause challenges a party can make.

Look for the negative in people.

In life, we are told to always look for the positive in people. But when selecting a jury, you need to look for the negative. Don't be seduced by someone you think will be great for your case. The better a potential juror appears for your case, the more likely she will be excused by the other side. Always ask, "How badly can this person hurt my case?" You will not end up with the jurors you want the most, because the other side will have excused them. Ideally, you will be left with the jurors most likely to give you a fair shot.

Think about the jurors as a group.

Keep in mind that you're not picking *individuals,* you're picking *a jury.* Think in terms of group dynamics. The verdict will be a result of the collective deliberation of this group of people. And it has to be unanimous. In other words, it will not be a vote that you want to win 5-3. So if you identify someone you think would be inclined to rule against you, but that person appears to be passive and not really interested in the process– i.e. a follower–they may not hurt you much, especially if you end up with a few good leaders on your side.

For example: Let's say you identify four people who would not be good jurors for you, but you only have three peremptory challenges to work with.

The first option is to see if you can get any of them excused for cause. You always want to get potential jurors excused for cause rather than by peremptory challenges if you can, because you have unlimited for-cause challenges but only a few peremptories.

The second option is to figure out which of these four potential jurors are likely to be leaders, and which are likely to be followers. Your first priority should be to excuse the bad jurors who are the most likely to be leaders. If you have to leave someone on the jury you don't like, aim for the followers, so they won't have as much influence on the group deliberations. Someone who is likely to find against you as an individual may not hurt you if that person is not a leader. They may just go with the flow. If that person does not appear to be interested in being there, they are less likely to hold up the deliberations if the majority want to rule in your favor.

So all other things being equal, you will want to save your peremptory challenges to excuse the people who you think don't like your case *and who are more likely to be invested in their opinions,* and who display leadership qualities. Those are the people who could really hurt your case. So, when you're dealing with limited resources, like peremptory challenges, figure out which of the "bad" potential jurors are more likely to make a difference, and prioritize them for your challenges.

You want to identify and excuse those potential jurors who would be inclined to find against you, *and* who would be willing to advocate and fight and argue to make sure the verdict is for the other side. These are the people who are likely to be elected jury foreperson and who are most likely to influence the ultimate verdict.

A party cannot excuse a potential juror for a discriminatory reason, such as race, ethnicity, or gender. If a party believes the other party has used its peremptory challenges in a discriminatory way, such as to reduce the number of black jurors, it can make what is called a *Batson* challenge, named for the case of *Batson v. Kentucky*, 476 U.S. 79 (1986), in which the U.S. Supreme Court held that the use of peremptory challenges to remove potential jurors from the jury pool in a criminal case based on race violates the Equal Protection Clause of the Fourteenth Amendment to the U.S Constitution.

The Supreme Court held in 1991 that the *Batson* reasoning also applied to civil cases. *See Edmonson v. Leesville Concrete Company*, 500 U.S. 614 (1991). The prohibition against discriminatory use of peremptory challenges has since been extended to gender *J.E.B v. Alabama ex rel T.B.*, 511 U.S. 127 (1994). Some courts have extended the *Batson* prohibition to religious affiliation and sexual orientation. Even though *Batson* only involved the issue of race, any objection to an allegedly discriminatory peremptory challenge is referred to as *Batson* challenge, regardless of whether the issue is race, gender, or religion.

In order to make a *Batson* challenge, a party must make the challenge at the time the peremptory challenge is made by the other party. Keep in mind,the party making a *Batson* challenge is challenging the other party's challenge. Try saying that three times fast. Once a party informs the judge it is making a *Batson* challenge, that party must explain the reasoning for why it believes the other party's peremptory challenge is discriminatory. If the judge believes the objecting party has raised an inference of discriminatory intent, the other party will have the opportunity to provide a neutral explanation for the basis for its challenge, and explain why the challenge is based on something other than the race, ethnicity, gender, or other prohibited basis. The judge will then decide whether the objecting party has proven by a preponderance of the evidence (more likely true than not) that the peremptory challenge was based on a prohibited reason. If a *Batson* challenge is sustained, the peremptory challenge to the potential juror will be disallowed, and that person who was subject to the peremptory challenge will be seated on the jury.

Jury Selection, Step By Step

1. Randomly selected potential jurors (i.e. jury pool or *venire*) enter the courtroom.

2. The judge makes an opening statement to the jury pool, explaining why they are there, and reads them the statement of the case and list of witnesses.

3. The judge and/or the parties (depending on what cout you're in) questions the jury pool. Usually, the judge will ask general questions to the entire group of potential jurors sitting in the jury box, and ask them to raise their hands to answer the questions. Then, the judge will question individual members of the pool. If there are any sensitive topics, such as criminal or medical history, or anything the potential juror does not want to discuss in front of everybody else, the judge will bring that person to the side and question them with the attorneys or parties present.

4. After all the potential jurors have been questioned, the judge will give the parties a few minutes to think about what potential jurors they want to excuse using peremptory or for-cause challenges.

5. The parties will usually make their challenges, outside the presence of the jury pool. The jury pool may be excused for a few minutes or for lunch, or the parties may make their challenges in the hallway outside the courtroom or in the judge's chambers. The judge will go through the list of potential jurors. After each name is read, the parties will either challenge or accept the potential juror. They do this until they have the right number of jurors – in other words, a jury.

6. The judge will call the jury pool back into the courtroom, or the judge and the attorneys and self-represented parties will return to the courtroom if they did the selection in the hallway or the judge's chambers, and announce which members of the jury pool are free to go. The remaining people are the jury. It is interesting to watch the faces of the people as they realize they have been excused or selected. There is often a visible reaction of relief when people are excused from jury duty.

7. If jury selection is over before lunch, the judge will often excuse
    everyone for lunch and then begin opening statements after
    lunch. If the jury is selected in the mid-afternoon, the judge may
    order opening statements to begin after a 5-10 minute break.
    But if it's later in the afternoon, the judge will most likely send
    everyone home and opening statements will begin first thing in
    the morning.

The specific procedures for jury selection can vary widely depending on
the judge. Some judges pick in panels of four, meaning the parties make
their challenges to the first four jurors. If any of those potential jurors are
excused for cause or due to peremptory challenges, their spots are filled by
the next potential jurors in line. Eventually, there will be four potential
jurors remaining after the challenges, and that is the first panel. They
will do this until enough jurors are chosen. Other judges pick using the
first 12 people in the jury box rather than a smaller panel. The judge will
explain how she handles jury selection at the final pre-trial conference.

***As jury selection proceeds, you will need a good way to keep track of
potential juror names and facts.*** You may hear from anywhere between
12 and 48 potential jurors. How will you remember who is who when it
comes time to make your challenges? There are several ways to go about
this, but most lawyers create some version of a chart with 12 boxes that
looks something like this:

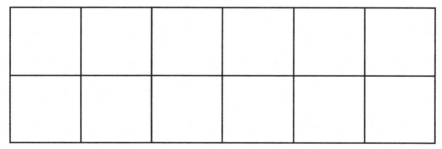

This chart represents the jury box, which will almost always have 6 seats
in front and six seats in back. Most judges will question 12 jurors at a
time, who will be seated in the jury box. This gets complicated when one
or more potential jurors get excused almost immediately for whatever
reason: for instance, if a juror has a plane ticket to travel the following
day, or a medical procedure scheduled, most judges will excuse them
immediately. In that case, the potential juror will leave the jury box, and

another potential juror will take her place in that same seat, or everyone will move over one seat and the new potential juror will sit on the end. Either way, your chart is now completely screwed up.

So how do you solve this problem?

Sticky notes!

Possibly one of the most revolutionary inventions of our time. Here's what you want to do:

→ Bring several over-sized pieces of paper to jury selection, and put six sticky notes on the top of each one and six on the bottom.

→ Write down the names of each potential juror based on where they sit in the jury box.

→ When someone gets excused, you can move the notes accordingly. You may still want to keep a separate list on a pad of paper for additional notes for each potential juror.

→ Once you determine which potential jurors you want to strike, you can write NO on those notes, or an X—whatever code you want to use.

→ You can also indicate which of the potential jurors you *don't* want to strike. Maybe you have a check-mark for the ones you do not want to strike, and an X for those you want to excuse.

→ When a potential juror is excused, I write **XFC** for Excused For Cause, **PX** for a peremptory challenge by the plaintiff, and **DX** for a peremptory challenge by the defendant.

→ Remember to keep track of each side's peremptory challenges, so you know when the other side has run out of challenges. And of course, you need to know how many challenges you have left.

You will be hearing from so many different potential jurors, it's important to keep track of who said what and which ones you want to excuse. Otherwise, you risk excusing the wrong person or failing to excuse the ones you need to excuse. When the time comes to make your challenges, you will be standing in front of an impatient judge with very little time to think about what you want to do. So take good notes and have a good idea of who you want off the jury before the time comes to make your challenges. Also, if the judge doesn't give you enough time to look at your notes and figure out who is who, ask for a few more minutes. But once you are standing in front of the judge making the challenges, you will be far less likely to get more time.

After all of the challenges are made and ruled on, the judge will name the remaining jurors, will excuse everyone else, and will swear the jury.

Opening Statements

An **opening statement** is a summary of the story you will be telling through the trial–the jury's introduction to the facts of the case. It's not an argument, although if the facts of your case are strong enough, and you construct your opening the right way, it can be (and definitely should be) very persuasive. If you are the plaintiff, you will be the first person to address the jury. This is a great advantage. While most courtroom dramas on TV or in the movies feature the climactic closing argument, many lawyers believe the opening statement is more important than the closing argument, because it is the first opportunity to frame the issues for the jury. It provides the lens through which the jury will evaluate the evidence as it comes in.

Opening Statements Can Determine Who Wins A Trial

By the time you make your closing argument at the end of the trial, most jurors will have heard the openings and sat through the evidence, and will have already made up their minds. Very few closing arguments change minds. In fact, studies show that most jurors make up their minds right after opening statements, and before they even hear the evidence! So make that opening statement a priority, and take time to make sure you construct it effectively.

Your case is constructed of a number of facts, like puzzle pieces that fit together to create the picture you want the jury to see. These facts will come from witnesses and exhibits, but not exactly the way you want. Evidence often comes out in a disjointed way, in dribs and drabs, because it comes out one witness at a time.

If you're telling the story of your case to someone, you tell the story by telling that person the facts in the order that makes sense so that person understands why you should win the case. You don't tell the person that Witness A will testify that blah, blah, blah, and then Witness B will say blah, blah, blah, and then

Witness C will show you a report that says blah, blah, blah. Instead, you will arrange the facts in a compelling way that draws from each witness.

That's not how it works in the evidentiary portion of a trial, where you put on each witness one at a time.

This is why the opening statement is so important. It allows you to tell the story of your case and arrange the facts in a way that makes the jury understand why you should win, fact by fact, not witness by witness. It also allows you to preview what each witness will say, so when the witnesses testify, the jury will have already heard you say it, and the witness testimony will simply reinforce the fact you want the jury to remember.

How Long Should The Opening Statement Be?

Most opening statements are 15 to 20 minutes at the most. Some judges will set a specific time limit on opening statements and closing arguments. Others will strongly suggest you keep them brief. While you may be tempted to make your opening longer, people have limited attention spans, and after about 15 minutes, they will lose focus. You want to keep your opening statement tight, keep it moving, and don't waste words with too many conclusions, opinions, or argumentative statements. You also want to avoid drawing objections which will interrupt the flow of your opening statement.

Facts v. Conclusions

To understand the importance of opening statements, you should know the difference between facts and conclusions.

Here is a test for you. Which one of these statements is a fact and which is a conclusion?

A: *The defendant drove his car unsafely.*

B: *The defendant drove his car 60 miles per hour on a quiet residential street and drove through the stop sign without slowing down.*

Spoiler alert: A is the conclusion and B is the fact.

Whether the defendant drove his car *unsafely* is an opinion, a.k.a. a conclusion. *The defendant's numerical speed and specific actions* are facts. They may be disputed facts–i.e. the other side may say the defendant was driving 20 miles per hour and stopped at the stop sign, which is why you're having a trial–but they are *objective facts,* not *subjective conclusions.* Facts arranged in a compelling way are far more persuasive than conclusions, even during closing arguments when you're allowed to use conclusions and allowed to argue the significance of the facts that came out during the trial.

The Best Storyteller Wins

The point of a trial is to tell a good story. Good stories don't just inform, they make us *feel* a certain way, whether it's afraid, happy, sad, or angry. When you hear a good story, it is because the facts were arranged in a way that allowed you to paint a picture in your mind of what happened.

When you hear that the defendant drove his car "unsafely," what picture do you see in your mind? Nothing! Because you have no idea what "unsafely" means. It could mean anything. But when you hear that "the defendant drove his black Chevy Camaro with the spoiler on the rear 60 miles an hour down Elm Street blasting 'Thunderstruck' by AC/DC," that paints a picture, right? (Especially if you are allowed to play "Thunderstruck" to the jury, which, depending on your musical taste, could be awesome.)

The trial is your story, but the opening statement is not Chapter One. ***Think of the opening statement as the Introduction to the story***, in which you lay out the most compelling facts supporting your case in the most effective way possible. You do this with facts.

However, the difference between facts and conclusions is not always perfectly clear. For instance, "Bob was angry." I would argue saying someone was angry is a conclusion, but we are so familiar with what people look like when they're angry, it sounds kind of factual. If you want pure fact, you could say,

"Bob was speaking very loudly, his face was red, and he kept jabbing his finger at my chest."

Of course, that paints a much more vivid picture than simply saying "Bob was angry", but you could probably get away with saying "Bob was angry" if it helps you tell your story. Whenever you say something during an opening statement that seems like it could be a conclusion, you should first say, "the evidence will show." In this example, you could even do a combination:

"The evidence will show that Bob was angry. He was speaking very loudly, his face was red, and he kept jabbing his finger at my chest."

Bottom line: Use your opening as a way to get the jury on your side before they hear a single witness. Do it briefly enough that they do not lose focus. Paint a picture for them using the facts of the case, and keep conclusions, if any, to a minimum. To the extent you want to use any conclusions, wait until the end of the opening where you can wrap up the story and bring it back into the courtroom:

"The evidence will show that by doing the things I just discussed – driving his car at an excessive rate of speed and failing to stop at a stop sign – Bob drove his car in an unsafe and negligent manner, causing me serious injuries. This is why at the end of the trial, I will speak with you again and ask you to return the only verdict supported by the evidence: a verdict in favor of the plaintiff. And I will ask you to enter an award that compensates me for the injuries I have sustained as a result of Bob's negligence."

There are definitely some conclusions in there, but they are wrapped up in a factual statement. You can usually get away with a few more conclusions at the end of your opening statement. But that's just between us – don't tell anyone I told you that.

Body Language Is Key

People are visual learners, meaning they take more from what they see, including a presenter's body language, than what they hear. As a result, your body language while you address the jury can be just as important as what you say.

When addressing the jury during jury selection, opening statements, or closing arguments, you should stand at least 3 to 5 feet away from the jury box. You should be close enough that people can hear you and see you, but not so close as to invade their personal space. Try not to move for the sake of moving. When you move, you distract the jury from what you're saying because you make it more difficult for the jury to follow, *unless* you move for a specific reason, such as to illustrate a point you are making:

Example: *"Bob testified he was a car length away from me when he heard me apologize for the accident. That's all the way over here."* (Walk 15 feet away.) *"I would have to be speaking pretty loud for him to hear me say anything"*, you say with a raised voice. *"I don't think his statement is credible."*

If you're going to move, move for a reason. Otherwise, try to stay in one place.

Hands!

One of the most challenging things for speakers, including trial lawyers, is finding something to do with their hands while they address the audience – in this case, the jury. Putting your hands in your pockets seems too casual, and can even be interpreted as disrespectful. Putting your hands on your hips can appear awkward or confrontational. Clasping your hands together in front of you below the waist makes you look passive and weak. Clasping your hands behind you can appear like you're hiding something. Finally, moving your hands all the time for no particular reason, like moving around the courtroom as discussed above, is distracting to a jury. And whatever you do, don't fold your arms in front of you: that'sthe ultimate sign of defiance and defensiveness.

So what should you do with your hands?

Here are a few suggestions:

→ Keep your hands above your waist.

→ Figure out (through practicing in front of the mirror) your neutral position - the position in which you are most comfortable.

→ If you are using a lectern or a podium, which I would avoid if you can, because it creates separation from the jury, you can put your hands on the side of the podium.

→ Hands at waist, palms up. This conveys honesty, showing the jury you have nothing to hide.

→ Use your hands purposefully. Just like your body movements, using your hands for specific reasons can be very helpful in keeping the jury's attention, and illustrating your story. If you're counting things, do it on your fingers.

Of course, you can mix it up and use a combination of these gestures as appropriate throughout your opening statement.

Pro tip: Practice your physical gestures as much as what you are going to say to the jury, and do it in front of a mirror, as painful as that sounds.

Case-In-Chief

Each party's case-in-chief is the meat of the trial. This is where the evidence is introduced.

Plaintiff's Case-In-Chief:

The plaintiff introduces evidence in his case-in-chief to support his claims. What kind of evidence? Primarily witness testimony and exhibits, like documents, photographs, diagrams, and video and audio footage. After the plaintiff introduces all of his evidence, the Plaintiff "rests", meaning the Plaintiff formally closes his case-in-chief.

Defendant's Case-In-Chief:

After the Plaintiff's case-in-chief, the defendant introduces evidence in its case-in-chief, to support its defense of the case. It should be noted that the defendant does not have to introduce any evidence at all, because it is the plaintiff who has the burden of proving the elements of her case. So, the plaintiff must make sure she introduces all of the evidence required to prove her case in her case-in-chief.

NOTE: Each party can introduce evidence in the other party's case-in-chief. For instance, the defendant can introduce exhibits during the plaintiff's case-in-chief if the defendant can lay the proper foundation (more on that later) using the plaintiff's witnesses, and *vice versa*. Also, any testimony elicited by one party while cross-examining the other party's witness is evidence, just like the witness's testimony on direct examination.

PRO TIP: GET YOUR WITNESSES READY TO GO

There are so many things to think about in a trial, it can be easy to forget the witnesses. Make sure you have your witnesses lined up and ready to go when your case begins. Have them in court in the order you expect to call them. Make sure you have your exhibits prepared and ready to go as well.

Admitting Evidence

When someone says "admit" or "introduce into evidence," they are talking about introducing a fact into the official court record. Things admitted into evidence are the guts of the case, the facts the jury or judge will rely on to make its decision. People may say "evidence admitted into the record," or "facts admitted into evidence," or similar combinations. These all mean the same thing.

Facts can be admitted into evidence in several ways:

1. Witness Testimony

2. Exhibits

3. Stipulation

4. Answers to Interrogatories, requests for admission

5. Evidence depositions

1. Witness Testimony

A witness testifies under oath from the witness stand or through an evidence deposition.

Witness testimony comes out in the form of direct examination and cross-examination. The party who calls the witness will normally use direct examination to question the witness, after which the other party may cross-examine the witness.

DIRECT EXAMINATION AND CROSS-EXAMINATION

When a party calls a witness, that party questions the witness using *open-ended questions* unless the witness is adverse or hostile. After the direct examination, the opposing party has the opportunity to cross-examine the witness using *leading questions*. The party who calls the witness may then have the opportunity for re-direct examination based on the cross-examination. The opposing party may then be able to re-cross examine the witness. This can go back and forth a few times, and the number of questions should be less and less each time. At some point, the judge may step in and stop the examination. Some judges do not allow re-cross examination at all.

- An **open-ended** question is one that does not suggest the answer. Examples include:

  "What color was the light?"

  "Please describe the person who struck you."

  "What happened next?"

- A **leading question** is one that suggests the answer:

  "The light was red, correct?"

  "The person who struck you was a Hispanic female, right?"

Yes or No questions are generally considered leading. For instance,

"Was the light red?" is a leading question, even though it is not as direct as the leading questions above.

When you conduct a *direct examination*, you are allowing your witness to tell their story. Because the witness is presumably on your side, you are not allowed to lead them, i.e. to ask leading questions. You ask them open-ended questions. Open-ended questions also help the jury to get to know the witness.

When you conduct a cross-examination, the witness should be simply affirming the facts you give him. You're the one who tells the story.

DIRECT EXAMINATION V. CROSS EXAMINATION

Direct Exam	Cross-Exam
• Please introduce yourself to the ladies and gentlemen of the jury.	• Your name is Roger Smith, correct?
• What is your occupation?	• You're a police officer?
• Who is your employer?	• You work for the Chicago Police Department?
• How long have you been an officer?	• You've been an officer for 17 years?
• On January 17, 2022, did you have occasion to make an arrest?	• You arrested my client on January 17, 2022, correct?
• Please tell me how you learned of the incident?	• You received a call from dispatch?
• How did the dispatcher describe the incident?	• The dispatcher said there was a bank robbery at 61st and Archer?
• Please describe the person who ran out of the store.	• The person who ran out of the store was 6-foot 4 with dark red hair?
• What did you do when you saw the person run out of the store?	• You immediately began to pursue the person who ran out of the store.

EXCEPTIONS TO OPEN-ENDED QUESTION RULE

There are some exceptions to the rule that you must use open-ended questions with the witness you call in your own case.

- **Preliminary questions:** Depending on the judge, you may be allowed to ask preliminary questions to move things along, especially when there is no dispute about the topic. For instance: "Let me direct your attention to January 17, 2022", or "At the time of this incident you were serving a 4-year term in prison?"

- **Adverse witness:** You are allowed to call the opposing party in your case-in-chief. It is assumed the opposing party will be adverse to your case, so you are allowed to treat that witness as if you are cross-examining them.

- **Hostile witness:** Even if the witness you call is not technically an adverse party, you may be able to conduct an adverse examination (essentially to cross-examine them), once it becomes clear that the witness is hostile to you or your questions. You will generally need to begin your examination with open-ended questions. After several hostile answers, you would request that you be allowed to treat the witness as a hostile witness. The judge will either allow you to cross-examine the witness, or the judge will deny your request, requiring you to continue examining the witness using open-ended questions.

- *Pro Se* **Testimony.** How does your judge handle testimony by a *self-represented* party? Some judges allow narrative testimony by self-represented parties. That means they allow the party to just tell his or her story without questions. Other judges require *pro se* parties to question themselves. They do this in order to allow the other side to make objections to certain questions before the testimony comes out.

Judges have discretion to decide what type of *pro se* testimony they will allow. Make sure you understand ahead of time whether your judge will allow narrative testimony or will require questions and answers. If you are required to testify by asking yourself questions, make sure you prepare your direct examination just like you would with any other witness. Do not assume that because you are asking yourself questions, it will have the correct order and flow. Prepare, prepare, prepare.

MIX IT UP ON CROSS-EXAMINATION

When cross-examining a witness, whether it is a witness called by the other party, or an adverse witness you have called, most of your questions should be leading questions. But you do not need to make every question a leading question. In fact, I would add some open-ended questions just to keep things interesting. If you know how the witness is going to answer the question, you can ask an open-ended question just to draw it out, make it more dramatic, or just mix up the flow of the questioning.

Remember, trial is theater, so you want to keep your audience interested if not entertained. If you ask 25 questions that end with, "Correct?" the jury will keep waiting for that last word and lose track of the content of each question. So mix up the pattern, the emphasis, and the form of the questions. And ask some open-ended questions just to keep it interesting, as long as you know the answer won't hurt you.

Should You Ever Ask A Question You Don't Know The Answer To?

Conventional wisdom says you should never ask a witness a question when you do not know how that witness will answer, as you may get an answer that hurts your case. But this is not always true. Sometimes, there is no good answer to a question, and whichever answer the witness gives will help you.

Here are some questions I like to ask officers, especially when their reports do not mention a fact they are now claiming was true:

"You were trained that your reports must be complete summaries of the arrest, and contain all information relevant to the arrest, correct?"

"Your report was a complete summary of the events of the arrest, containing all relevant information, correct?"

If the officer answers "No" to either question, he'll sound ridiculous, and you can ask him an entire line of questions about what kind of relevant information he routinely leaves out of his reports.

If he answers "Yes" (and in my experience they always say "Yes"), you make him admit there is no mention of you resisting arrest in his report, strongly suggesting that you did not resist arrest.

WHAT MAKES GOOD TESTIMONY

The best way for you and your witnesses to testify is to testify *truthfully* and *reasonably*. The goal in any trial is to capture the hearts and minds of the jurors or the judge, but primarily, the hearts.

- You do that the way any storyteller grabs his or her audience–by being relatable.

- You want the jury to see the case through your eyes—you want them to relate to you.

- You don't accomplish this by being overly dramatic or exaggerating, and you certainly don't do it by fudging the truth.

- There is *nothing* that will hurt you more in the eyes of a jury than if they think you're lying to them.

A witness should have the same demeanor and body position regardless of who is questioning her–a "friendly" attorney or the opponent. No matter what position the witness has or which side her testimony might favor, she should answer all questions with the same level of sincerity and respect. You should not be able to tell from how a witness is testifying which side has called her. She should testify as a straight fact witness. As a *pro se* witness, of course, you should answer the questions of the opposing lawyer as sincerely and respectfully as if it was your own attorney questioning you – assuming you had an attorney.

ADVERSE EXAMINATION

One thing that's advantageous about being the plaintiff is that you can call any of the defendants in your case-in-chief, and you get to cross-examine them before they even testify for the defense. This is something you should think long and hard about before you make the decision. I like calling certain defendants in my case when their testimony is particularly helpful to my client's case. Also, when you call a defendant in your case, they do not get to set up their testimony the way they would prefer to do.

When a party calls its own witness, that witness is able to tell the story the way that is most effective for their side. This includes humanizing the witness in front of the jury–telling the jury about themselves–why they decided to become a police officer, how long they have been a police officer, or whatever the case may be.

When a plaintiff calls the defendant in her case, the defendant does not get to set up his testimony the way he wants. The plaintiff can cherry-pick only the most effective questions to ask the defendant. Once that happens, the defense must decide if they want to simply complete the full testimony during the plaintiff's case in chief, or ask a few questions during the plaintiff's case, and then choose to call the defendant *again* in the defense case-in-chief. When they do that, the plaintiff can cross-examine the defendant again. When I was a defense attorney, I used to hate it when the plaintiff would call my client in their case-in-chief.

But as I said earlier, you should think very carefully about whether it makes sense to call the defendant in your case-in-chief. Think about your cross-examination of the defendant. *Do not call the defendant unless you know doing so will help your case.*

If you do it right, calling the other side in your case is like capturing their flag. It also can be like judo, in which you use your opponent's strength against him. But this only works if there is something you know the defendant will have to admit that will advance your case. *Do not do it just to do it.*

For instance, if two defendants have significantly inconsistent testimony about the incident in question, you can call each of them to compare their stories and show the inconsistencies. If one defendant's testimony is inconsistent with what he wrote in a report, you can highlight this by calling him in your case.

You may decide that even if you have some good stuff you want to use from one or more of the defendants, it makes more sense to elicit that testimony on cross-examination after the defendants testify in their own case-in-chief. The decision whether to call a defendant in the plaintiff's case-in-chief is simply part of your overall thought process about how you want to structure your case.

Keep in mind the defendant can call the plaintiff as an adverse witness in the defense case, although that rarely happens, because the plaintiff has already testified in direct and cross-examination.

2. Exhibits

An exhibit is any physical thing, such as a document, a photograph, drawing, video or audio footage, etc. In order for an exhibit to be considered by the fact-finder, it must be admitted into evidence.

An exhibit may be admitted *substantively* or *demonstratively*. A **substantive exhibit** is like trial testimony–it may be admitted to prove or disprove a certain fact. For instance, a contract or a video clip of the incident in question may be considered substantive evidence.

On the other hand, a **demonstrative exhibit** is used to assist a witness in explaining what happened. Examples of demonstrative exhibits include a map of an intersection, or a photo of an intersection taken at a different time than the incident in question. This allows witnesses to point to where certain things were at different times during the incident. An exhibit that has been admitted demonstratively may be referenced by any party throughout the trial, including opening statements and closing arguments.

If you want to use something as a demonstrative exhibit, you should show it to the opposing side before trial begins. If they do not object, you can use it. If there is an objection, you have to present it to the judge to decide if the exhibit can be used. A demonstrative exhibit will generally be allowed if the judge believes it will be helpful to the jury's understanding of the facts of the case.

3. Stipulations

Sometimes the parties will agree, or stipulate, that a certain relevant fact is true. This is called a stipulation, and it can be published or stated to the jury as substantive evidence. For instance, the parties may stipulate that the moon was full, or that the park was scheduled to close at 9:00 p.m. on the night in question. This can streamline the trial by eliminating unnecessary testimony.

4. Answers To Requests for Admission of Facts, Answers to Interrogatories

These are a combination of testimony and exhibits. They are contained in documents that may be introduced as exhibits, but they contain sworn statements by the parties, which is essentially testimony. More often than not, specific answers to requests to admit or interrogatories are published by reading them to the jury or questioning the party who gave the answer while that party is on the stand.

5. Evidence Depositions

Under certain circumstances, a witness can testify in an evidence deposition, as opposed to a discovery deposition). The witness's deposition testimony will then be read by a live reader or played by video to the jury during the trial.

In federal court, all deposition testimony is considered trial testimony, so a discovery deposition can be read to the jury at trial just like an evidence deposition. But the format of discovery depositions is different from the format of evidence depositions. Evidence depositions are just like trial testimony: witnesses are asked questions formally as if they are testifying live at trial. Discovery depositions, while still Question and Answer format, are less structured, because discovery depositions are about discovering facts rather than testifying at trial. So, even in federal court, you may want to get a specific evidence deposition for a witness who cannot testify live in court. You will probably need to file a motion for leave to take an evidence deposition, unless all parties agree.

Note that there can be a difference between exhibits that are admitted and published to the jury, and exhibits that are "sent back" to the jury during jury deliberations. Not all admitted exhibits are sent back to the jury. Some documents that were admitted into evidence may contain irrelevant material or material that has been excluded by the judge. That material may be blacked out (known as being **redacted**), or the entire document may simply not go back to the jury. The discussion of what evidence goes back to the jury normally takes place after the jury is instructed and sent to deliberate.

Rule 50 Motion For Directed Verdict (FRCP 50)

After the plaintiff rests her case, the defendant may make a motion for directed verdict, a.k.a. a **Rule 50 Motion**, or a motion for judgment as a matter of law. In this type of motion, the defendant argues that even if the court views the plaintiff's evidence in the light most favorable to the plaintiff, there is still insufficient evidence for any reasonable jury to find in the plaintiff's favor. This is known as a Rule 50 motion, because it is based on FRCP 50.

In most cases, the judge will listen to brief arguments on the Rule 50 motion. The judge will allow the parties to submit written briefs if they want, but normally will deny the Rule 50 motion almost immediately. This is because the jury is still sitting in the jury room, and the judge will not want to delay the jury from considering the case and finishing its job. Obviously, the judge can also grant the Rule 50 motion. If this happens, the jury will be excused, and will be done with its service, and the judge will enter judgment as a matter of law in favor of the defendant. But judges rarely grant Rule 50 motions, for a couple reasons.

First, if the plaintiff does not have sufficient evidence to meet her burden of proof, it is more likely the judge would have granted the defendant's motion for summary judgment before the case went to trial. If the case reaches trial, either the defendant never filed a motion for summary judgment, or the defendant's motion for summary judgment was denied, meaning the judge found sufficient evidence for a reasonable jury to find in favor of the plaintiff. In that case, assuming the plaintiff introduces the necessary evidence during the trial, the judge will most likely allow the case to go to the jury.

The second reason judges are more likely to deny a directed verdict motion is that it is far more difficult for an appellate court to overturn a jury's verdict than it is to overturn a judge's granting of a Rule 50 motion. The law places a great deal of weight on a jury's verdict. In order for an appellate court to overturn a jury verdict, it must find that the verdict was "against the manifest weight of the evidence.". This is a very high standard. One thing to understand about judges is that they do not like to be reversed by an appellate court. The best way to avoid being reversed is to let the jury decide the case.

The third reason judges rarely grant directed verdict motions is that the jury is already there–you might as well let them decide the case, and the judge can still grant the motion after the jury returns its verdict. In fact, if a judge thinks the directed verdict motion may have some merit, she may reserve ruling on the motion, and let the jury decide the case. If the jury finds in favor of the defendant, there is no reason to revisit the directed verdict motion–the defendant won anyway, and the jury verdict is stronger and more likely to survive an appeal than a judge's decision granting a directed verdict motion. If the jury finds in favor of the plaintiff, the judge can always grant the directed verdict motion after the fact. However, that is unlikely, because judges do not like to invalidate a jury's verdict.

It is important to note that the plaintiff must still make sure she introduces sufficient evidence into the record to support her case. While it is somewhat rare, judges do grant directed verdict motions. Also, if you don't have enough evidence to support your case, the jury is likely to find against you anyway.

Jury Instruction Conference

After the defense case-in-chief, the court may send the jury home so the court can rule on the parties' proposed jury instructions. As noted above, jury instructions are the jury's instruction manual for how to evaluate the facts and decide the case. The instructions tell them what specific facts – often referred to as **elements** – must be proven. This informs the jury about the standard of proof. It explains the different types of damages and under what circumstances the damages should be awarded. It also contains the verdict forms the jury will complete after they have decided the case to indicate who won and how much money should be awarded, if any.

Many of the jury instructions will be undisputed, but you should still pay close attention to each one. You will normally have two sets of proposed instructions: marked and clean. Marked jury instructions will usually contain the title of the instruction at the top, followed by the text of the instruction, and then, at the bottom of the page, a little paragraph that looks like this:

Source: Seventh Circuit Pattern 1.01 (modified)

Plaintiff's Instruction Number 1

___ **Given**

___ **Refused**

___ **Withdrawn**

This little paragraph provides the source of the instruction, the number of the instruction for reference, and allows you to indicate what happened with the proposed instruction. If you submit a non-pattern instruction that comes from a case, you would substitute the case name and citation for the Pattern designation, so it looks like this:

Source: *Smith v. Jones,* 784 F.3d 99, 103 (1986)

Plaintiff's Instruction Number 1

___ **Given**

___ **Refused**

___ **Withdrawn**

Once the judge rules on jury instructions, the court staff may take a set of marked, approved instructions and make them "clean," or delete the title and the bottom paragraph, leaving only the text of the instruction. One or two sets of clean instructions will be provided to each party, and the jury will receive either one or multiple sets of clean instructions right before they go into the jury room to deliberate. The judge will read the instructions to the jury either right before or right after closing arguments.

WARNING: Dealing with the actual, physical jury instructions can be very confusing if you are not super-organized. They are essentially a whole bunch of sheets of white paper with similar looking blocks of text. But, of course, each one is different, and each one has an instruction that you want to include and argue for, or exclude and argue against. The jury instruction conference is relatively quick. The conference often happens after a full trial day, and the parties want to go home (or to their hotel rooms) to finalize their closing arguments.

Often, the judge will modify one or more of the proposed instructions, and one of the parties may have to go back to change the instruction according to the judge's orders, and make clean copies. The moral of this story is to make sure you have a good system for organizing the instructions as they come up in the jury instruction conference, and that you have a good set of accepted instructions after the judge rules on them. As a *pro se* litigant, I imagine the judge and the other attorneys will make sure you have some help organizing everything.

I suggest having a set of colored folders:

- Green for approved instructions

- Red for refused instructions

- Yellow for instructions that need to be modified

- Blue for withdrawn instructions

As soon as each proposed instruction is ruled on, it goes into the appropriate folder.

PRO TIP

If you're in an area with a law school, try going to the law school a couple of months ahead of your trial and letting them know you're a self-represented litigant who could use a law student to help you in your trial. Because law students are not yet lawyers, it is doubtful you can get one of them to represent you or try your case with you, but it could be helpful to have someone who knows a little bit about the law to assist you in preparing your case. Many law schools have clinics in which law students can represent you in certain kinds of cases under the supervision of a law professor, so you might as well ask about that too.

Closing Arguments

Finally—the climax of the trial, the closing arguments! You've made it to the point where you can explain directly to the jury why you should win your case. This is a big moment. I still believe a well-crafted opening statement is more influential in determining whether you will win or lose a case, but there's nothing like a closing argument to help you focus on the best parts of your case and actually *argue* to the jury about what happened in the case.

Remember, an opening statement can only include facts that you expect to come out at the trial, and you have to be very careful about how you structure the statement so the facts are as compelling as possible without having to argue. But in a closing *argument,* you get to let loose a little bit and tell the jury what you believe the facts *mean,* how they apply to the law contained in the jury instructions, and why you should win the case.

Because you are not an attorney, you will have some leeway in how you present your closing argument, but you should still sit down ahead of time, think about what you want to say, and think about the best way to structure it. When I am preparing a closing argument, I have a bunch of issues and facts rolling around in my head that I need to put in an order that makes sense. So, before I begin to write the outline, I write each fact on an index card. I also write each jury instruction I will want to address. But you have to be able to boil down a fact, an issue, or an instruction into 2-3 words that will fit on the card. This process will help you focus on what exactly you want to say, and once you can boil down an entire issue into a few words, you won't need a script, because you'll have thought it through.

Then, I sit at my desk or dinner table and literally put all my cards on the table. I move them around into different positions to see what works. I find it is more efficient than cutting and pasting and rearranging phrases on a computer or a pad of paper. Once you've figured out a good order, you can write it down, or you can just use the index cards as a guide. I think having a final outline is probably better because:

a) if your index cards get rearranged somehow, you have to figure out the order again, or you'll be lost, and;

b) you don't want to be fidgeting with cards while you're speaking to a jury.

But of course it all depends on your own comfort level.

The key to a closing argument is to provide the jury with a road map to find in your favor. Explain the key jury instructions and then bring in the facts, and explain why the facts and the law together require a finding for you.

Length Of Closing Argument

The length of closing arguments generally depends on the complexity and length of the case, but judges will want you to be brief–maybe 20-30 minutes. You should practice your closing argument at home before trial in front of a mirror or your family, and time yourself.

In a sense, you should be writing your closing argument throughout the case, as issues come up, as you conduct discovery, as things occur to you. Think about having a specific document called "Closing Thoughts", and jot down anything that comes to mind. Ask yourself why you filed this case in the first place.

Format Of Closing Arguments

In closing arguments, as in opening statements, the plaintiff addresses the jury first. Then the defendant addresses the jury. But unlike in opening statements, the plaintiff gets to go *again,* and offer a rebuttal to the defense closing. This is another reason it's fun to be a plaintiff. The plaintiff gets a rebuttal because it is the plaintiff who has the burden of proof, and so the theory is the plaintiff should get the last word. The rebuttal argument should be shorter than the main argument, maybe five minutes.

Instead of addressing every single argument the defense attorney makes during her closing argument, I recommend picking one or two things that tie into the larger themes of the case, and just hit those. When I was a defense attorney, I often saw the plaintiff's attorney do his closing rebuttal by just checking things off on his notes, as if it were a shopping list. It was very boring and not compelling. Don't be boring. Be compelling.

Jury Deliberation

After closing arguments, the judge will read the jury instructions to the jury. This is called **instructing the jury.** Once this happens, the jurors will be taken into the jury room to deliberate. Some judges instruct the jury right before closing arguments rather than after. I think instructing the jury before closing arguments is better, because the arguments make more sense once the jury has been instructed on the law.

Once the jury goes into the jury room to deliberate, the parties and the judge will decide which exhibits were admitted, and which exhibits should go back to the jury room so the jurors can use them to help decide the case. Then the judge's deputy will probably ask everyone for their cell phone numbers so they can call everyone if the jury has a question or if there is a verdict. Normally, you will have to leave the courtroom at that point. I recommend not going too far, just in case there's a question or a quick verdict. FYI a quick verdict is usually a defense verdict. A plaintiff's verdict will normally take a little longer, because once they decide on liability, they have to decide how much damages to award. The joke is that if the jury asks for a calculator, you're in good shape.

Trial Concepts

Before you try a case, you should understand some basic trial concepts. The first thing to understand is that we are moving from the Federal Rules of Civil Procedure (FRCP) to the **Federal Rules of Evidence (FRE).** The FRCP will still come up during trial, for instance in Rule 50 motions (motions for directed verdict), or Rule 59 motions (motion for a new trial). But, in a trial where evidence is king, you need to understand the rules of evidence.

Here are some key concepts to learn before you begin your trial:

Burden Of Proof

Generally, the plaintiff has the burden of proving her case by a *preponderance of the evidence.* That means the plaintiff must prove that any fact necessary to win her case is *more likely (or more probably) true than not true.* If you picture a scale of justice, the plaintiff must make the scale tilt just the tiniest bit toward her side. Contrast this with the criminal burden of proof, which requires the prosecution to prove *beyond a reasonable doubt* the defendant is guilty. The criminal burden of proof is the highest and most difficult in the law. On the other hand, the civil burden of proof is one of the lowest.

If the defendant sets forth any affirmative defenses, it is the defendant's burden to prove those affirmative defenses by a preponderance of the evidence–the same standard the plaintiff needs to prove his case. Usually, those affirmative defenses do not come into play until the plaintiff has met his burden of proof.

Relevance (a.k.a. Probative Value) vs. Prejudice

Determining what evidence will be allowed into the record for the jury to consider often boils down to relevance vs. prejudice. So, let's take a look at both concepts.

RELEVANCE (FRE 401, 402)

In order for evidence to be admissible (legally acceptable to be made part of the official court record which will be considered by the factfinder), it must be: 1) relevant and; 2) reliable.

Relevance means in court what it means to the rest of us on the outside: it has to be factually related to one or more of the issues in the case. Under Federal Rule of Evidence 401, which defines relevance, evidence is relevant if:

1) it has a tendency to make a fact more or less probably true than not true, and;

2) the fact is of consequence in determining the action.

In plain English, this means that a certain piece of evidence is relevant if it makes a fact more or less true, if that fact is necessary to prove one of the elements the law says must be proven for a party to succeed in the case.

For Example:

In Bob's traffic accident lawsuit against Adam, if Bob can prove his light was green at the time of the accident, he has a much better chance to win the case. Evidence that other cars were proceeding through the intersection along with Bob at the same time he was going through the intersection would make it more likely that his light was green. This is relevant evidence. However, evidence that other cars were proceeding through the intersection 25 minutes before the accident would probably not be relevant, because that has nothing to do with the color of Bob's traffic light at the time of the accident.

PREJUDICE

Outside of court, when we say someone is prejudiced, we normally mean they are bigoted, i.e. racist. They are prejudiced against a group of people. But in court, "prejudice" means harm. In litigation, if you say you would be prejudiced by the introduction of certain evidence, it means that it would hurt your case. Of course, that is exactly why the other side wants to admit the evidence, right? They want to hurt your case. That is the adversarial process. There is a joke we lawyers make sometimes: when someone tries to introduce evidence, the other side stands up and says, "Objection, judge." The judge says, "What is the basis for your objection?" The objecting lawyer says, "It hurts my case, judge." Jokes like these are why most funny people people do not become lawyers, and why most lawyers do not become comedians. One exception is my friend Paul Farahvar. Check him out.

In order for evidence to be barred or **prohibited** based on prejudice, that evidence must be *unfairly* or *unduly* prejudicial, a.k.a it must result in *unfair prejudice*. This is normally defined as "more prejudicial than probative." In other words, the **prejudice**–the harm to one party– outweighs the value of the evidence to prove or disprove a relevant fact.

So, let's say in our accident case, Bob's opponent, Adam, wants to introduce evidence that two years before the accident, Bob received a traffic ticket for speeding. Adam says this is relevant because it shows Bob has a history of disobeying traffic laws. But Bob says:

1) what happened two years ago has nothing to do with what happened on the date of the accident;

2) receiving a ticket does not necessarily mean someone is guilty, and;

3) speeding is not the same thing as violating a red light.

These are all reasons why the speeding ticket evidence is not very relevant. Also, Bob will argue that the prejudice to him will be far greater than the tiny bit of relevance it may have. In all likelihood, the speeding ticket evidence would be barred by the judge because the prejudice outweighs the probative value, i.e. the relevance.

Reliability

Even if evidence is relevant, it will not be admissible unless it is also *reliable.* That means the evidence must be trustworthy. **Hearsay evidence** (discussed later in this chapter) is normally not admissible because it lacks reliability. It is an out of court statement by someone who is not present at trial, introduced to prove the truth of the matter asserted in the statement.

So, when Bob testifies he heard Jane tell a police officer she saw that his light was green, he is essentially bringing in another witness on his behalf, except this witness will not be able to be cross-examined by the other side, because she won't be in court.

Also, Bob does not have personal knowledge of what Jane saw. Thus, Bob's testimony about Jane's statement is not sufficiently reliable to be admitted into evidence. However, if Jane comes to court, and testifies that she saw that Bob's light was green, that is reliable because she has personal knowledge of what she saw, and she can be cross-examined on her testimony.

Foundation

Foundation is related to reliability. In order for evidence to be reliable, it must have the proper **foundation.** It must be able to "stand up" on its own. Think of a house without a proper foundation. It is weak, and is likely to fall over or collapse. It is not reliable. For instance, if Bob wants to testify that his light was green, he will have to *lay the foundation* for his statement. In other words, he will have to explain how he knows his light was green. He would normally do this by first testifying that he observed the light as he drove toward the intersection. Without that foundation, the fact finder has no way of knowing if they can trust Bob's statement. For all they know, some random, unknown person told Bob the light was green.

So Bob must first explain how he knows his light was green before he testifies it was green. He must lay the foundation for his testimony that the light was green.

Foundation also comes into play with expert testimony. Someone who testifies as an expert witness must first lay the foundation for her expertise. This means she must describe her qualifications–her education, experience, and training – that allows her to be considered an expert on the subject of her testimony.

Practically speaking, the provision that comes into play most often when it comes to admission of relevant evidence is FRE 403, which states that "[t]he court may exclude relevant evidence if its probative value is substantially outweighed by a danger of one or more of the following: unfair prejudice, confusing the issues, misleading the jury, undue delay, wasting time, or needlessly presenting cumulative evidence."

Rule 403 says that relevant and admissible evidence may be barred (a.k.a. prohibited) if its probative value–meaning its importance in proving one fact or another–is outweighed by the prejudice to one of the parties.

Here's a classic example:

Criminal convictions of a party or a witness can sometimes be admitted under the theory that someone who has committed a crime may be more willing to lie than someone who has not committed a crime. Some people think this is a very overbroad and speculative assumption, but that is the theory courts use. The admissibility of criminal convictions is spelled out in FRE 609, which we will discuss in a later section. In any event, the theory is that certain convictions may have some probative value in assisting the jury to evaluate the credibility of the witness.

But let's say the witness was convicted of murder. Surely, that witness– and the party who calls that witness–will suffer **prejudice** (i.e. harm) because people tend not to like people who commit murders. Jurors may think, "I don't care what he says, I won't listen to a murderer," or if the plaintiff was convicted of murder, some jurors may be unwilling to award money to a convicted murderer even if he proves his case under the law. The judge may decide the danger of unfair prejudice to the plaintiff is greater than the limited probative value of the conviction. In that case, the conviction will be excluded. In other words, the other side will not be able to mention it during the trial. Another option is for the judge to allow the fact that the witness committed a felony but not identify the type of felony it was.

Hearsay (FRE 801-807)

A hearsay statement is defined as an out-of-court statement introduced for the truth of the matter asserted. *See* FRE 801. Let's break that down a bit.

In our traffic accident case, Plaintiff Bob wants to testify that he heard his friend Jane tell a police officer after the accident that Bob's light was green as he approached the intersection. He wants to testify about this in order to convince the jury that his light was green and he is not at fault for the accident.

This is a hearsay statement, because it involves an out-of-court statement (Jane telling the officer Bob's light was green) introduced for the truth of the matter asserted (Bob's light was, in fact, green).

Hearsay is normally not allowed because it is considered not reliable enough for the jury to hear, especially if Jane will not be a witness and she cannot be asked about the statement on the witness stand. It would be too easy for Bob to make up the statement.

WHAT IS *NOT* A HEARSAY STATEMENT?

Let's say the accident resulted in serious injuries to the other driver, and Bob was arrested for reckless driving, including running a red light. Bob sues arresting officer Smith for false arrest, claiming the officer had no probable cause to believe Bob's light was red. Bob wants to testify that Jane told the officer Bob's light was green. It's the same statement as in our last example.

Is this hearsay?

No.

Why?

In this case, the question is not whether Bob's light was actually green. The question is whether the officer *had reason to believe* his light was green. If Jane told the officer Bob's light was green, that is relevant to whether the officer had probable cause to believe Bob ran a red light, *even if Jane's statement was false.* The issue is the officer's knowledge, not whether the light was actually green or red. So, Bob is introducing Jane's statement for the fact that the statement was made, not for the truth of whether his light was green. Bob is allowed to testify to that because he observed Jane make the statement.

Another statement that is not hearsay under the rules is the statement of a party-opponent of the side asking the questions (see FRE 801(d)(1)). So, Plaintiff Bob can ask any witness about a statement made by Defendant Officer Smith.

Remember: HEARSAY IS NOT ALLOWED.

(Except when it is. See below.)

HEARSAY EXCEPTIONS

FRE 803 and 807 contain all of the Hearsay exceptions. These are categories of statements that do not violate the Hearsay rule, even if they are hearsay. There are 24 of these exceptions—we're not going to go into them now—so check out these rules before trial.

Authenticity

In order to be admitted, evidence must not only be relevant, it must be reliable. Most exhibits need to be authenticated before they can be admitted into evidence. This normally means an exhibit must be supported by sworn testimony. For instance, an attorney or a party cannot just admit into evidence a jail record with the plaintiff's name on it without someone from the jail laying the foundation—i.e. authenticating the record.

So, a witness from the jail would testify to certain facts about the record so the jury can be satisfied that it was not just a made-up document. Many documents can be authenticated as business records, in what is known as the *business records exception* to the hearsay rule, which is covered by FRE 803(6). Under this rule, a business record may be admitted into evidence if it can be established that the record:

1) was made in the ordinary course of business at such-and-such organization (jail, office, hospital, etc.)

2) it was one of the normal functions of that organization to make records such as the record in question, and;

3) the information contained in the record was documented at or near the time it was received.

These are basic factors that are supposed to ensure that the record is what it appears to be. The logic of this exception is that there is less of a reason to believe a record has been falsified if it was a routine record produced by an organization that routinely generates the same type of record.

Impeachment

To **impeach** a witness is to undermine her credibility by introducing evidence of a statement she made before trial that is inconsistent with the statement she is making at trial. Witnesses are often impeached with their deposition testimony from earlier in the case, but you can use any sworn testimony to impeach a witness, including depositions in other cases, or testimony in other proceedings, such as criminal trials.

You can also use other statements to impeach a witness. For instance, if Officer Bob says one thing on the witness stand, you can impeach him by pointing out that he stated something different in his arrest report,or any other report he wrote. You can also call another witness to impeach the first witness. For example, in a traffic accident case, Frank testifies his light was green. You can call the officer who investigated the accident to testify Frank told him his light was red. These are what we call **prior inconsistent statements**.

Example of impeachment by using deposition testimony:

"Q. Mr. Smith, you just testified that your light was green as you approached the intersection?

A. That is correct.

Q. You gave a deposition in this case?

A. Yes, I did.

Q. That was on December 21, 2022?

A. Yes.

Q. In that deposition, you were asked questions about the accident.

A. Yes.

Q. Before you testified in that deposition, you took an oath to tell the truth?

A. Correct.

Q. That was the same oath that you took today before you testified.

A. Yes.

Q. And at your deposition, you did tell the truth.

A. Of course.

Q. At your deposition, you were asked the following question, and you gave the following answer:

Q. *"Mr. Smith, what color was your light as you approached the intersection?"*

A. *"I couldn't see the light because I was too busy trying to change the radio station in my car."*

A. Yes, that's what I said.

Boom. Impeachment.

This is just an example of how I like to handle impeachments. They don't have to be exactly like this. For instance, you don't have to point out that the witness was under oath at his deposition, or that he told the truth, but I believe these questions make for a more effective impeachment.

Remember: if you have a really good prior inconsistent statement, you want to use it to the greatest effect possible. You want to build it up, take some time, and make sure the jury knows you believe this is a big deal. So, you ask a few more questions than you have to.

The basic elements are:

1) that the witness gave a deposition (or testified in another proceeding);

2) that he was under oath, and;

3) that he gave X answer to X question.

It is important that the prior testimony be actually inconsistent with the testimony he gives in court, otherwise you may get an objection for "Not Impeaching," as in the prior testimony was not inconsistent with the current testimony, so it is not impeaching.

Having said that, if you are cross-examining the opposing party, his prior statements do not have to be inconsistent. You can ask him about anything he said in the past, assuming it is relevant to the case, because he is a party opponent, and it is admissible as a statement of a party opponent.

Movement & Positioning While Examining a Witness

When questioning a witness, make sure the jury can hear your questions and the witness's answers. If the witness speaks softly, try moving further away so that the witness knows to speak loud enough so you can hear her—that way, the jury will hear her as well. I will often move to where the farthest juror is seated to make sure all the jurors can hear the witness.

Often, a witness will need to leave the witness stand and into the **well of the courtroom** (that means the center of the courtroom) in order to demonstrate something physical or to testify about an exhibit,such as a photograph or a map, on an easel. When this happens, you need to make sure the witness is facing the jury so they hear what she is saying. You need to make sure your questions are loud enough for them to hear. And, of course, you need to make sure the jury can see the exhibit. Generally the most effective way to do this is to place the easel a few feet away and directly in front of the jury box, and you and the witness stand on either side of the easel. Also, be aware of the court reporter who has to hear everything and is probably sitting on the side of the judge.

If you want to approach the witness on the witness stand to provide her an exhibit or for some other reason, some judges require that you ask permission: "Your Honor, may I approach the witness?" While we're on the subject, any time you want to address the judge during the trial, you ask, "Your Honor, may I approach the bench?"

Additional Considerations For *Pro Se* Litigants At Trial

Here are some other considerations when thinking about how you want to structure your case:

Primacy And Recency

People tend to remember the first and the last things they heard more than what they heard in the middle. For this reason, consider calling your most impactful witnesses first and last. Any weak or not particularly exciting witnesses you may want to call in the middle of your case. The best way to get the jurors to fall asleep is to play a video deposition after lunch. The lights get dimmed, if the testimony is not captivating, this will be a perfect time for a little nap.

Make Sure You Get Subpoenas Out In Time

Do you need to subpoena a witness? If so, you need to think about that a month or two before the trial so you can get that witness served with a **subpoena**. Remember, witnesses are not required to testify in a proceeding unless they are properly served with a subpoena. Review FRCP 45 to learn about how to do this.

Admission of Criminal Convictions

The admissibility of criminal convictions to impeach a witness's credibility is governed by FRE 609. It is based on very specific facts. Generally, a felony conviction that is less than 10 years old at the time of the trial, or a conviction that resulted in a sentence that ended less than 10 years before the trial–whichever is later–must be admitted, subject to FRE 403–which means that a judge may bar the conviction if she believes it is more **prejudicial** (harmful to the witness) than **probative** (relevant).

If more than 10 years has passed since the conviction or since the witness was released from confinement, whichever is later, a felony conviction is admissible only if its probative value, supported by specific facts and circumstances, substantially outweighs its prejudicial effect, and the proponent gives an adverse party reasonable written notice of the intent to use it so that the party has a fair opportunity to contest its use.

If the witness was convicted of a crime involving dishonesty, such as fraud, perjury, or knowingly writing a bad check, *the conviction must be admitted,* whether it is a felony or misdemeanor.

Impeachment by a criminal conviction is based on the idea that someone who has committed a felony or a crime that involves dishonesty would be more willing to lie under oath than someone who has not been convicted. The 10-year rule embodied in FRE 609 is based on the idea that the more distant the conviction or the incarceration, the less likely it is going to affect the witness's credibility.

Trial Objections

Objections during a trial are like those you might make during a deposition, except when you're on trial, you have a judge ruling on the objections immediately. There are more objections available at trial.

- When making an objection at trial, try to stay away from speaking objections when you can. As in a deposition, stick to legal objections. A **speaking objection** is a wordy objection that gets into the specifics of the testimony, and it can start to be argumentative. **Legal objections**, on the other hand, are specific categories of objections without additional commentary. Most judges are experienced and will understand your legal objection without you having to explain it.

- If you believe you need to explain the full basis of your objection, ask to approach the bench or for a sidebar.

- When you make an objection, stand up and make your objection clearly, confidently, and loud enough for the judge to hear. But use a neutral tone. No yelling, no dramatics. As a *pro se* litigant, you will be allowed some leeway in terms of how you phrase your objections. But, you should still try to be as accurate as you can.

- Direct your attention to the judge, not the other side.

- Do not address the opposing attorney or party directly. Always address the judge.

- Keep in mind that you do not need to object to everything you can. In fact, you probably should *not* object to everything you can. You don't want to give the jury the idea that there is something you don't want them to hear. Only object to things you think are objectionable and will hurt your case somehow.

Here are the most common trial objections:

• **Asked and Answered** (sometimes referred to as **"cumulative"**)

The other attorney or party is repeatedly asking the same question to the witness, hoping for a different answer. Sometimes, the witness doesn't actually answer the question, or offers an evasive answer. In those situations, you can ask the question more than once.

• **Leading**

When the other side asks a leading question of its own witness. Remember, you are *not* allowed to ask leading questions of any witness you call, except those you call as adverse witnesses. Having said that, you are generally allowed to ask leading questions that are preliminary in order to keep things moving.

• **Calls for Hearsay**

Question calls for a hearsay statement, i.e. "What color did she say the light was?"

• **Disclosure**

This objection is made when the objecting party believes that the witness has testified to a fact that has not been disclosed by the other side. When someone makes a disclosure objection, the judge will normally call the parties to the bench (where the judge sits) and ask the party seeking to admit the evidence – sometimes called the **proponent of the evidence** – to prove that the information was disclosed.

• **Compound**

Generally, you are not allowed to ask multiple questions in one question. For example: "How did you get to the park, what time did you get to the park, and what happened when you got to the park?" These are three questions, and should be asked as three separate questions. Otherwise, it creates a very confusing record, and is confusing for the witness and the jury.

• Narrative

Witnesses are generally not allowed to speak about something for more than a sentence or two before being asked another question. It should be Question-Answer, Question-Answer, Question-Answer. If the answer gets too long, the other side may object to the testimony as a narrative.

As a *pro se* litigant, you may be allowed to testify narratively, because there is no one to question you. Some judges allow narrative testimony by *pro se* litigants, but others require that the *pro se* litigant ask himself questions and answer them. This sounds silly, but it makes a certain amount of sense. (Check out the Woody Allen movie *Bananas* for a classic take on this issue.)

• Argumentative

When the question is more of an argument. Sometimes, an aggressive cross-examination can turn into an argument, especially if the questioner and the witness are going back-and-forth quickly.

• Move to Strike

Sometimes, the question is perfectly fine, but the witness says something objectionable. For instance, the question is, "what color was your light?" and the witness says, "pretty sure it was green—at least that's what I was told." At this point, you would object to hearsay, and request that the court strike the testimony by saying, "objection, hearsay, move to strike." If the judge agrees with you and sustains the objection, the judge will most likely say something like, "the testimony is stricken, and the jury is instructed to disregard the testimony."

Of course, the damage has been done, and the jury cannot "un-hear" the testimony. If you believe the testimony is so damaging that it severely harms your case, you can move for a **mistrial**. If the judge grants the mistrial, the trial is over, the jury is excused, and the trial must start over again on a new date. Judges will rarely grant a mistrial, but there's no harm in asking if you truly believe the testimony has affected your ability to receive a fair trial.

• Outside the Scope

Generally, a cross-examination must stay within the scope of issues discussed during the direct examination. One exception to this rule is when a plaintiff calls a defendant as an adverse witness. Sometimes, the parties agree that the defense attorney can go "outside the scope of the direct" during his cross-examination in order to complete all questioning of the defendant. That way, the defense does not need to call the defendant again.

• Relevance

The question is seeking information not relevant to the case.

• Calls for Speculation/Foundation

"Calls for speculation" and "foundation" are two sides to the same coin. They are not always identical, but they are related. A question that calls for **speculation**, like,"what did you think he meant when he said…" does not seek information, but the witness's uneducated assumption about something. It calls for the witness to speculate.

A "Foundation" objection essentially argues that the witness has no factual basis to answer the question. For example, a witness testifies she has eaten at McDonald's on and off throughout her life. The attorney asks, "At what temperature are McDonald's hamburgers cooked?" The questioner has not demonstrated that the witness has any reason to know at what temperature the hamburgers are cooked. The questioner will have to lay the foundation for that question by asking the witness about her experience or training about how McDonald's cooks its hamburgers. Without that foundation, the witness would be speculating about the temperature of McDonald's hamburgers.

• Timeframe

This objection is for questions that seek information from an undefined point in time during the incident. "What did you see?" can mean one thing when the witness is driving toward the intersection, and another when she is standing outside her car after the accident.

• Calls for a Legal Conclusion

This is essentially a foundation objection, but a bit more specific. The objector is claiming that the witness lacks the qualifications (i.e. the foundation) to be able to offer an opinion on a legal question.

General Approach & Demeanor Throughout The Case

It may seem easy for opposing lawyers to have a respectful and civil relationship. They all know how the process works, they are all professionals, and none of them were personally involved in the underlying incident. But staying civil and respectful may be more difficult for you as a *pro se* litigant because you are the one personally affected by what happened. Whatever happened, happened *to you*. To make matters worse, you are in a foreign environment where almost everyone else works on a daily basis and went to school to learn how to do what they're doing. You're the outsider, and you have a distinct disadvantage.

Regardless, you must keep your composure and act professionally throughout the lawsuit, and especially at trial. A trial is a battle for the hearts and minds of the jury. It is harder to win those hearts and minds when you're acting disrespectfully.

And remember that you have a secret weapon: you care more than they do. This case means far more to you than it means to the lawyers who will go on to a different case when this one is over, and in fact are probably dealing with other cases right now.

Here's another secret weapon: you're the underdog, and everyone wants to root for the underdog. You may also get more leeway from jurors because you're up against professional lawyers, which is all the more reason to conduct yourself professionally. The better you act in court, the more credit you'll get from the jury.

So keep your cool, work hard, and show up prepared. Stay civil and respectful, especially with the judge. Most judges will bend over backward to make sure you get a fair trial despite your obvious disadvantage, and they will be more inclined to help you if you conduct yourself respectfully and reasonably. You will blow away the jury, which is expecting you to be unprepared, maybe volatile–a courtroom amateur. No one has to know you read this awesome book that prepared you to kick ass in the courtroom.

But, the fact is you are an amateur. You are not a professional court person. So, use that to your advantage. You can be a little bit (*little* bit) more casual than the lawyers. After all, you don't know this legal stuff. You're just an everyday Joe or Jane, telling it like it is. You can even say it like this:

"Hey, I'm not a fancy lawyer like these people. All I have on my side is the truth. All I can do is tell you what happened, and hope you see this for what it is, and not get sidetracked by what the lawyers are telling you."

But this approach will only work if you maintain a sense of dignity and respect for everyone. You can get a little laugh by teasing the fancy lawyers, but if it starts to get bitter or disrespectful, you can lose that jury and confirm their stereotypes about unrepresented people in court.

Chapter Recap

Jury Selection

The Seventh Amendment guarantees Americans a jury trial in civil cases, a right unique to few countries. In federal court, a civil jury must contain at least six people, up to 12, with a unanimous verdict unless parties agree otherwise.

Jury selection is where potential jurors are questioned by judges or attorneys. The goal of jury selection is to de-select jurors unfavorable to your case, using peremptory and for-cause challenges.

- **Peremptory challenges** allow dismissing jurors without explanation, usually limited to 3 or 5.

- **For-cause challenges** involve showing a juror's inability to be fair and impartial.

- **Batson challenges** prevent discriminatory use of peremptory challenges based on race, gender, or other factors.

Jury selection proceeds in steps, including questioning, challenges, and finalizing the jury. Strategies include excluding potential jurors based on negatives and considering group dynamics. Practical methods like using sticky notes help in tracking potential jurors during selection.

Opening Statements

An **opening statement** is a summary of the case's story, not an argument, serving as the jury's introduction to the facts. It frames the issues for the jury and can be more crucial than closing arguments, setting the tone for how evidence will be evaluated. Studies suggest jurors often make up their minds after opening statements.

Body Language

Body language is crucial when addressing the jury, as people are visual learners and pay attention to what they see.

→ Maintain an appropriate distance from the jury box (3 to 5 feet).

→ Avoid unnecessary movement, as it can distract the jury unless used purposefully to illustrate a point.

→ When moving, do so with intention, such as to emphasize a specific argument or point.

→ Avoid casual or defensive hand positions like putting hands in pockets, on hips, clasping behind back, or folding arms.

→ Keep hands above the waist in a comfortable neutral position or use the podium's sides if necessary.

→ Practice both verbal delivery and physical gestures, including hand movements, in front of a mirror to refine your presentation skills.

Case-In-Chief

The case-in-chief is the main part of the trial where each party presents evidence to support their claims or defenses. Each party can introduce evidence during the other party's case-in-chief if they can establish the necessary foundation.

PLAINTIFF'S CASE-IN-CHIEF

The plaintiff introduces evidence to support their claims, primarily through witness testimony and exhibits such as documents, photographs, diagrams, and audiovisual recordings.

After presenting all evidence, the plaintiff formally "rests" their case-in-chief.

DEFENDANT'S CASE-IN-CHIEF

Following the plaintiff's case-in-chief, the defendant presents evidence to support their defense. It's important to note that the defendant is not obligated to introduce evidence since the burden of proof lies with the plaintiff. However, they may choose to do so to bolster their defense.

PREPARE YOUR WITNESSES

Ensure that witnesses are ready and available when needed during the trial. Organize witnesses in the expected order of their appearance and have exhibits prepared and readily accessible.

Admitting Evidence

When someone refers to "admitting" or "introducing into evidence," they're discussing the process of officially including a fact in the court record.

Ways to admit evidence:

- Witness Testimony

- Exhibits

- Stipulation

- Answers to Interrogatories, requests for admission

- Evidence depositions

DIRECT EXAMINATION AND CROSS-EXAMINATION

During direct examination, the party calling the witness asks open-ended questions. Cross-examination allows the opposing party to ask leading questions. While most questions during cross-examination should be leading, incorporating some open-ended questions can add interest and drama to the proceedings. Re-direct and re-cross examination may follow.

EXCEPTIONS TO OPEN-ENDED QUESTION RULE

Preliminary questions and dealing with adverse or hostile witnesses may warrant deviations from open-ended questioning.

RULE 50 MOTION FOR DIRECTED VERDICT

After the plaintiff rests their case, the defendant may file a Rule 50 Motion, also known as a motion for judgment as a matter of law. This motion argues that even with the evidence presented, no reasonable jury could find in favor of the plaintiff. Reasons for rare granting including:

- **Prior Evidence:** If evidence was insufficient, a summary judgment might have been granted earlier.

- **Appellate Difficulty:** It's harder for appellate courts to overturn a jury's verdict than a judge's ruling.

- **Jury's Presence:** It's more practical to let the jury decide since they're already present.

Jury Instruction Conference

After the defense presents its case-in-chief, the court may adjourn for a jury instruction conference. Here, the judge reviews proposed jury instructions, which serve as a guide for the jury in deciding the case.

PURPOSE OF JURY INSTRUCTIONS

- Outline specific facts ("elements") required for a verdict.

- Clarify the standard of proof.

- Explain types of damages and when they should be awarded.

- Provide verdict forms.

PROCESS

Parties submit two sets of proposed instructions: marked and clean. The judge reviews and may modify proposed instructions. You can organize your instructions using colored folders

Marked: Includes source, instruction number, and status (given, refused, withdrawn).

Clean: Text only, without additional markings.

Closing Arguments

In the culmination of the trial, closing arguments allow you to directly persuade the jury of your case's merits.

- Craft your argument by organizing key facts and issues on index cards, then arranging them for the most effective structure.

- Keep your presentation concise, focusing on key themes rather than addressing every defense argument.

- As the plaintiff, you'll address the jury first, followed by the defendant, with a shorter rebuttal opportunity.

- Engage the jury effectively to emphasize your points and provide a clear roadmap to support your case.

Jury Deliberation

Following closing arguments, the judge instructs the jury on the law before sending them into deliberation. Parties and the judge decide which exhibits to send back to aid the jury's decision-making process. Be prepared to await the jury's decision nearby, as a quick verdict may indicate a defense victory, while a plaintiff's verdict may take longer, especially if damages need to be decided. Stay readily available for questions or a verdict, as the jury's decision could come swiftly.

Trial Concepts

Before proceeding with a trial, it's crucial to grasp fundamental trial concepts, particularly the transition from the Federal Rules of Civil Procedure (FRCP) to the Federal Rules of Evidence (FRE). While the FRCP still applies in certain motions during trial, understanding the rules of evidence is paramount as evidence plays a central role in trial proceedings.

BURDEN OF PROOF

In civil cases, the burden of proof typically rests with the plaintiff, requiring them to establish their case by a preponderance of the evidence, meaning the facts are more likely true than not. Affirmative defenses introduced by the defendant also require proof by a preponderance of the evidence.

RELEVANCE VS. PREJUDICE

Admissibility of evidence hinges on its relevance and reliability. Evidence must tend to make a fact more or less probable and be of consequence in the case. Unfair harm or disadvantage caused by the admission of certain evidence.

AUTHENTICITY AND IMPEACHMENT

Evidence must be authenticated to ensure its reliability, often through sworn testimony. Impeachment involves undermining a witness's credibility through prior inconsistent statements or other means.

MOVEMENT & POSITIONING WHILE EXAMINING A WITNESS

Ensure clear communication between you, the witness, and the jury, particularly when witnesses demonstrate physical actions or testify about exhibits. Be mindful of the jury's ability to hear and see, especially when using exhibits or approaching the witness.

Additional Considerations

PRIMACY AND RECENCY

Jurors remember the first and last things heard the most, so place impactful witnesses first and last, weaker ones in the middle. Pro tip: avoid dull video depositions after lunch; jurors may lose focus.

SUBPOENAS

Plan to serve subpoenas a month or two before trial. Witnesses must be properly served to testify in court.

Admission of Criminal Convictions

Admission of criminal convictions is governed by FRE 609, based on specific facts. Felony convictions within 10 years or released within 10 years are generally admissible. Convictions for crimes involving dishonesty must be admitted, regardless of type or timing.

Trial Objections

- Make objections clearly and confidently.

- Avoid speaking objections; stick to legal objections.

- Direct objections to the judge, not opposing counsel.

- Common objections include leading questions, hearsay, and relevance.

- Move to strike testimony if necessary; request a mistrial if testimony severely harms the case.

General Approach & Demeanor Throughout the Case

- Maintain composure and act professionally.

- Embrace the role of the underdog; jurors may root for you.

- Stay civil and respectful, especially with the judge.

- Leverage your amateur status to connect with jurors, but maintain dignity and respect.

PART III

Statutes of Limitations

Heck v. Humphrey, 512 U.S. 477 (1994)

Statutes of limitations are so important they deserve their own chapter. Statutes of limitations are strict deadlines for filing cases. If you file after the applicable statute of limitations expires, your case will probably be **dismissed with prejudice**, which means you cannot file it again. In other words, if you don't file in time, you will be forever barred from filing your lawsuit. There is no wiggle room for judges to give someone a break.

> **See Chapter 15 for filing deadlines in employment cases.**

Statutes of limitations can be tricky. There is no federal statute of limitations for civil rights claims. Instead, the federal courts in each state use the most relevant statute of limitations in that state. Different states have different statutes of limitations. Most state statutes of limitations for federal civil rights claims are two or three years from the date of accrual. But remember, laws and statutes of limitations can change.

If you want to include state law claims in your federal lawsuit against a local unit of government, the statute of limitations may be different. For instance, in Illinois, the personal injury statute of limitations is two years. But if you are suing a municipality, or an employee of a municipality, under state law, *you only have one year to file.* See the Illinois Tort Immunity Act, 745 ILCS 10/8-101.

So in Illinois, you have two years to file a *federal* claim against a municipality or municipal employee, but only one year to file a *state* law claim against the same municipality or municipal employee.

Also, many states have strict **notice requirements** in which you must make a claim to the municipality in a very specific way, often within six months of the date of the incident. This only affects claims under state law, not federal law. Make sure you check the law in your state to figure out whether that state has notice requirements.

For example, the statute of limitations in Illinois for personal injury lawsuits is two years from the date of **accrual.** That means federal claims in a federal civil rights lawsuit in Illinois must be filed within two years of the date of accrual.

What is an "accrual," you ask? Read on.

Make sure you confirm the statute of limitations in your state when investigating a possible claim.

Know Your Accrual Date

To determine when the statute of limitations expires, you must know when the limitations period begins. The beginning date of a limitations period is called an "accrual date." The limitations period does not start until the cause of action *accrues*–that is, it becomes a viable (legally recognized) claim as a matter of law. Not all causes of action accrue on the date of the first incident, such as the arrest.

False Arrest & Unlawful Detention Claims

A false arrest or unlawful detention claim accrues on the date of the arrest or detention. If you believe you were arrested without probable cause, otherwise known as a **false arrest,** or temporarily detained without reasonable suspicion, known as an **unlawful detention**, your accrual date is the date of the arrest or detention. Your statute of limitations starts running on *that* day. If you were arrested in Illinois on January 20, 2020, you must file your lawsuit on or before January 20, 2022.

Malicious Prosecution Claims

If you file a lawsuit claiming **malicious prosecution**, meaning there was no probable cause for your prosecution in a case where you were convicted, that lawsuit would call into question the validity of your criminal conviction. You cannot file such a claim until and unless your conviction is invalidated, reversed, or overturned. For instance, if you were convicted of robbery and you have appealed that conviction, you cannot file a claim for malicious prosecution or wrongful conviction until and unless that conviction is reversed or vacated, either by the trial court or an appellate court. **Vacating a conviction** is like erasing it so it no longer exists.

If an appellate court reverses the trial court's finding, it may **vacate** the conviction and send the case back down to the trial court to re-try it. Or, if the trial court determines that newly discovered evidence warrants a new trial, it will vacate its own judgment of conviction. So, until your conviction has been vacated or otherwise invalidated, you cannot file yet.

Another way of saying this is that a malicious prosecution claim does not accrue or become legally viable until the conviction is overturned, reversed, or vacated. So, your statute of limitations period does not begin until that date. Let's say you appeal your conviction, and the appellate court reversed the conviction on April 7, 2021. If this took place in Illinois, you will now have two years–until April 7, 2023–to file your federal claims, and only one year–until April 7, 2022–to file a malicious prosecution claim under state law. Both state law and federal law recognize malicious prosecution claims. If you file within the statute of limitations, you can file state law and federal law malicious prosecution claims both in the same suit.

Unless your conviction was vacated, reversed, or otherwise invalidated, you cannot file a lawsuit that even suggests the conviction is invalid. This is the federal courts' way of honoring state court convictions.

What The *Heck?*

The main case in this area is *Heck v. Humphrey*, 512 U.S. 477 (1994), a U.S. Supreme Court decision that says a criminal defendant cannot claim damages for an allegedly unconstitutional conviction or imprisonment without showing that the conviction or sentence has been overturned in some way. If the conviction has not been vacated or reversed, the federal court will not allow you to pursue any lawsuit that would question the validity of the conviction. If you cite this case, resist the urge to make a bad pun using the case name like I did here.

If you are waiting for your criminal trial, sitting in jail, or out on bond, you cannot file a malicious prosecution case under federal law (or state law in most states) *until and unless the case ends in your favor*. Under federal law, that does not have to be an acquittal. Anything that is not a conviction will do the trick, including a dismissal of the charges for any reason or no reason. For instance, if a witness refuses to cooperate or the prosecutor believes it cannot prove its case, the prosecution will dismiss the charges, usually without stating the reason why. *Thompson v. Clark*, 142 S. Ct. 1332 (2022).

Some states, like Illinois, have different standards. For instance, in Illinois, a case must be dismissed in a manner *indicative of the innocence of the accused*. "[T]he abandonment of the criminal proceedings must compel an inference that there existed a lack of reasonable grounds to pursue the criminal prosecution." So, if a prosecutor dismisses a case by *Nolle Prosequi* (Latin for "not wish to prosecute"), it is considered a favorable termination only if the reason is the weakness of the case or the innocence of the accused. *Swick v. Liautaud,* 169 Ill. 2d 504 (Ill. 1996).

A dismissal based on any of the following is not indicative of the innocence of the accused, and therefore not sufficient to institute a *state law* malicious prosecution case in Illinois:

* An agreement or compromise with the accused,

* Misconduct on the part of the accused for the purpose of interfering with a trial (such as intimidating or threatening a prosecution witness),

* Mercy requested or accepted by the accused,

* The institution of new criminal proceedings, or,

* The impossibility or impracticability of bringing the accused to trial.

Remember to research your specific state law to make sure you know how your state handles these issues. Many states handle malicious prosecution cases similarly, but there may be key differences.

Because you cannot even file a malicious prosecution lawsuit until a favorable termination of the criminal case (or until an already-existing conviction is overturned), the statute of limitations clock does not begin to run–in other words, the claim does not accrue and cannot be filed–until the favorable termination of your criminal case or an existing conviction is overturned.

While malicious prosecution claims do not accrue until the case ends in favor of the accused, other types of claims, like false arrest and excessive force claims, accrue at the time of arrest. So, while you cannot file a *malicious prosecution* claim until after the criminal case terminates in favor of the accused or the conviction is overturned, you *must* file a *false arrest* claim within two years (or whatever your state's statute of limitations is) of the arrest, *even if the criminal case is still pending.*

What do you do if you get arrested on January 1, 2020, and you are acquitted (or your conviction is overturned) on March 8, 2023?

If you want to preserve your false arrest claim in Illinois, you must file your lawsuit within two years of your arrest or within whatever the applicable statute of limitations period is in your state. Your false arrest claim will probably be **stayed** – i.e., suspended–while your criminal case proceeds. In other words, the false arrest lawsuit will just sit there doing nothing until the criminal case has concluded. That is because the court hearing your civil lawsuit does not want to do anything that might interfere with the decisions of the criminal court. This is known as the *Younger* **doctrine of abstention**, based on the U.S. Supreme Court's decision in *Younger v. Harris,* 401 U.S. 37 (1971).

Special Statute of Limitations Rules
For Minors
& Disabled People

If you are a minor, or if you are under a legal disability, the rules may be different depending on your state. For instance, in Illinois, the statute of limitations for minors does not begin running until the minor's 18th birthday. So, if the cause of action accrues when you're 15 years old, you have until your 20th birthday (two years after you turn 18) to file your lawsuit. This also applies to death cases where at least one of the beneficiaries (i.e., the child of the person who died) is a minor. Under Illinois law, if you are under a legal disability, the statute of limitations does not begin running until that disability is removed. A **legal disability** is a physical or mental disability that makes it impossible for the person to manage their person or estate. See 5 ILCS 70/1.06. (No, a broken leg does not render you "legally disabled").

Even if you qualify for a longer statute of limitations, it doesn't mean you should wait that long. The idea behind statutes of limitations is that the longer you wait to file a lawsuit, the less people remember and the greater the likelihood that witnesses will die, or move away, or that documents or other evidence will be lost or destroyed. I prefer to file as soon as it becomes clear there is a basis for the lawsuit. Lawsuits can take years, so you should start the process as soon as you can.

Finally, and perhaps most importantly, the statute of limitations applies to individual defendants. In other words, you have to file within the statute of limitations for every defendant you want to sue. Under § 1983, one lawsuit against multiple defendants is really multiple individual lawsuits combined into one. Filing a lawsuit against one defendant within the statute of limitations does not allow you to sue additional defendants *after* the statute of limitations expires. You need to name everyone you need to sue before the statute of limitations expires.

Chapter Recap

Statutes of limitations are critical deadlines for filing lawsuits. Missing these deadlines generally means your case will be dismissed permanently. Filing your case after the statute of limitations expires typically results in dismissal with prejudice, preventing any future attempt to file the lawsuit. There is no uniform federal statute of limitations for civil rights claims. Federal courts use the state's relevant statute of limitations, which varies by state and can change over time. All defendants must be named before the statute of limitations expires.

Accrual Dates

The statute of limitations countdown starts on the "accrual date," the moment a claim becomes legally actionable, or viable. Always confirm your state's current statute of limitations and understand when your claim accrues. Different types of claims may accrue differently, affecting when the statute of limitations begins.

→ False Arrest/Unlawful Detention: These claims accrue at the time of the arrest or detention.

→ Malicious Prosecution: This claim accrues when a criminal case ends favorably for the defendant or a conviction is overturned.

→ *Heck v. Humphrey*: A plaintiff cannot challenge a conviction's constitutionality in a civil lawsuit without showing the conviction was reversed or vacated.

→ *Younger* Doctrine: Civil claims like false arrest might be paused while criminal proceedings are ongoing, to avoid interfering with state court proceedings.

Special Statute of Limitations Rules

In some states, the statute of limitations (statute of limitations) for minors doesn't start until they reach 18. This means a minor has until their 20th birthday to file a lawsuit if the cause of action accrued before they turned 18. The statute of limitations is also paused for individuals under a "legal disability," defined as a physical or mental incapacity that prevents managing one's affairs. The statute of limitations clock starts once the disability is removed.

Motions and Legal Research

Motions are how parties ask the court for specific rulings, orders, or judgments (known generally as "requested relief"). A party can file a motion to dismiss a case, a motion to compel another party to answer discovery, a motion for leave (permission) to file a specific document, like an amended complaint, or a motion for summary judgment, among others.

Motions are generally written and filed with the court. This is less true during trials, when parties often make oral motions based on events occurring in real time. For instance, if a witness says something irrelevant, a party can make an oral motion to strike the testimony, and the court will either grant or deny the motion on the spot. Some motions are simple, and can be ruled on quickly, but most motions require the parties to file briefs in support of and against the motion. The party filing the motion is known as the *movant.* The party opposing the motion is referred to as the *non-movant,* the *respondent,* or the *responding party.*

Often, when a party files a motion, the court will enter an order setting a **briefing schedule,** which is a set of deadlines for the parties to file their briefs. The moving party will file his motion, and the responding party will file her response brief by the date specified in the briefing schedule. Some courts allow the moving party to file a **reply brief** to respond to arguments made by the responding party. Other courts do not allow a reply brief unless the court grants the movant leave to file a reply. How does the movant request leave to file a reply brief? Through a motion, of course!

PRO TIP: KEEP IT SIMPLE

When you're writing or responding to a motion, you are attempting to persuade the judge to decide the issue in your favor, just like you hope to persuade a jury to decide the case in your favor if you get to trial. In order to persuade someone to agree with you, use clear, simple language, and a clear, simple argument. I've seen too many *pro se* briefs and pleadings peppered with fancy legal terms, often used improperly, in an attempt to come across as more lawyerly. You're not going to fool the judge into thinking you're a lawyer by using a lot of fancy legal terms, and you shouldn't want to do that anyway. To the extent it is necessary to use legal terms to make the argument, of course you should do so, but make sure you do it correctly. If a 10-cent word gets the idea across as well as a five-dollar word, go with the 10-cent word and save your money.

PRO TIP: AVOID EMOTIONAL ARGUMENTS

Resist the urge to use sarcasm or attack the motivations of the other side in your briefs (known as an *ad hominem* attack). You will be more successful when you stick to the specific facts and legal arguments and leave emotion out of your briefs. The judge is not likely to be moved by appeals to emotion, and will probably be turned off by sarcasm or by questioning the motivations of your opposing lawyers. Stick to criticizing or attacking the actions of the opposing party that give rise to the lawsuit, if relevant to the motion.

Legal Research & Authorities

As you may recall from Chapter 4, the federal court system contains three different levels of courts: the district courts,which are the trial courts, the appellate courts, which are divided into 13 appellate circuits, and the U.S. Supreme Court. State courts have similar systems, with trial courts, appellate courts, and state supreme courts.

STATE COURT SYSTEMS

The structures and titles of state courts vary from state to state. For instance, the highest state court in New York is called the Court of Appeals, and the level *below* the Court of Appeals is the Supreme Court. (You read that right: The New York Supreme Court is *below* the Court of Appeals.) In Arizona, the *Superior Court* is the trial court for most cases, the *appellate courts* are above the Superior Court, and above them all is the Arizona Supreme Court. For information on each state court, check out the National Center for State Courts website:

https://www.ncsc.org/information-and-resources/state-court-websites

As you might imagine, the U.S. Supreme Court is the final word on any given legal question. In other words, U.S. Supreme Court decisions are "controlling." But, the Supreme Court only accepts a fraction of the cases heard in the federal and state courts, and there are many legal questions that have not yet been addressed (and may never be addressed) at that level. So, the bulk of precedential case law is at the federal and state appellate level. **Precedential** means that the holding of a particular appellate opinion will govern the outcome of similar cases.

There are 13 federal appellate circuits in the U.S., including 12 regional circuits, and one "federal" circuit (how confusing is that?), which handles very specific types of cases from all over the U.S. and its territories.

Chart of federal appellate circuits

Circuit	Region
Dist. of Columbia	District of Columbia
Federal	All federal judicial districts – only handles certain types of cases
First	Maine, Massachusetts, New Hampshire, Puerto Rico, Rhode Island
Second	Connecticut, New York, Vermont
Third	Delaware, New Jersey, Pennsylvania, Virgin Islands
Fourth	Maryland, North Carolina, South Carolina, Virginia, West Virginia
Fifth	District of the Canal Zone, Louisiana, Mississippi, Texas
Sixth	Kentucky, Michigan, Ohio, Tennessee
Seventh	Illinois, Indiana, Wisconsin
Eighth	Arkansas, Iowa, Minnesota, Missouri, Nebraska, North Dakota, South Dakota
Ninth	Alaska, Arizona, California, Idaho, Montana, Nevada, Oregon, Washington, Guam, Hawaii
Tenth	Colorado, Kansas, New Mexico, Oklahoma, Utah, Wyoming
Eleventh	Alabama, Florida, Georgia

There are many legal questions that are answered differently by different federal circuits, so make sure you check the law in your own circuit. Also, just as there are many more cases from the appellate courts than from the Supreme Court, there are many more cases at the district court level than there are at the appellate court level. While district court cases have no precedential value–in other words, they are not binding on other courts– they can be persuasive. If one judge sees that her fellow judge in the same district decided a case one way, that might persuade her to decide a similar case the same way.

How Do You Refer To Specific Cases In A Brief?

Identifying a specific case you rely on in a legal brief is known as "citing" a case. Case citations have very specific rules, but they usually go like this:

1. Volume number

2. Abbreviation of reporter

3. First page number of case

4. Specific page for cited language

5. Year of decision

Here is an example of a U.S. Supreme Court case citation:

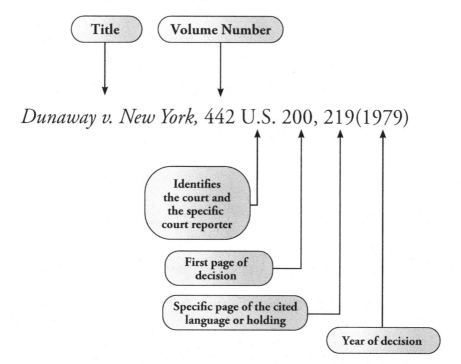

If you want to cite to a specific statement or legal proposition in a case on a specific page, you would include the specific page number, like this:

Dunaway v. New York, 442 U.S. 200, 219 (1979).

"Dunaway v. New York" is the name of the case. Case names in citations should be italicized. Or they can be underlined, but courts prefer italics to underlining, and italics look better.

"442" is the volume number. Back when books were the primary source of legal opinions, they were published by volume. This case is contained in the 442nd volume of the Supreme Court reporter.

"U.S." tells us this is a U.S. Supreme Court case. This is an abbreviation for **United States Reports**, the official, and preferred, Supreme Court reporter.

"200" is the first page of the decision within the 442nd volume.

"219" is the page number of the specific statement or holding you are citing.

It can take years for a Supreme Court decision to be published in the United States Reports. For instance, *Nieves v. Bartlett,* a 2019 Supreme Court decision, has not yet been published in the United States Reports as of June 2023.

In cases where the decision has not yet been published in the United States Reports, you would use the **Supreme Court Reporter,** which is cited like this:

Nieves v. Bartlett, 139 S. Ct. 1715 (2019).

Cite to a specific page like this:

Nieves v. Bartlett, 139 S. Ct. 1715, 1725 (2019).

Appellate cases are cited a bit differently than Supreme court decisions. They look like this:

Jenkins v. Keating, 147 F.3d 577 (7th Cir. 1998)

Jenkins v. Keating is the name of the case, which you've probably figured out by now.

147 is the volume number

F.3d is the abbreviation for the reporter, called the Federal Reporter. We are now on the third series of federal reporters, so it is abbreviated "F.3d."

577 is the first page of the case within that volume.

(7ᵗʰ Cir. 1998) refers to the specific federal circuit that decided the case, and the year of decision.

There are plenty of other citation rules (like how to cite state law cases) we won't get into here. The recognized authority for legal citations is called *The Bluebook (A Uniform System of Citation)*. You can purchase this on Amazon for $30 and up, or you can find it at a public law library. You can also see how cases are cited in published case law.

Legal Research Options

But where and how do you find these cases? How do you look them up? Most of us have heard about major legal research software like Westlaw, Lexis, and Casetext, but these programs can be expensive–up to hundreds of dollars a month.

So what is a non-rich non-lawyer to do? One answer is **Google Scholar** (https://scholar.google.com/), which contains articles and case law on different topics. And, of course, there's plain old **Google.** I often go to Google first before I use my legal research software, just to see what's out there. There's so much online: cases, articles, and summaries. Many of the more important cases are featured in Wikipedia. Google can be a solid starting point, though you cannot rely on any old thing you found on Google in a legal brief. Don't cite an article about a case (and *definitely* do not cite a Wikipedia article) when you can cite the case itself.

Another option is your local public law library. Many of these libraries are contained in local courthouses. For a directory of public law libraries by state, check out the **American Association of Law Libraries** website: https://www.aallnet.org/advocacy/government-relations/online-legal-information/. Many local law libraries have terminals where you can research the law using one of the major legal research programs like Westlaw or Lexis-Nexis.

Also, many **law school libraries** are open to the public. Public law school libraries should be open to the public, and some private law school libraries may be as well. Call ahead to see if they're open to the public before heading out. Some law school libraries, like the University of Chicago Law School Library, don't even allow other students in from the same school unless they're law students.

If you are incarcerated, your correctional facility may have a library, and most correctional facilities should have access to some form of computerized legal research, either in the law library or on a kiosk.

Chapter Recap

Parties use **motions** to request specific rulings, orders, or judgments from the court. Motions are crucial tools for legal advocacy, requiring clear and persuasive writing.

Types of motions include motions to dismiss, compel, for leave to file certain documents, and for summary judgment. They're generally filed in writing, except during trials where parties often make oral motions.

The motion process often involves a briefing schedule, which contains deadlines for the movant (the party making the motion) and the respondent (the party opposing the motion) to submit their written arguments.

Use clear and simple language to make your point effectively.

Stick to facts and legal arguments without resorting to sarcasm or questioning the other side's motives.

Legal Research & Authorities

The Federal Court System comprises district courts (trial courts), appellate courts (13 circuits), and the U.S. Supreme Court. State Court Systems vary by state but generally include trial courts, appellate courts, and a supreme court. U.S. Supreme Court decisions are controlling, but appellate and district court decisions also play significant roles.

Citing Cases in Legal Briefs

Proper citation is essential for referencing legal authorities in briefs and arguments. Citation format includes the volume number, reporter abbreviation, case page, specific page for cited language, and decision year.

Legal Research Options

Google Scholar and other online databases offer access to case law and legal articles.

Public law libraries are a valuable resource for accessing legal databases and research materials. Some law school libraries are open to the public as well. For incarcerated individuals, correctional facilities usually provide access to legal research tools.

Forms Of Relief:
What Can I Get
Out Of My Lawsuit?

FRCP 65: Injunctions and Restraining Orders

You believe your rights were violated, so you want to sue someone.

But why?

Before you go through the hassle of a lawsuit, ask yourself what you want out of the lawsuit.

What's your goal?

Some people want their day in court–they want to be heard. Others want the defendant to be held accountable somehow for what he, she, or it did. Most want both.

However, as a legal matter, there are only two categories of relief a court can award to someone who files a lawsuit: **money damages** and **injunctive relief.**

Let's talk about them.

Money Damages

Lawsuits seeking money damages are far more common than actions seeking injunctive relief.

There are three types of money damages that can be awarded in federal court: Compensatory damages, punitive damages, and nominal damages.

Compensatory Damages

As its name implies, **compensatory damages** are intended to compensate the plaintiff for the harm caused by the defendant if there is a finding that the defendant violated the plaintiff's rights. In federal court, the different categories of compensatory damages follow the laws of the state in which the lawsuit takes place.

Generally, compensatory damages include 1) **special damages,** which are objective and easily quantifiable damages, such as medical expenses and lost wages, and 2) **general damages**, such as pain and suffering and mental anguish. General damages are more subjective and more difficult to calculate.

Punitive Damages

Punitive damages, also known as exemplary damages, are not intended to compensate a plaintiff. Instead, they are designed to punish a defendant and discourage future bad acts by the defendant and others. Punitive damages are only available in certain kinds of cases and under specific conditions. For instance, in civil rights cases, punitive damages can be awarded only where the plaintiff proves the defendant's conduct involved reckless or callous indifference to the plaintiff's federally protected rights, or when the defendant's conduct was motivated by evil motive or intent.

Nominal Damages

Sometimes, a plaintiff suffers no actual harm as a result of the defendant's violation of his rights other than the violation itself. **Nominal damages**, often as little as one dollar, are intended to demonstrate that the defendant violated the plaintiff's rights, but the plaintiff suffered no actual damages. Instead, nominal damages are intended to commemorate the plaintiff's vindication of his rights in court. They are only awarded in certain types of cases where the rights in question are deemed to be special, such as constitutional rights. In most state law **tort actions** (such as a personal injury case), a plaintiff must prove he sustained damages in order to win the case.

Injunctive Relief

Injunctive relief, also known as equitable relief, is where a court *requires* a party to do something or *restrains* a party from doing something. Injunctive relief can only be granted by a judge, not a jury. In other words, there is no right to a jury trial when seeking injunctive or equitable relief.

Examples of injunctive relief include improving prison conditions and prohibiting the enforcement of an unconstitutional law. Injunctive relief is considered a very extreme measure, as courts do not tell people or institutions what to do and what not to do without a very good reason.

Because injunctive relief is such a coercive measure, there are a number of safeguards to protect parties from unreasonable orders.

Injunctive relief is available only when two conditions are met:

1) There is a likelihood that the plaintiff will suffer substantial and immediate "irreparable" harm and;

2) There exists no other remedy to adequately address this threat of harm.

In other words, failure to grant the requested relief will harm the plaintiff in ways that cannot be repaired, and money damages are insufficient to protect the plaintiff from experiencing the harm. Where money damages are intended to compensate the plaintiff for harm experienced in the past, injunctive relief is forward-looking, and intended to protect the plaintiff (and, often others in similar circumstances) from experiencing harm in the future.

The first step in obtaining injunctive relief is to seek a **preliminary injunction,** also known as a **temporary restraining order ("TRO"),** which is available only if the party seeking the relief can prove four things:

1. Irreparable injury in the absence of an order granting the

injunctive relief;

2. That the threatened injury to the moving party outweighs the harm to the opposing party resulting from the order;

3. That the injunction is not adverse to public interest; and

4. That the moving party has a substantial likelihood of success on the merits.

If granted, the TRO will go into effect immediately while the lawsuit goes through the litigation process. A plaintiff can sue for injunctive relief and money damages in the same lawsuit. In that case, the judge will decide the injunctive relief issue and the jury will decide whether to award money damages, assuming at least one side has requested a trial by jury.

It is very difficult to obtain injunctive relief, even with an attorney. But it is much more difficult on your own.

Chapter Recap

When considering a lawsuit, understanding the potential outcomes and what you aim to achieve is crucial. The legal system provides different forms of relief for successful litigants, primarily categorized into two: money damages and injunctive relief.

Money Damages

Money damages are the most common form of relief sought in lawsuits. They are intended to compensate the plaintiff for the harm caused by the defendant's actions. There are three main types of money damages:

- **Compensatory Damages** - These aim to compensate the plaintiff for actual losses, including both special damages (quantifiable losses like medical expenses and lost wages) and general damages (more subjective losses like pain and suffering).

- **Punitive Damages** - These are not compensatory but are designed to punish the defendant for particularly egregious behavior and deter similar future conduct.

- **Nominal Damages** - Awarded when the plaintiff's rights are violated but no substantial harm is suffered, nominal damages symbolize the vindication of rights rather than financial compensation.

Injunctive Relief

Injunctive relief, or equitable relief, involves a court order requiring a party to do or refrain from doing specific actions. It's a measure taken to prevent irreparable harm that cannot be adequately remedied by monetary compensation. Injunctive relief is sought when:

1. The plaintiff faces a substantial and immediate risk of irreparable harm.

2. No other remedy (such as money damages) can adequately prevent this harm.

Injunctive relief is forward-looking, aiming to protect the plaintiff (and sometimes others in similar situations) from future harm. Obtaining this type of relief begins with a request for a preliminary injunction or a temporary restraining order (TRO), which demands proof of:

1. **Irreparable injury** if the injunction isn't granted.

2. **Balance of harms** favors the party seeking the injunction.

3. **Public interest** is not harmed by the injunction.

4. **Likelihood of success** on the merits of the case by the party seeking the injunction.

Achieving injunctive relief is challenging and typically requires the expertise of an attorney. Those considering pursuing this path on their own should carefully evaluate the likelihood of success and the potential impact on their case. Given the complexity and challenges of obtaining injunctive relief, individuals without legal representation should consider the feasibility and potential effectiveness of their legal action.

Prisoner Litigation

Filing a lawsuit as a prisoner has its own challenges. Obviously, there are limitations you have in prison or jail you do not have on the outside.

Prison Litigation Reform Act

The first thing you should know about is the Prison Litigation Reform Act (PLRA). The PLRA is a series of federal laws enacted by Congress in 1996 to limit prisoner litigation.

When Does the PLRA Apply?

The PLRA governs cases filed by *current inmates or detainees* in any jail or prison. The specific language is "any person incarcerated or detained in any facility who is accused of, convicted of, sentenced for, or adjudicated delinquent for, violations of criminal law or the terms and conditions of parole, probation, pretrial release, or diversionary program." 42 U.S.C. § 1997e.

In other words, as long as the plaintiff is incarcerated or detained *at the time of the filing,* the lawsuit will be governed by the PLRA–even if the plaintiff is released from custody a day later. However, if the lawsuit is filed *after the plaintiff is released from custody,* the PLRA does not apply, even if the lawsuit relates to something that happened while the plaintiff was detained or incarcerated in a jail or prison.

Generally, if you are on parole, probation, or some form of in-home custody such as electronic monitoring, the PLRA will not apply, because you are not a "prisoner" as defined by the PLRA. But you should check your federal circuit case law to confirm this.

If you know you will be released soon, you may want to wait before filing your lawsuit until after you are released to avoid the limitations imposed by the PLRA. Of course, you need to make sure you file the lawsuit within the relevant statute of limitations, or else you will be barred from filing at all. So, if the statute of limitations will expire before you are released, you have to file before you are released.

Here Are The Key Provisions Of The PLRA:

FILING FEES

28 U.S.C. 1915(b)

It used to be that any person living below the poverty line–including a prisoner–could file *in forma pauperis* (in the form of a pauper), and not have to pay filing fees, which are around $400. However, under the PLRA, prisoners are now required to pay full filing fees. If the prisoner-plaintiff is approved to proceed *in forma pauperis,* the payments can be stretched out over time and deducted from the prisoner's prison account until the full fee is paid.

FRIVOLOUS LAWSUITS

The PLRA establishes a **three-strikes rule** for frivolous lawsuits. Prisoners who have had three or more previous lawsuits dismissed as frivolous, malicious, or for failure to state a claim cannot file new lawsuits without prepaying the full filing fee, unless they are in imminent danger of serious physical injury.

LIMITATIONS ON INJUNCTIVE RELIEF

The PLRA places restrictions on courts' ability to issue **injunctive relief** (orders to change prison conditions). The standard to award injunctive relief is higher under the PLRA. Courts must find that ongoing violations of prisoners' rights exist and that no other remedy will suffice before ordering injunctive relief.

EXHAUSTION OF ADMINISTRATIVE REMEDIES

42 U.S. Code § 1997e(a)

Prisoners must exhaust all available administrative remedies set by the jail or prison before filing a lawsuit in federal court. This means they must first go through the jail or prison's grievance procedures and complete them before seeking relief in court. This includes all administrative appeals. If you file a lawsuit before your grievance process is completed, your case may be dismissed.

Grievance rules can be very specific. You must file your grievance on time according to prison or jail rules, and you must name all people you believe are responsible for violating your rights. If you cannot name them, you must identify them as specifically as possible in order to preserve your right to file a lawsuit once your grievance process is complete. The statute of limitations will not begin to run until after you have completed the grievance process. So, if your rights are violated on January 1, 2022, and you file a grievance, and the grievance process concludes on March 8, 2022, your statute of limitations clock will begin running on March 8, 2022.

SPECIAL MASTERS

In some cases, the PLRA allows courts to appoint special masters (volunteer attorneys) to oversee aspects of prison conditions, such as overcrowding or mental health services. This provision is designed to address systemic issues in prisons.

ATTORNEY FEE LIMITATIONS

42 U.S. Code § 1997e(d)

The PLRA limits the attorneys' fees that can be awarded to prisoners who prevail in lawsuits. Attorneys' fees are capped at 150% of the monetary judgment or injunctive relief obtained by the prisoner. It also limits the hourly rate an attorney can claim. This makes it less attractive for an attorney to handle a prisoner case, and more difficult for prisoners to obtain counsel.

Also, in civil rights cases, a prevailing plaintiff's attorney can submit a petition to the court requesting reasonable attorneys' fees. In non-prisoner cases, the fees awarded by the court are paid by the defendant. Under the PLRA, the court may order some percentage of those fees to be paid from the plaintiff's damages award.

NO EMOTIONAL DISTRESS DAMAGES WITHOUT PHYSICAL INJURY

42 U.S. Code § 1997e(e)

The PLRA restricts prisoners from recovering damages for emotional distress without a showing of physical injury. This limitation is intended to prevent prisoners from filing lawsuits solely for emotional distress claims.

MERIT REVIEW

42 U.S. Code § 1997e(c)

After a prisoner files a lawsuit against a government employee or entity, the next thing to happen will be a **merit review** conducted by the district court judge, who will identify legally valid claims and dismiss claims she determines are frivolous, malicious, or which fail to state a claim upon which relief may be granted. 28 U.S.C. 1915A. This is different than with non-prisoners, in which the defendant may (or may not) file a motion to dismiss. With prisoner lawsuits, the court's review is automatic.

If the court allows one or more claims to stand, the court will arrange for service of the complaint and summons on the defendants, either by direct service or using waivers of service. In other words, the incarcerated prisoner does not have to serve the defendants himself.

Chapter Recap

Enacted in 1996, the Prison Litigation Reform Act (PLRA) was designed to limit prisoner lawsuits by imposing several restrictions, including the requirement for prisoners to pay filing fees and exhaust administrative remedies, before heading to court.

The PLRA applies to individuals incarcerated or detained at the time the lawsuit is filed. The act does not apply if the lawsuit is filed after the plaintiff's release.

Under the PLRA, prisoners must pay the full filing fees, even if proceeding *in forma pauperis*, with payments deducted from their prison accounts over time. Prisoners with three or more dismissed lawsuits for being frivolous or malicious lose the privilege to file without prepaying fees, unless in imminent danger of serious physical injury.

The PLRA sets a higher bar for courts to grant injunctive relief, requiring proof of ongoing rights violations and the insufficiency of other remedies. PLRA requires prisoners to complete the prison's grievance procedures before filing a federal lawsuit, with specific rules on timely filing and naming responsible parties. It also restricts prisoners' ability to claim damages for emotional distress unless accompanied by physical injury, aiming to reduce claims based solely on emotional distress.

CHAPTER

14

Dismiss Your Own Case

The possibilities and dangers of the voluntary nonsuit

Under certain circumstances, a plaintiff can voluntarily dismiss his own case and **refile,** or file it again, at a later time. This is called a **dismissal without prejudice**. A dismissal "without prejudice" means a case has been dismissed–either by a judge or by the plaintiff–with **leave**, or permission, to refile the complaint within a certain amount of time.

Why Would I Want To Dismiss My Own Case?

Under certain circumstances, plaintiffs can dismiss their own lawsuits. But why would a plaintiff want to dismiss his own lawsuit?

There are several possible reasons you might want to dismiss your lawsuit. One reason has to do with the Prison Litigation Reform Act (PLRA), which we discuss in the Prisoner Litigation chapter. The PLRA contains numerous limitations on a plaintiff's ability to file suit or to collect damages. But, the PLRA only applies if the plaintiff is incarcerated in a jail or a prison *at the time she files her lawsuit*. If she files her lawsuit any time after being released–even if the lawsuit is about what happened in that jail or prison–the PLRA limitations do not apply.

A prisoner can file a lawsuit while he is in jail, then voluntarily dismiss his lawsuit when she gets released, and refile the lawsuit a day (or more) later. The new case will not be subject to the PLRA limitations.

There may be other reasons to **voluntarily dismiss** (or "nonsuit") your case. Maybe you're having health or family problems, and you don't have the time or the resources to pursue your case. You can dismiss the case and refile when you're in a better position to prosecute your case. Maybe you were represented by an attorney, but that attorney withdrew from the case, and you want to find another attorney. Normally, the judge will allow you 30 to 45 days to find another attorney, but if you're still having trouble finding an attorney, you can dismiss the case to give yourself some more time.

In federal court, the dismissal rule is FRCP 41. Rule 41(a)(1) provides that a plaintiff may dismiss his own case without prejudice by filing a notice of dismissal before the opposing party serves an answer or a summary judgment motion, or by stipulation of the parties. In other words, if all the parties agree, and file a written stipulation (agreement).

If the defendant has already answered the complaint, the plaintiff must file a motion requesting leave of the court to dismiss her case without prejudice. There are specific criteria the court will examine to determine if a voluntary dismissal would result in "plain legal prejudice" to the defendant.

State courts have similar provisions for voluntary dismissals, but as you know by now, state laws and rules differ, so you need to check your own state court rules to see how they handle voluntary dismissals.

Be aware!

Here are the things to know about voluntarily dismissing your case without prejudice:

First, if you nonsuit your case, you generally have one year to refile it as a new case. When you refile it, it is a new case, even though it is based on the same issues as the first lawsuit. It will have a new case number and you will have to serve the defendants with the summons and complaint just like you did the first time.

Second, you can only dismiss your case without prejudice **one time**. If you want to dismiss your case a second time, it must be with prejudice. In other words, you will not be able to refile that case again.

Third, be very careful of statutes of limitations (time limits for filing lawsuits). As we discuss in the statutes of limitations chapter, different states have different rules regarding statutes of limitations. For instance, Illinois has something called a **savings statute**, which allows a plaintiff to file a lawsuit within the remaining statute of limitations, or, if the statute has expired, within one year after a voluntary dismissal. But other states don't have the same rule, so if you dismiss your case after the original statute of limitations has expired, you may not be able to refile it.

Chapter Recap

A voluntary dismissal is a legal process where a plaintiff can dismiss their own case without prejudice, allowing them to refile the case later under certain conditions. Reasons to voluntarily dismiss a case include avoiding PLRA limitations by filing after release from incarceration, personal issues that hinder case management, or changes in legal representation.

Federal Rule (FRCP 41) allows plaintiffs to dismiss their cases without prejudice before the opposing party serves an answer or motion for summary judgment, or by mutual agreement. A case can only be dismissed without prejudice once; subsequent dismissals must be with prejudice, preventing refiling.

Careful consideration must be given to statutes of limitations, as dismissal and refiling must adhere to state-specific rules and timelines, including savings statutes that may allow refiling within a set period after dismissal.

Employment Discrimination Claims

Note: This chapter applies to the following federal laws:

- Title VII of the Civil Rights Act of 1964, which prohibits employment discrimination based on race, color, religion, sex and national origin

- The Americans with Disabilities Act (ADA)

- The Age Discrimination in Employment Act

- The Pregnancy Discrimination Act of 1978

There are very specific rules for filing employment discrimination cases in federal and state courts. A plaintiff claiming employment discrimination under federal law–and under most state laws–must exhaust administrative remedies before filing a lawsuit.

This means filing a claim, known as a **charge,** with the U.S. Equal Opportunity Commission (EEOC) **within 300 days of the alleged discriminatory action,** and waiting for the EEOC to issue a **right-to-sue letter.** The best resource for this is the EEOC website, https://www.eeoc.gov/filing-charge-discrimination.

The exception to this requirement are claims under the **Equal Pay Act (EPA).** If you're filing a claim under the EPA, you can go right to court without filing a claim with any administrative agency.

Most states, as well as many cities and counties, have their own employment discrimination laws and regulations, and their own agencies that enforce those laws, just like the EEOC enforces the federal laws. The state agencies are known as **Fair Employment Practices Agencies (FEPAs).**

The cool thing is that when you file a claim with either the EEOC or your local FEPA, the agency you file with will automatically cross-file with the other agency. For instance, if you file with the EEOC, it will cross-file with the local FEPA, assuming it has a worksharing agreement with the local FEPA, and if you file with your local FEPA, it will cross-file with the EEOC, if the basis for the claim is recognized under federal law. Some states' discrimination laws are broader than federal law. That way you can eventually file your claim in state court or federal court.

If you are thinking of filing in state court, you will want to familiarize yourself with the specific rules and laws in the state where the discrimination occurred. They are often similar to but not necessarily the same as the EEOC rules.

How The EEOC (And Likely Many PETAs) Works

1. You file your charge using the EEOC public portal, https://publicportal.eeoc.gov/Portal/Login.aspx.

2. You wait while the EEOC investigates.

3. The EEOC may decide the case is a good candidate for mediation. If they do, I highly suggest you take advantage of the opportunity. At a minimum, this allows you to "look under the hood" of the defendant employer to see what their arguments are, and how seriously they're taking your charge. Of course, you may be able to settle it as well. *Both parties must consent to mediation.*

4. The investigation can take a long time, but after 180 days, you can request a right-to-sue letter from the agency. You will have 90 days after receiving the right-to-sue letter to file your lawsuit in federal court.

Chapter Recap

Plaintiffs must exhaust administrative remedies by filing a charge with the U.S. Equal Employment Opportunity Commission (EEOC) within 300 days of the alleged discriminatory action and must wait for a "right-to-sue" letter before filing a lawsuit, except for claims under the Equal Pay Act (EPA), which do not require this step.

Claims should be filed either with the EEOC or a local Fair Employment Practices Agency (FEPA), which will cross-file the claim with the other agency if applicable, providing the option to pursue the claim in state or federal court.

The process involves filing a charge via the EEOC's public portal, awaiting investigation, possibly participating in mediation, and, after 180 days, requesting a right-to-sue letter, which then allows 90 days to file a lawsuit in federal court.

Conclusion

I would tell you that this book is literally the tip of the litigation iceberg, but despite how casually we use the term "literally" these days, we both know that there is no iceberg here, and this is just a book. But "tip of the iceberg" is a pretty good way to understand how much you still have to learn if you decide to pursue litigation.

Nevertheless, I hope you can now see the rough outlines of this complicated process. It can be helpful to see something from a distance, see how its parts fit together and relate to each other, get to know the main characters, and understand how the machinery operates, so when you're inside of it, engaged in the process, you know what's happening.

Now you know what you're getting yourself into before you make the decision to go forward.

Despite all the information in this book, and more that you will have to learn, I hope you realize that you can do this alone–if you must–but it will not be easy and it will not be quick. The fact that you took the time to purchase and read this book means that you have the desire and commitment to understand and effectively navigate the court system. This puts you ahead of many of your fellow *pro se* litigants.

I hope you can understand the reasoning behind the many rules and procedures you will have to learn, so it is no longer a foreign, seemingly random series of requirements, but rather something that makes sense and has logic.

Whatever you take away from this book, remember that the courts are for all of us–lawyers and non-lawyers alike, even if the system was designed by, and–let's face it–designed for lawyers. Indeed, as noted in the Introduction, the United States Code specifically references *pro se* litigants when it states that "[i]n all courts of the United States the parties may plead and conduct their own cases personally or by counsel…" 28 U.S.C. Sec. 1654.

It is no surprise that a legal profession has evolved to attempt to master this unmasterable system. The legal profession at its best is a true embodiment of the desire to serve others–and make a living doing it. It is an honorable profession, and I have been proud to make it my career. But the courthouse doors cannot be closed to others who–for whatever reason–cannot or will not hire a lawyer to represent them. The courts exist for all of us, and must be truly–not just technically–available to everyone, represented or not. Apologies to Judge Wapner, Judge Judy and all the other TV judges, but the American legal system is the true People's Court, even if it doesn't always operate that way. Don't let anyone tell you or even suggest that you are burdening the system by litigating on your own. It is the job of the legal system to accommodate all who play by the rules, just as it is the job of all litigants to learn and abide by those rules.

As Indiana University Professor Andrew Hammond wrote in a 2022 law review article, "the federal courts cannot fulfill the aspirations of a national forum for all Americans until these courts address the needs of those who walk through their courthouse doors without a lawyer."

Professor Hammond's words apply just as forcefully to state courts as they do to federal courts. So, go forth and try your case. Or don't. But make your decision wisely and with full knowledge of what it takes to be a player in this amazing, complicated, not completely fair system.

Glossary

Term	Definition
Absolute Immunity	An immunity that shields a potential defendant from civil liability, that applies regardless of the facts, as long as the defendant performed a specific function, such as prosecuting a case.
Accrue	To become a legally viable and enforceable claim.
Accrual Date	The beginning date of a limitations period, when a legal claim becomes viable.
Admissible	Capable of being admitted into evidence.
Admit into Evidence	To make part of the official court record that the factfinder may consider in deciding the case.
Affidavit/ Declaration	A written statement made under oath.
Affirmative Defense	A factual and/or legal assertion by a defendant that the defendant asserts defeats the plaintiff's claim, even if the plaintiff's allegations are true. Usually filed as part of an answer to the complaint.

Answer	Formal written response filed by a defendant in a civil lawsuit in which the defendant admits or denies the allegations in the complaint.
Authenticate	To prove to be real, true, or genuine.
Bates Stamp	When parties produce documents in discovery, the documents will often be bates-stamped, meaning each page will be stamped with a specific number so that they can be easily identified during discovery or at trial. This is not required, but it is a helpful way to identify and refer to specific documents.
Batson Challenge	An argument by a party during jury selection that another party unlawfully excused a potential juror for a prohibited reason, such as the person's race, ethnicity, or gender.
Battery	Generally defined as harmful or offensive contact by one person against another without the consent of that person under state law.
Boilerplate Objections	The same objections to all discovery requests regardless of the substance of the requests.
Breach	The violation of a defendant's duty to a plaintiff.
Brief	Document submitted to a court containing legal arguments, often in favor of or opposing a motion.
Briefing Schedule	A briefing schedule is a schedule containing due dates for the parties to file motions, response briefs, and reply briefs.

Burden of Proof	A party's duty to produce sufficient evidence to support an allegation or argument.
Case in Chief	The portion of a trial in which a party puts on evidence.
Citation	Specific identification of a case or law that a party uses to support a legal argument.
Causation	The cause-and-effect relationship between a defendant's conduct and a plaintiff's injury. Also known as "proximate cause".
Cause of Action	A recognized set of facts that the law allows a plaintiff to bring as a lawsuit, such as false arrest, employment discrimination, or breach of contract.
Civil Cover Sheet	A document filed with a complaint in federal court containing all the basic information about the case being filed.
Closing Argument	A closing argument is an opportunity for each party to remind jurors about key evidence presented and to persuade them to adopt an interpretation favorable to their position. The parties or their attorneys may argue reasonable inferences from the evidence that came out during the trial.
Common Law	A body of law consisting of cases decided by judges over time. Also known as "case law".
Compensatory Damages	Money awarded by a judge or jury intended to compensate the plaintiff for the harm caused by the defendant if there is a finding that the defendant violated the plaintiff's rights.

Complaint	The initial document filed by the plaintiff to initiate a civil lawsuit.
Counterclaim	A claim filed by a defendant against a plaintiff arising out of the same facts as the plaintiff's complaint against the defendant.
Court of Claims	A court where a person can file an action against the state itself for damages.
Credibility	Believability.
Damages	Money a plaintiff seeks from a defendant as a result of the defendant's alleged violation of the plaintiff's rights.
Deliberation	Discussion and/or evaluation of a case by a judge or a jury to decide the outcome of a case.
Demonstrative Exhibit	An item, such as a document, map, or photograph used by a witness to explain the witness's testimony.
Deposition Subpoena	A discovery device consisting of a court order requiring a non-party witness to appear for a deposition.
Deposition	Discovery device consisting of oral questioning of a party or witness under oath, typically transcribed by a court reporter.
Discovery	Formal part of a case in which the parties seek information from other parties and non-parties related to the lawsuit.
Dismissal with Prejudice	Dismissal of a case without the ability to re-file the case.
District Courts	The first level of courts in the federal court system. Often used in state court as well.

Diversity Jurisdiction	A means of getting a case into federal court if all of the parties on one side of the case are from a different state than all of the other parties, and the amount in controversy is greater than $75,000.
Document Subpoena	A court order issued by a lawyer or party requiring a non-party to produce documents or other tangible items.
Duty	The legal obligation of a party in a lawsuit to act or refrain from acting in a certain way.
Evidentiary Record	Collection of all the evidence related to a case, including exhibits and testimony.
Exculpatory Evidence	Evidence that is favorable to the criminal defendant.
False Arrest	Cause of action under the Fourth Amendment to the U.S. Constitution in which the plaintiff is allegedly arrested without probable cause.
Federal District Judges	Article III judges, primary judges in the district courts.
Federal Question Jurisdiction	Federal jurisdiction based on an alleged violation of a federal law, including the U.S. Constitution, a federal statute, or a federal regulation.
Final Pretrial Conference	A meeting between the parties, their attorneys, and the judge to discuss trial procedures and resolve any outstanding issues.
Final Pretrial Order (FPTO)	A document filed jointly by all parties. A road map for the trial, including witness and exhibit lists, statement of the case, and legal and factual disputes and stipulations.

For Cause Challenge	A party's motion to excuse a potential juror during jury selection, arguing that the potential juror would not be fair and impartial.
Foundation	The factual basis for evidence to be admitted or for a witness to testify about a certain topic or event.
General Damages	Financial damages for intangible injuries such as pain, suffering, and mental anguish.
Group Pleading	Suing a group of defendants without distinguishing between them and explaining what each of them did to violate the plaintiff's rights.
Hearsay	An out-of-court statement introduced to prove the truth of the matter asserted in the statement.
Impeachment	To impeach a witness in court is to attack the witness's credibility (i.e. believability or truthfulness) by introducing evidence contradicting her testimony in court.
Indemnification	The agreement of an employer to pay any civil judgment against an employee for actions taken within the scope of that person's employment.
Injunctive Relief	Also known as equitable relief, where a court requires a party to do something or restrains a party from doing something. Injunctive relief can only be granted by a judge, not a jury.
Intentional Torts	Unreasonable intentional conduct, such as a false arrest or a battery.

Interrogatories	Written questions by each party to other parties that must be answered under oath, in writing.
Irreparable Injury	Harm or injury that cannot be adequately compensated or remedied by any monetary award.
Jurisdiction	The legal authority of a specific court to try cases and rule on legal matters within a particular geographic area and/or over a certain type of legal case.
Jurors	A group of people selected by the parties who will make findings of fact and render a verdict in a lawsuit.
Jury Verdict	Decision rendered by a jury after a trial.
Legal Disability	A physical or mental disability that makes it impossible for a person to manage their own affairs.
Legal Standard	The portion of a legal brief that informs the court of the primary legal principles governing that particular type of motion.
Limitations Period	The period of time in which a case may be filed, after the cause of action accrues (becomes legally viable), and before the statute of limitations expires.
Litigation	Generally refers to the process of filing and pursuing a disputed matter in court. Also describes the application of the relevant facts of a case to the governing law.

Magistrate Judge	A federal judge who can hear cases just like district judges if all the parties to a lawsuit agree. Magistrate judges supervise discovery, decide discovery disputes, and conduct settlement conferences. Magistrate judges work closely with the parties to try to settle cases or move them along.
Malicious Prosecution	Cause of action alleging a wrongful prosecution, which generally requires a plaintiff to prove a lack of probable cause and malice by a defendant who initiates or continues a criminal action.
Material Fact	A fact that would change the outcome of the case under the law.
Merit Review	Review of a prisoner lawsuit by a federal judge (as required by the Prisoner litigation Reform Act), to identify legally valid claims and dismiss claims she determines are frivolous, malicious, or fail to state a claim upon which relief may be granted.
Monell Claim	A claim that alleges that a municipal defendant caused the plaintiff's rights to be violated because of a written or unwritten policy, custom or practice.
Money Damages	The most common type of damages awarded to a party who prevails in a lawsuit. Money damages can be used to compensate an injured party (compensatory damages) or to punish the wrongdoer (punitive damages).
Motion for Summary Judgement	A request made by a party for the court to rule in its favor based on the evidence presented during the discovery phase without the need for a trial.

Motion to Compel	A written motion asking the court to require another party to do something, like answering discovery within a certain amount of time or allowing a site visit.
Motion to Dismiss	A request by the defendant to dismiss the complaint because the complaint contains some defect, such as failing to state a valid claim.
Motion	A request to the court by a party for certain specific relief. Motions are usually written but can be made orally in certain circumstances.
Motion *in Limine*	Request by a party to exclude certain evidence or arguments during the trial based on specific legal grounds.
Negligence	Unreasonable non-intentional conduct, such as driving too fast or failing to take proper precautions when doing an activity.
Nominal Damages	Symbolic award after a trial (such as a dollar), intended to demonstrate that the defendant violated the plaintiff's rights, but the plaintiff suffered no actual damages.
Non-Parties	People and organizations who are not part of the lawsuit but who may possess information relevant to the lawsuit.
Notice of Deposition	Written notice announcing a party's intention to take the deposition of someone.
Offer of Judgment	An offer made by a civil defendant pursuant to Federal Rule of Civil Procedure 68, offering to accept a judgment against it in exchange for the plaintiff accepting a certain amount of money.
Opening Statement	A non-argumentative summary of the evidence a lawyer or party expects will come out at trial.

Original Jurisdiction	Jurisdiction of an appellate court, such as a supreme court, to hear matters directly, rather than by an appeal.
Otherwise Plead	To file a pleading in response to a complaint other than an answer. Usually a motion to dismiss the complaint.
Outside Counsel	Private law firm hired by a corporate or government defendant to represent that defendant in court.
PACER	The federal electronic docket and filing system.
Pendant Claim	A supplemental state law claim filed in federal court in a case that also includes at least one federal claim.
Peremptory Challenge	A request by a party to excuse or dismiss a potential juror without having to explain the basis of the request.
Pleadings	Generally used to define documents filed in court. Also used to refer to filed documents such as a complaint and answer, which define the legal and factual issues in a case.
Post Trial Motion	Motion to alter or set aside the judgment, seeking a new trial or adjustment of the jury's decision based on claims of errors made during the trial.
Precedent	Legal principle established by case law that governs the outcome of similar cases in certain jurisdictions.
Prejudice	The harm to a party in a case.

Preliminary Injunction	An order issued by a judge early in a lawsuit to stop a defendant from continuing their allegedly harmful actions while the court evaluates the merits of the case.
Propound	To formally issue or serve discovery requests to the other parties in a lawsuit.
Pretext	Fictional reason offered by an employer for an adverse action taken against an employee.
Pretrial Phase	The period right before the trial, when the parties make final preparations for the trial and submit pretrial documents to the court.
Prison Litigation Reform Act (PLRA)	A set of federal laws that place restrictions on the ability of prisoners to file federal lawsuits.
Procedural	Relating to court proceedings.
Prosecutorial Immunity	A doctrine shielding criminal prosecutors from civil liability for actions taken during the judicial phase of a criminal case.
Punitive Damages	Also known as exemplary damages, these damages are not intended to compensate a plaintiff. They are designed to punish a defendant and discourage future bad acts by the defendant and others.
Qualified Immunity	A doctrine that protects public officials from civil liability for constitutional violations if the law was not "clearly established" at the time of the alleged conduct.
Redact	Block out certain text from a document so that it cannot be seen.

Relevance	The quality of being related to an issue in a case. The tendency of a given item of evidence to prove or disprove a fact, in other words to make a fact more or less likely.
Removal	The transfer of a lawsuit containing at least one federal claim from a state court to federal court based on a motion by one of the parties (usually the defendant).
Request for Admission	Written request by one party to another, asking the recipient to admit or deny certain alleged facts.
Request for Production	Request by one party to another to produce specific documents, reports, records, or other evidence, like video footage.
Respondeat Superior	A doctrine allowing plaintiffs to sue employers for the actions of their employees if they are acting within the scope of employment.
Rider	A document attached to a subpoena that explains exactly what a party seeks by virtue of that subpoena.
Rule 16 Conference	A meeting between the judge and the attorneys or unrepresented parties to discuss case deadlines and scheduling.
Savings Statute	A state law that allows a plaintiff to file a lawsuit within the remaining statute of limitations, or, if the statute has expired, within a certain amount of time after a voluntary dismissal.
Scheduling Order	An order that contains deadlines for specific actions, such as completing discovery, amending the complaint, and naming additional parties.

Service of Process	The formal delivery of the summons and complaint to the defendant.
Settlement Conference	A voluntary process in which a judge facilitates settlement discussions between the parties.
Settlement Statement	A document submitted before a settlement conference, in which the parties explain their theories of liability and damages.
Sidebar	A conference between the judge and the attorneys and/or *pro se* parties away from the jury, so the jury does not hear what they are saying. If a party or an attorney wants to discuss a particular matter that comes up during trial, they will ask the court for a sidebar.
Sovereign Immunity	The immunity of states and the federal government from being sued.
Speaking Objection	An objection that is not a concise legal objection, that exceeds the necessary basis for the objection. A speaking objection often suggests to the witness how the attorney or party would like them to answer.
Special Damages	Objective and easily quantifiable damages, such as medical expenses and lost wages.
Standing Order	An order by a particular judge applying to all cases of a certain type. Standing orders can be found on the Court's website.
Status Report	A report filed with the Court to provide specific information about the status of the case to the judge.
Statutory Law	General description of law (i.e. statutes) established by an act of a legislative body, such as a state legislature or Congress.

Statement of Material Fact	A list of facts that a party asserts are undisputed that support the party's position in a summary judgment motion.
Statement of the Case	A brief, neutral summary of the case, including the date and location of the incident, the parties involved, and the claims and defenses, prepared prior to trial, to be read during jury selection.
Statute of Limitations	The time limit set by law that governs when a claim may be filed.
Stipulation	Formal agreement of the parties regarding a particular legal or factual issue in a case.
Strict Liability	When a person or company is held responsible for an injury even if it had no knowledge or intent to injure, such as product liability.
Subpoena	Order to a non-party to produce documents or to testify in a deposition, hearing, or trial. (A "non-party" is a person or an entity that is not a plaintiff or a defendant in the lawsuit but has information relevant to the case.)
Summons	A legal document notifying the defendant of the lawsuit.
Temporary Restraining Order (TRO)	A type of short-term injunction issued to prevent a party from taking a certain action until the court is able to evaluate the merits of a claim.
Tort	A wrongful act that may form the basis of a lawsuit. Not a pastry, which would be a torte.

Transcript	A word-for-word record of everything that was said on the record in a legal proceeding, such as a deposition or a trial.
Trial	The formal presentation of evidence and arguments to determine the outcome of a civil or criminal case.
Trier of Fact	The judge in a bench trial or the jury in a jury trial that determines which facts are true in a trial and renders a verdict after the trial.
Unlawful Detention	Temporary detention of an individual by law enforcement without reasonable suspicion to believe that person committed a crime.
Venire	A group of potential jurors, also known as the jury pool. A jury is eventually chosen from the venire.
Waive	Forfeit an argument or a right to object because it was not raised at the right time.
Waiver of Service	A defendant's written, signed agreement that she does not require the complaint to be served on her in accordance with the formal service requirements of the Federal Rules of Civil Procedure.
Well of the Courtroom	Center of the courtroom.
With Prejudice	Description of the dismissal of a complaint or the denial of a motion meaning that whatever was dismissed or denied cannot be re-filed.

Without Prejudice	Description of the dismissal of a complaint or the denial of a motion meaning whatever was dismissed or denied can be re-filed under certain circumstances. Dismissal of a complaint without prejudice means the plaintiff is allowed to file an amended complaint within a specified time frame that complies with the court's ruling. Denial of a motion without prejudice means the party who brought the motion can bring it again if circumstances change.
Witness Statements	Written accounts from witnesses collected by law enforcement.
Zebra	An animal in a zoo. Or out of a zoo. Nothing to do with litigation.

Appendix

This appendix is a selection of forms and sample documents you might find helpful to see what these things look like. Some of them – particularly the court forms – are pretty much the way they have to look. They are taken straight from the district courts' websites. Other documents, such as pleadings, motions, letters, etc., are just examples, and you have some leeway to craft them in a way you think is effective. Be creative and strategic but do so within the applicable rules.

Many of the appendix documents are drawn from real cases, but the names have been changed to protect the innocent (and probably the guilty too). I have created a fictional case, *Fred Smith v. Village of Sunnyside and Robert Jones.* The attorneys are fictional as well. Any similarity to people with the same names, as they say, is purely coincidental.

Most of these documents can be used in any federal district court, although some jurisdictions have specific formatting rules. For instance, the Federal District of Nevada requires numbered lines and other very specific items in submitted briefs. A sample page of a Nevada complaint is included in the appendix.

As an added bonus, I have included a chart of open records laws by state. Go to **www.tryyourowncase.com/resources** for MS Word and fillable PDF versions of these documents.

Enjoy!

APPENDIX
TABLE OF CONTENTS

THE UNITED STATES DISTRICT COURT
FOR THE NORTHERN DISTRICT OF ILLINOIS
EASTERN DIVISION

FRED SMITH,

Plaintiff,

v.

No. 22-cv-7749

Jury Trial Demanded.

VILLAGE OF SUNNYSIDE,
a Municipal Corporation, and
Sunnyside Police Detective
ROBERT JONES,

Defendants,

**DEFENDANTS' ANSWER AND AFFIRMATIVE DEFENSES
TO PLAINTIFF'S FIRST AMENDED COMPLAINT AT LAW**

NOW COME the Defendants, VILLAGE OF SUNNYSIDE, a Municipal Corporation, and Sunnyside Police Detective ROBERT JONES, and for their Answer and Affirmative Defenses to Plaintiff's First Amended Complaint at Law, state as follows:

1.   This action arises under the Constitution of the United States, particularly the Fourth and Fourteenth Amendments to the Constitution of the United States, under the laws of the United States, particularly the Civil Rights Act, Title 42 of the United States Code, §§ 1983 and 1988, and under the laws of the State of Illinois.

ANSWER: Defendants admit that this Honorable Court has jurisdiction over this matter but deny that Defendants violated the Fourth or Fourteenth Amendments to the Constitution, the Civil Rights Act, 42 U.S.C. § 1983, the laws of the State of Illinois, or any other law, and deny that they committed any wrongdoing whatsoever.

2.   The jurisdiction of this Court is invoked under the provisions of Title 28 of the United States Code, §§ 1331 and 1343. Plaintiff also invokes the supplemental jurisdiction of this Court pursuant to Title 28 of the United States Code, Section 1367.

ANSWER: Defendants admit that this Honorable Court has jurisdiction over this matter but deny that Defendants violated any law or committed any wrongdoing whatsoever.

3.   This Court has jurisdiction over this action pursuant to Title 28 of the United States Code §§ 1331 and 1367, as Plaintiff asserts claims under federal law and the state law claims arise out of the same facts as the federal claims. Venue is proper in the United States District Court for the Northern District of Illinois under Title 28 of the United States Code, § 1391(b)(2), as the events complained of occurred within this district.

ANSWER: Defendants admit that this Honorable Court has jurisdiction over this matter and that venue is proper, but deny that Defendants violated any law or committed any wrongdoing whatsoever.

4.   Plaintiff Fred Smith (hereinafter "Fred") is a decorated U.S. Marine veteran who served five combat tours in Iraq and Afghanistan and received a Purple Heart after being injured by enemy gunfire in the line of duty. At all times relevant, Fred was a resident of Cook County, Illinois.

ANSWER: Defendants lack knowledge or information sufficient to form a belief as to the truth of the allegations of this paragraph and therefore deny same.

5.   Defendant Village of Sunnyside is a government entity operating within the State of Illinois. Village of Sunnyside is responsible for the actions of its employees while acting within the scope of their employment. At all times relevant to this action, Village of Sunnyside was the employer of Defendant Jones.

ANSWER: Defendants admit that the Village of Sunnyside is a government entity operating within the State of Illinois. Defendants further admit that the Village of Sunnyside is the employer of Defendant Robert Jones. The remaining allegations of this paragraph call for a legal conclusion to which no answer is required. To the extent an answer is required, Defendants deny the remaining allegations of this paragraph.

2

6.   Defendant Robert Jones is sued in his individual capacity and was at all times relevant, a sworn police officer employed by Defendant Village of Sunnyside, and was acting within the scope of his agency, service and/or employment with the Village of Sunnyside, and was acting under color of the statutes, ordinances, regulations, customs, and usages of the State of Illinois.

ANSWER: Defendants admit that Defendant Robert Jones is a sworn police officer employed by Defendant Village of Sunnyside. Defendants further admit that Defendant Robert Jones was acting under color of law and within the scope of his employment during his interactions with Plaintiff. Defendants deny the remaining allegations of this paragraph.

7.   On April 25, 2022, Fred received an "Accident Notice" (hereinafter "notice") from the Village of Sunnyside, stating the Village received a report of a hit and run accident on April 2, 2022, involving his vehicle. The Notice stated, "It is your obligation to contact the Police Department and complete the accident report," and directed him to contact Defendant Jones. The Notice further informed Fred that "[t]his is the only notice you will receive. You must contact the Officer named below. Failure to do so will result in either a criminal complaint filed against you or a report filed with the Department of Transportation which could result in Suspension or Revocation of your driver's license or license plates."

ANSWER: Defendants admit that an accident notice was sent to Plaintiff's alleged address. Defendants further admit that the accident notice stated Plaintiff's vehicle was involved in a hit and run accident on April 2, 2022, and instructed Plaintiff to contact Defendant Robert Jones. Defendants lack knowledge or information sufficient to form a belief as to the truth of the remaining allegations of this paragraph and therefore deny same.

8.   On April 25, 2022 – the same day he received the notice – Fred left a voicemail message for Defendant Jones, and sent him an email, stating, "I just received a letter from you informing me that my vehicle was involved in hit and run accident. I assure you that my vehicle was not. No one drives it but me, and I, nor it were involved in an accident. On 4/2/22, I don't believe I left my

3

property on the Southside of Chicago. I'd like to resolve this as quickly as possible. Please call me ANYTIME at xxx-xxx-xxxx."

ANSWER: Defendants admit that Plaintiff left Defendant Robert Jones a

voicemail and sent Defendant Robert Jones an email on April 25, 2022. Defendants lack knowledge or information sufficient to form a belief as to the truth of the remaining allegations of this paragraph and therefore deny same.

9.   Defendant Jones called Fred the next day and told him that in order to clear things up, he just needed to take some photographs of Fred's car.

ANSWER: Defendants admit that Plaintiff and Defendant Robert Jones spoke on the telephone on April 26, 2022, and that Plaintiff agreed to come to the Sunnyside Police Department. Defendants deny the remaining allegations of this paragraph.

10.   On May 3, 2022 Fred drove to the Sunnyside Police Department so that Defendant Jones could photograph his car.

ANSWER: Defendants admit that Plaintiff drove to the Sunnyside Police Department on May 3, 2022. Defendants deny the remaining allegations of this paragraph.

11.   In fact, Defendant Jones had no interest in photographing Fred's car, and there was no hit and run accident on April 2. Jones sent the notice to Fred as a ruse in order to lure him into custody.

ANSWER: Defendants admit that Defendant Robert Jones used deception to lure Plaintiff from his home in order to effectuate a lawful arrest for which there was probable cause. Defendants deny the remaining allegations of this paragraph.

12. Defendant Jones unlawfully detained Fred for more than seven hours.

ANSWER: Defendants admit that Defendant Robert Jones took Plaintiff into custody when Plaintiff arrived at the Sunnyside Police Department. Defendants deny the remaining allegations of this paragraph.

4

13.   Defendant Jones refused to explain why he was detaining/arresting Fred unless he signed a Miranda waiver, which Fred refused to do.

ANSWER: Admit.

14.   Jones had no probable cause or reasonable suspicion that Fred had been involved in criminal activity.

ANSWER: Deny.

15.   Defendant Jones confiscated Fred's telephone without seeking or obtaining a warrant.

ANSWER: Defendants admit that Defendant Robert Jones took custody of Plaintiff's cell phone because probable cause existed that it contained evidence of criminal activity. Defendants deny the remaining allegations of this paragraph.

16.   Defendant Jones had no probable cause or reasonable suspicion to believe Fred's phone contained evidence of criminal activity.

ANSWER: Deny.

17.   Defendant Jones eventually released Fred without charges but refused to return Fred's telephone.

ANSWER: Defendants admit that Plaintiff was released from custody without charges on May 3, 2022. Defendants further admit that Defendants temporarily retained custody of Plaintiff's cell phone because probable cause existed that it contained evidence of criminal activity. Defendants deny the remaining allegations of this paragraph.

18.   Fred retained a criminal defense attorney, who contacted Defendant Jones in order to set up a time for Fred to come into the police station to provide whatever information he could regarding the accident.

ANSWER: Defendants admit that an attorney claiming to represent Plaintiff contacted Defendant Robert Jones on or about May 3, 2022 and scheduled an appointment for Plaintiff

to meet with Defendant Robert Jones. Defendants deny the remaining allegations of this paragraph.

19.   Fred and his attorney made an appointment to see Defendant Jones on May 10, 2022 at 4:00 p.m. at the Sunnyside police station.
ANSWER: Admit.

20.   When Fred and his attorney arrived, Defendant Jones informed them there had been no accident – the notice was simply a ruse to get Fred into custody.
ANSWER: Defendants admit that on May 10, 2022, Defendant Robert Jones told Plaintiff and his attorney that the accident notice was a ruse to get Plaintiff to come to the Sunnyside Police Department. Defendants deny the remaining allegations of this paragraph.

21.   Defendant Jones asked Fred where he was on December 19, 2021.
ANSWER: Admit.

22.   Fred informed Defendant Jones he had no idea where he was on that date and would have to check his calendar and other items to determine his whereabouts on that date.
ANSWER: Deny.

23.   Although Fred was willing to answer any additional questions, Defendant Jones stated he had no further questions for Fred.
ANSWER: Deny.

24.   Fred's attorney demanded the return of Fred's phone, but Defendant Jones refused.
ANSWER: Admit.

25.   Fred's attorney noted that Jones had no warrant to seize or search the phone. Jones replied that he was in the process of obtaining a warrant.

ANSWER: Admit.

26.   Fred stated that without his phone, it would be more difficult to determine where he was and what he did on December 19, 2021. Jones still refused to return Fred's phone.

ANSWER: Defendants admit that Defendants temporarily retained custody of Plaintiff's cell phone because probable cause existed that it contained evidence of criminal activity. Defendants deny the remaining allegations of this paragraph.

27.   Fred and his attorney left the police station without being informed of any allegations, and without Fred being arrested or charged.

ANSWER: Admit.

28.   As of the date of this filing, Fred has not been arrested, and his phone has not been returned.

ANSWER: Deny.

<u>COUNT I – FEDERAL CLAIM</u>
<u>FALSE ARREST</u>
<u>DEFENDANT JONES</u>

29.   Each paragraph of this Complaint is incorporated as if restated fully herein.

ANSWER: Defendants restate their answers to each paragraph of this Complaint as though fully restated herein.

30.   Defendant Jones caused Fred to be arrested without probable cause to believe he had committed a crime, in violation of the Fourth Amendment to the U.S. Constitution.

ANSWER: Deny.

31.   At all times relevant, Defendant Jones was acting under color of the statutes, ordinances, regulations, customs, and usages of the State of Illinois, and within the scope of his employment as a Sunnyside police officer.

ANSWER: Admit.

32.   As a proximate result of Defendant's misconduct, Fred suffered loss of liberty, fear, mental anguish, and emotional pain and suffering.

ANSWER: Deny.

WHEREFORE, Defendants respectfully request that this Honorable Court enter judgment in favor of Defendants and dismiss Plaintiff's claims with prejudice.

COUNT II – FEDERAL CLAIM
UNLAWFUL DETENTION
DEFENDANT JONES

33.   Each paragraph of this Complaint is incorporated as if restated fully herein.

ANSWER: Defendants restate their answers to each paragraph of this Complaint as though fully restated herein.

34.   Defendant Jones caused Fred to be detained without probable cause or reasonable suspicion to believe he had committed, or was committing, a crime, resulting in deprivation of his liberty, in violation of the Fourth Amendment to the U.S. Constitution.

ANSWER: Deny.

35.   As a proximate result of Defendant's misconduct, Fred suffered loss of liberty, fear, mental anguish, and emotional pain and suffering.

ANSWER: Deny.

WHEREFORE, Defendants respectfully request that this Honorable Court enter judgment in favor of Defendants and dismiss Plaintiff's claims with prejudice.

COUNT III – FEDERAL CLAIM
ILLEGAL SEIZURE
DEFENDANT JONES

36.   Each paragraph of this Complaint is incorporated as if restated fully herein. **ANSWER: Defendants restate their answers to each paragraph of this Complaint as though fully restated herein.**

37.   Defendant Jones seized and/or caused Fred's property to be seized without legal process or probable cause to believe the property contained evidence of a crime, in violation of the Fourth Amendment to the U.S. Constitution.

ANSWER: Deny.

38.   As a proximate result of Defendant's misconduct, Fred suffered loss of his property, inconvenience, disruption, mental anguish, emotional pain and suffering, and loss of income.

ANSWER: Deny.

WHEREFORE, Defendants respectfully request that this Honorable Court enter judgment in favor of Defendants and dismiss Plaintiff's claims with prejudice.

COUNT IV – STATE CLAIM
FALSE ARREST/WRONGFUL IMPRISONMENT
VILLAGE OF SUNNYSIDE

39.   Each paragraph of this Complaint is incorporated as if restated fully herein.

ANSWER: Defendants restate their answers to each paragraph of this Complaint as though fully restated herein.

40.   Defendant Village of Sunnyside, by and through its agent, Defendant Jones, caused Fred to be restrained, detained, seized, imprisoned, and/or arrested without having reasonable grounds to believe he had committed any crime or offense.

ANSWER: Deny.

41.   As a proximate result of Defendant's misconduct, Fred suffered loss of liberty, fear, mental anguish, and emotional pain and suffering.

ANSWER: Deny.

WHEREFORE, Defendants respectfully request that this Honorable Court enter judgment in favor of Defendants and dismiss Plaintiff's claims with prejudice.

COUNT V – STATE CLAIM
CONVERSION
VILLAGE OF SUNNYSIDE

42.   Each paragraph of this Complaint is incorporated as if restated fully herein.

ANSWER: Defendants restate their answers to each paragraph of this Complaint as though fully restated herein.

43.   Defendant Village of Sunnyside, by and through its agent, Defendant Jones, wrongfully asserted control, dominion, and/or ownership of Fred's property without legal justification or authorization.

ANSWER: Deny.

44.   Fred had an absolute right in the property, and a right to immediate, absolute, and unconditional possession of the property.

ANSWER: Deny.

45.   Fred demanded possession of the property, which Defendant Village of Sunnyside, by and through its agent Defendant Jones, refused.

ANSWER: Defendants admit that Defendants temporarily retained custody of Plaintiff's cell phone because probable cause existed that it contained evidence of criminal activity. Defendants deny the remaining allegations of this paragraph.

46.   As a proximate result of Defendant Village of Sunnyside's misconduct, Fred suffered and continues to suffer inconvenience, disruption, frustration, mental anguish, and emotional pain and suffering.

ANSWER: Deny.

WHEREFORE, Defendants respectfully request that this Honorable Court enter judgment in favor of Defendants and dismiss Plaintiff's claims with prejudice.

COUNT VI – STATE CLAIM
INTENTIONAL INFLICTION OF EMOTIONAL DISTRESS
VILLAGE OF SUNNYSIDE, JONES

47.   Each paragraph of this Complaint is incorporated as if restated fully herein.

ANSWER: Defendants restate their answers to each paragraph of this Complaint as though fully restated herein.

48.   The conduct of Defendant Jones and Defendant Village of Sunnyside, by and through its agent, Defendant Jones, as set forth herein, was extreme and outrageous.

ANSWER: Deny.

49.   Defendants intended to cause or recklessly or consciously disregarded the probability of causing emotional distress, and Fred suffered severe emotional distress as a proximate result of Defendants' actions.

ANSWER: Deny.

50.   As a proximate result of Defendants' misconduct, Fred suffered severe anxiety, mental anguish, and emotional pain and suffering.

ANSWER: Deny.

WHEREFORE, Defendants respectfully request that this Honorable Court enter judgment in favor of Defendants and dismiss Plaintiff's claims with prejudice.

COUNT VII – STATE LAW CLAIM
INDEMNIFICATION
VILLAGE OF SUNNYSIDE

51.   Each paragraph of this Complaint is incorporated as if restated fully herein.

ANSWER: Defendants restate their answers to each paragraph of this Complaint as though fully restated herein.

52.   At all relevant times, Village of Sunnyside was the employer of Defendant Jones. **ANSWER: Admit.**

53.   Defendant Jones committed the acts alleged above under color of law and in the scope of his employment as an employee of the Village of Sunnyside.

ANSWER: Defendants admit that Defendant Robert Jones was acting under color of law and within the scope of his employment during his interactions with Plaintiff. Defendants deny the remaining allegations of this paragraph and deny that Defendant Robert Jones violated any law or committed any wrongdoing whatsoever.

54.   Illinois law provides that government entities are directed to pay any tort judgment for any damages for which employees are liable within the scope of their employment activities.

ANSWER: This paragraph calls for a legal conclusion to which no answer is required. To the extent an answer is required, Defendants deny the allegations of this paragraph.

55.   Should Defendant Jones be found liable on one or more of the claims set forth above, Plaintiff Fred Smith demands, pursuant to Illinois law, that his employer, Defendant Village of Sunnyside, be found liable for any judgment plaintiff obtains against Defendant Jones, as well as attorney's fees and costs awarded, and for any additional relief this Court deems just and proper.

ANSWER: Deny.

12

AFFIRMATIVE DEFENSES

Defendants, VILLAGE OF SUNNYSIDE, a Municipal Corporation, and Sunnyside Police Detective ROBERT JONES, by and through their attorney, Jeffrey C. Johnson of Johnson Law Firm, P.C., and for their Affirmative Defenses to Plaintiff's First Amended Complaint at Law, state as follows:

1.   Probable cause existed to arrest Plaintiff. The existence of probable cause is an absolute defense to any federal or state law claim against a police officer for false arrest, false imprisonment, unlawful detention, or unlawful seizure.

2.   "The use of deception to lure a defendant from his home in order to effectuate an arrest without a warrant has been held not to violate fundamental fairness." *U.S. v. Vasiliavitchious,* 919 F. Supp. 1113, 1117 (N.D. Ill. 1996) (*quoting People v. Witherspoon,* 216 Ill. App. 3d 323, 332 (1st Dist. 1991)). "[I]t is perfectly acceptable for law enforcement officers to lure someone suspected of a crime to a location so that he may be arrested." *Nesbitt v. Jaisca,* 2012 U.S. Dist. LEXIS 116367, *15 (N.D. Ill. Aug. 17, 2012). Therefore, Defendant Robert Jones's use of deception to lure Plaintiff from his home in order to effectuate a lawful arrest was legal and did not violate the U.S. Constitution or any law.

3.   Defendant Robert Jones is entitled to qualified immunity because he did not violate any of Plaintiff's clearly established statutory or constitutional rights of which a reasonable person would have known.

4.   Plaintiff's cell phone was confiscated as part of a criminal investigation. Probable cause existed that Plaintiff's cell phone contained evidence of criminal activity.

5.   Defendants have returned the cell phone to Plaintiff.

6.   Defendant Robert Jones cannot be liable for any acts or omissions taken in the execution or enforcement of any law unless such acts or omissions constitute willful and wanton conduct. 745 ILCS 10/2-202.

7.   The actions of Defendant Robert Jones were not extreme and outrageous or intended to cause Plaintiff emotional distress. Additionally, Defendant Robert Jones did not recklessly or consciously disregard the probability of causing Plaintiff emotional distress.

8.   To the extent Plaintiff failed to mitigate any of his claimed injuries or damages, any verdict or judgment obtained by Plaintiff must be reduced by application of the principle that a plaintiff has a duty to mitigate his damages.

9.   Defendant Village of Sunnyside is not liable for an injury resulting from an act or omission of its employee where the employee is not liable. 745 ILCS 10/2-109.

10.   To the extent sought by Plaintiff, Plaintiff is precluded from obtaining punitive damages against the Village of Sunnyside for any claim asserted. 745 ILCS 10/2-102.

JURY DEMAND

Defendants demand trial by a jury of twelve.

Respectfully Submitted,

VILLAGE OF SUNNYSIDE and

ROBERT JONES

By: /s/ Jeffrey C. Johnson

Their Attorney

Jeffrey C. Johnson
Johnson Law Firm, P.C.
780 South Elm Street
Sunnyside, IL 60987
Tel: (312) 663-2626
Fax: (312) 663-2627
jjohnson@johnsonlawfirm.com

14

ILND 44 (Rev. 08/23)

CIVIL COVER SHEET

The ILND 44 civil cover sheet and the information contained herein neither replace nor supplement the filing and service of pleadings or other papers as required by law, except as provided by local rules of court. This form, approved by the Judicial Conference of the United States in September 1974, is required for the use of the Clerk of Court for the purpose of initiating the civil docket sheet. *(See instructions on next page of this form.)*

I. (a) PLAINTIFFS

DEFENDANTS

(b) County of Residence of First Listed Plaintiff
(Except in U.S. plaintiff cases)

County of Residence of First Listed Defendant
(In U.S. plaintiff cases only)
Note: In land condemnation cases, use the location of the tract of land involved.

(c) Attorneys *(firm name, address, and telephone number)*

Attorneys *(If Known)*

II. BASIS OF JURISDICTION *(Check one box, only.)*

☐ 1 U.S. Government Plaintiff

☐ 3 Federal Question
(U.S. Government not a party.)

☐ 2 U.S. Government Defendant

☐ 4 Diversity
(Indicate citizenship of parties in Item III.)

III. CITIZENSHIP OF PRINCIPAL PARTIES *(For Diversity Cases Only.)*
(Check one box, only for plaintiff and one box for defendant.)

	PTF	DEF		PTF	DEF
Citizen of This State	☐ 1	☐ 1	Incorporated or Principal Place of Business in This State	☐ 4	☐ 4
Citizen of Another State	☐ 2	☐ 2	Incorporated and Principal Place of Business in Another State	☐ 5	☐ 5
Citizen or Subject of a Foreign Country	☐ 3	☐ 3	Foreign Nation	☐ 6	☐ 6

IV. NATURE OF SUIT *(Check one box, only.)*

CONTRACT	TORTS		PRISONER PETITIONS	LABOR	OTHER STATUTES
☐ 110 Insurance	**PERSONAL INJURY**	**PERSONAL INJURY**	☐ 510 Motions to Vacate Sentence	☐ 710 Fair Labor Standards Act	☐ 375 False Claims Act
☐ 120 Marine	☐ 310 Airplane	☐ 365 Personal Injury - Product Liability	☐ 530 General	☐ 720 Labor/Management Relations	☐ 376 Qui Tam (31 USC 3729 (a))
☐ 130 Miller Act	☐ 315 Airplane Product Liability ☐ 320 Assault, Libel & Slander	☐ 367 Health Care/ Pharmaceutical Personal Injury	☐ 535 Death Penalty	☐ 740 Railway Labor Act	☐ 400 State Reapportionment ☐ 410 Antitrust
☐ 140 Negotiable Instrument ☐ 150 Recovery of Overpayment & Enforcement of Judgment	☐ 330 Federal Employers' Liability ☐ 340 Marine ☐ 345 Marine Product Liability	Product Liability ☐ 368 Asbestos Personal Injury Product Liability	**Other:** ☐ 540 Mandamus & Other ☐ 550 Civil Rights	☐ 751 Family and Medical Leave Act ☐ 790 Other Labor Litigation	☐ 430 Banks and Banking ☐ 450 Commerce ☐ 460 Deportation
☐ 151 Medicare Act ☐ 152 Recovery of Defaulted Student Loan (Excludes Veterans)	☐ 350 Motor Vehicle ☐ 355 Motor Vehicle Product Liability ☐ 360 Other Personal Injury	**PERSONAL PROPERTY** ☐ 370 Other Fraud	☐ 555 Prison Condition ☐ 560 Civil Detainee - Conditions of Confinement	☐ 791 Employee Retirement Income Security Act	☐ 470 Racketeer Influenced and Corrupt Organizations ☐ 480 Consumer Credit
☐ 153 Recovery of Veteran's Benefits	☐ 362 Personal Injury - Medical Malpractice	☐ 371 Truth in Lending		**PROPERTY RIGHTS**	☐ 485 Telephone Consumer
☐ 160 Stockholders' Suits		☐ 380 Other Personal Property Damage		☐ 820 Copyright	Protection Act (TCPA)
☐ 190 Other Contract ☐ 195 Contract Product Liability ☐ 196 Franchise		☐ 385 Property Damage Product Liability		☐ 830 Patent ☐ 835 Patent - Abbreviated New Drug Application ☐ 840 Trademark	☐ 490 Cable/Sat TV ☐ 850 Securities/Commodities Exchange
				☐ 880 Defend Trade Secrets Act of 2016 (DTSA)	☐ 890 Other Statutory Actions ☐ 891 Agricultural Arts
REAL PROPERTY	**CIVIL RIGHTS**	**BANKRUPTCY**	**FORFEITURE/PENALTY**	**SOCIAL SECURITY**	☐ 893 Environmental Matters
☐ 210 Land Condemnation	☐ 440 Other Civil Rights	☐ 422 Appeal 28 USC 158	☐ 625 Drug Related Seizure of Property 21 USC 881	☐ 861 HIA (1395ff)	☐ 895 Freedom of Information Act
☐ 220 Foreclosure	☐ 441 Voting	☐ 423 Withdrawal 28 USC 157	☐ 690 Other	☐ 862 Black Lung (923)	☐ 896 Arbitration
☐ 230 Rent Lease & Ejectment	☐ 442 Employment			☐ 863 DIWC/DIWW (405(g))	☐ 899 Administrative Procedure
☐ 240 Torts to Land	☐ 443 Housing/Accommodations	**IMMIGRATION**		☐ 864 SSID Title XVI	Act/Review or Appeal of
☐ 245 Tort Product Liability	☐ 445 Amer. w/ Disabilities- Employment	☐ 462 Naturalization Application		☐ 865 RSI (405(g))	Agency Decision
☐ 290 All Other Real Property	☐ 446 Amer. w/Disabilities- Other	☐ 463 Habeas Corpus - Alien Detainee (Prisoner Petition)		**FEDERAL TAXES** ☐ 870 Taxes (U.S. Plaintiff or Defendant)	☐ 950 Constitutionality of State Statutes
	☐ 448 Education	☐ 465 Other Immigration Actions		☐ 871 IRS—Third Party 26 USC 7609	

V. ORIGIN *(Check one box, only.)*

☐ 1 Original Proceeding
☐ 2 Removed from State Court
☐ 3 Remanded from Appellate Court
☐ 4 Reinstated or Reopened
☐ 5 Transferred from Another District (specify)
☐ 6 Multidistrict Litigation - Transfer
☐ 8 Multidistrict Litigation - Direct File

VI. CAUSE OF ACTION (Enter U.S. Civil Statute under which you are filing and write a brief statement of cause.)

VII. PREVIOUS BANKRUPTCY MATTERS (For nature of suit 422 and 423, enter the case number and judge for any associated bankruptcy matter previously adjudicated by a judge of this Court. Use a separate attachment if necessary.)

VIII. REQUESTED IN COMPLAINT: ☐ Check if this is a **class action** under Rule 23, F.R.CV.P. Demand $ **CHECK Yes only if demanded in complaint:** Jury Demand: ☐ Yes ☐ No

IX. RELATED CASE(S) IF ANY *(See instructions.)* Judge _____ Case Number _____

X. Is this a previously dismissed or remanded case? ☐ Yes ☐ No If yes, Case # _____ Name of Judge _____

Date: _____ Signature of Attorney of Record _____

INSTRUCTIONS FOR ATTORNEYS COMPLETING CIVIL COVER SHEET FORM JS 44

Authority for Civil Cover Sheet

The ILND 44 civil cover sheet and the information contained herein neither replaces nor supplements the filings and service of pleading or other papers as required by law, except as provided by local rules of court. This form, approved by the Judicial Conference of the United States in September 1974, is required for the use of the Clerk of Court for the purpose of initiating the civil docket sheet. Consequently, a civil cover sheet is submitted to the Clerk of Court for each civil complaint filed. The attorney filing a case should complete the form as follows:

I.(a) **Plaintiffs-Defendants.** Enter names (last, first, middle initial) of plaintiff and defendant. If the plaintiff or defendant is a government agency, use
  (b) **County of Residence.** For each civil case filed, except U.S. plaintiff cases, enter the name of the county where the first listed plaintiff resides at the
  (c) **Attorneys.** Enter the firm name, address, telephone number, and attorney of record. If there are several attorneys, list them on an attachment, noting in this section "(see attachment)".

II.   **Jurisdiction.** The basis of jurisdiction is set forth under Rule 8(a), F.R.Cv.P., which requires that jurisdictions be shown in pleadings. Place an "X" United States plaintiff. (1) Jurisdiction based on 28 U.S.C. 1345 and 1348. Suits by agencies and officers of the United States are included here. United States defendant. (2) When the plaintiff is suing the United States, its officers or agencies, place an "X" in this box. Federal question. (3) This refers to suits under 28 U.S.C. 1331, where jurisdiction arises under the Constitution of the United States, an amendment Diversity of citizenship. (4) This refers to suits under 28 U.S.C. 1332, where parties are citizens of different states. When Box 4 is checked, the citizenship of the different parties must be checked. (See Section III below; **NOTE: federal question actions take precedence over diversity cases.**)

III. **Residence (citizenship) of Principal Parties.** This section of the JS 44 is to be completed if diversity of citizenship was indicated above. Mark this section for each principal party.

IV.   **Nature of Suit.** Place an "X" in the appropriate box. If there are multiple nature of suit codes associated with the case, pick the nature of suit code that is most applicable. Click here for: Nature of Suit Code Descriptions.

V.   **Origin.** Place an "X" in one of the seven boxes.
Original Proceedings. (1) Cases which originate in the United States district courts.
Removed from State Court. (2) Proceedings initiated in state courts may be removed to the district courts under Title 28 U.S.C., Section 1441.
Remanded from Appellate Court. (3) Check this box for cases remanded to the district court for further action. Use the date of remand as the filing date.
Reinstated or Reopened. (4) Check this box for cases reinstated or reopened in the district court. Use the reopening date as the filing date.
Transferred from Another District. (5) For cases transferred under Title 28 U.S.C. Section 1404(a). Do not use this for within district transfers or multidistrict litigation transfers.
Multidistrict Litigation – Transfer. (6) Check this box when a multidistrict case is transferred into the district under authority of Title 28 U.S.C.
Multidistrict Litigation – Direct File. (8) Check this box when a multidistrict case is filed in the same district as the Master MDL docket.
PLEASE NOTE THAT THERE IS NOT AN ORIGIN CODE 7. Origin Code 7 was used for historical records and is no longer relevant due to changes in statue.

VI.   **Cause of Action.** Report the civil statute directly related to the cause of action and give a brief description of the cause. **Do not cite jurisdictional statutes unless diversity.** Example: U.S. Civil Statute: 47 USC 553 Brief Description: Unauthorized reception of cable service

VII. **Requested in Complaint.** Class Action. Place an "X" in this box if you are filing a class action under Rule 23, F.R.Cv.P.
Demand. In this space enter the actual dollar amount being demanded or indicate other demand, such as a preliminary injunction.
Jury Demand. Check the appropriate box to indicate whether or not a jury is being demanded.

VIII. **Related Cases.** This section of the JS 44 is used to reference related pending cases, if any. If there are related pending cases, insert the docket numbers and the corresponding judge names for such cases.

Date and Attorney Signature. Date and sign the civil cover sheet.

THE UNITED STATES DISTRICT COURT
FOR THE NORTHERN DISTRICT OF ILLINOIS
EASTERN DIVISION

FRED SMITH,	
Plaintiff,	
v.	
VILLAGE OF SUNNYSIDE, a Municipal Corporation, and Sunnyside police officer ROBERT JONES	No. 23-cv-3456
Defendants	*Jury Trial Demanded.*

COMPLAINT AT LAW

NOW COMES Plaintiff FRED SMITH, by his attorney, Law Office of Susan Miller, complaining

of the Defendants, VILLAGE OF SUNNYSIDE, a Municipal Corporation, and Sunnyside police

officer ROBERT JONES, and states the following:

JURSDICTION AND VENUE

1. This action arises under the Constitution of the United States, particularly the Fourth and

Fourteenth Amendments to the Constitution of the United States, under the laws of the United States,

particularly the Civil Rights Act, Title 42 of the United States Code, Sections 1983 and 1988, and

under the laws of the State of Illinois.

2. The jurisdiction of this Court is invoked under the provisions of Title 28 of the United States

Code, Sections 1331 and 1343. Plaintiff also invokes the supplemental jurisdiction of this Court

pursuant to Title 28 of the United States Code, § 1367.

1

3. This Court has jurisdiction over this action pursuant to Title 28 of the United States Code §§ 1331 and 1367, as Plaintiff asserts claims under federal law and the state law claims arise out of the same facts as the federal claims. Venue is proper in the United States District Court for the Northern District of Illinois under Title 28 of the United States Code, § 1391(b)(2), as the events complained of occurred within this district.

PARTIES

4. At all times relevant herein, Plaintiff FRED SMITH (hereinafter "Fred") was a resident of the County of Cook, State of Illinois, and a citizen of the State of Illinois.

5. Defendant VILLAGE OF SUNNYSIDE is a governmental entity operating within the State of Illinois. The VILLAGE OF SUNNYSIDE is responsible for the actions of its employees while acting within the scope of their employment. At all times relevant to this action, VILLAGE OF SUNNYSIDE was the employer of Defendant ROBERT JONES (referred to as "Jones").

6. Defendant JONES is sued in his individual capacity and was at all times relevant, a sworn police officer employed by Defendant VILLAGE OF SUNNYSIDE, and was acting within the scope of his agency, service and/or employment with the VILLAGE OF SUNNYSIDE, and was acting under color of the statutes, ordinances, regulations, customs, and usages of the State of Illinois.

FACTUAL ALLEGATIONS

7. On April 25, 2022, Fred received an "Accident Notice" (hereinafter "notice") from the Village of Sunnyside, stating the Village received a report of a hit and run accident on April 2, 2022, involving his vehicle. The Notice stated, "It is your obligation to contact the Police Department and complete the accident report," and directed him to contact Defendant Jones. The Notice further informed Fred that "[t]his is the only notice you will receive. You must contact the Officer named

below. Failure to do so will result in either a criminal complaint filed against you or a report filed with the Department of Transportation which could result in Suspension or Revocation of your driver's license or license plates."

8. On April 25, 2022 – the same day he received the notice – Fred left a voicemail message for Defendant Jones, and sent him an email, stating, "I just received a letter from you informing me that my vehicle was involved in hit and run accident. I assure you that my vehicle was not. No one drives it but me, and I, nor it were involved in an accident. On 4/2/22, I don't believe I left my property on the Southside of Chicago. I'd like to resolve this as quickly as possible. Please call me ANYTIME at xxx-xxx-xxxx."

9. Defendant Jones called Fred the next day, and told him that in order to clear things up, he just needed to take some photographs of Fred's car.

10. On May 3, 2022 Fred drove to the Sunnyside Police Department so that Defendant Jones could photograph his car

11. In fact, Defendant Jones had no interest in photographing Fred's car, and there was no hit and run accident on April 2. Jones sent the notice to Fred as a ruse in order to lure him into custody.

12. Defendant Jones unlawfully detained Fred for more than seven hours.

13. Defendant Jones refused to explain why he was detaining/arresting Fred unless he signed a Miranda waiver, which Fred refused to do.

14. Jones had no probable cause or reasonable suspicion that Fred had been involved in criminal activity.

15. Defendant Jones confiscated Fred's telephone without seeking or obtaining a warrant.

3

16. Defendant Jones had no probable cause or reasonable suspicion to believe Fred's phone contained evidence of criminal activity.

17. Defendant Jones eventually released Fred without charges but refused to return Fred's telephone.

18. Fred retained a criminal defense attorney, who contacted Defendant Jones in order to set up a time for Fred to come in to the police station to provide whatever information he could regarding the accident.

19. Fred and his attorney made an appointment to see Defendant Jones on May 10, 2022 at 4:00 p.m. at the Sunnyside police station.

20. When Fred and his attorney arrived, Defendant Jones informed them there had been no accident – the notice was simply a ruse to get Fred into custody.

21. Defendant Jones asked Fred where he was on December 19, 2021.

22. Fred informed Defendant Jones he had no idea where he was on that date, and would have to check his calendar and other items to determine his whereabouts on that date.

23. Although Fred was willing to answer any additional questions, Defendant Jones stated he had no further questions for Fred.

24. Fred's attorney demanded return of Fred's phone, but Defendant Jones refused.

25. Fred's attorney noted that Jones had no warrant to seize or search the phone. Jones replied that he was in the process of obtaining a warrant.

26. Fred stated that without his phone, it would be more difficult to determine where he was and what he did on December 19, 2021. Jones still refused to return Fred's phone.

27. Fred and his attorney left the police station without being informed of any allegations, and without Fred being arrested or charged.

28. As of the date of this filing, Fred has not been arrested, and his phone has not been returned.

COUNT I - FEDERAL CLAIM
42 U.S.C. § 1983 FALSE ARREST
DEFENDANT JONES

29. Each paragraph of this Complaint is incorporated as if restated fully herein.

30. Defendant Jones caused Fred to be arrested without probable cause to believe he had committed a crime, in violation of the Fourth Amendment to the U.S. Constitution.

31. At all times relevant, Defendant Jones was acting under color of the statutes, ordinances, regulations, customs, and usages of the State of Illinois, and within the scope of his employment as a Sunnyside police officer.

32. As a proximate result of Defendant's misconduct, Fred suffered loss of liberty, fear, mental anguish, and emotional pain and suffering.

WHEREFORE, the Plaintiff, FRED SMITH, prays for judgment against Defendants in a fair and reasonable amount, including compensatory and punitive damages, attorney's fees and costs, and for any additional relief this Court deems just and proper.

COUNT II - FEDERAL CLAIM
42 U.S.C. § 1983 UNLAWFUL DETENTION
DEFENDANT JONES

33. Each paragraph of this Complaint is incorporated as if restated fully herein.

34. Defendant Jones caused Fred to be detained without probable cause or reasonable suspicion to believe he had committed, or was committing, a crime, resulting in deprivation of his liberty, in violation of the Fourth Amendment to the U.S. Constitution.

35.   As a proximate result of Defendant's misconduct, Fred suffered loss of liberty, fear, mental

anguish, and emotional pain and suffering.

WHEREFORE, the Plaintiff, FRED SMITH, prays for judgment against Defendants in a fair and

reasonable amount, including compensatory and punitive damages, attorney's fees and costs, and for

any additional relief this Court deems just and proper.

COUNT III – FEDERAL CLAIM
42 U.S.C. § 1983 ILLEGAL SEIZURE
DEFENDANT JONES

36.   Each paragraph of this Complaint is incorporated as if restated fully herein.

37.   Defendant Jones seized and/or caused Fred's property to be seized without legal process or

probable cause to believe the property contained evidence of a crime, in violation of the Fourth

Amendment to the U.S. Constitution.

38.   As a proximate result of Defendant's misconduct, Fred suffered loss of his property,

inconvenience, disruption, mental anguish, emotional pain and suffering, and loss of income.

WHEREFORE, the Plaintiff, FRED SMITH, prays for judgment against Defendants in a fair and

reasonable amount, including compensatory and punitive damages, attorney's fees and costs, and for

any additional relief this Court deems just and proper.

COUNT IV – STATE LAW CLAIM
FALSE ARREST/WRONGFUL IMPRISONMENT
DEFENDANT VILLAGE OF SUNNYSIDE

39. Each paragraph of this Complaint is incorporated as if restated fully herein.

40. At all relevant times, VILLAGE OF SUNNYSIDE was the employer of Defendant JONES.

6

41. Defendant Village of Sunnyside, by and through its agent, Defendant Jones, caused Fred to be restrained, detained, seized, imprisoned, and/or arrested without having reasonable grounds to believe he had committed any crime or offense.

42. As a proximate result of Defendant's misconduct, Fred suffered loss of liberty, fear, mental anguish, and emotional pain and suffering.

WHEREFORE, the Plaintiff, FRED SMITH, prays for judgment against Defendants in a fair and reasonable amount, including compensatory and punitive damages, attorney's fees and costs, and for any additional relief this Court deems just and proper.

COUNT V – STATE LAW CLAIM
CONVERSION
DEFENDANT VILLAGE OF SUNNYSIDE

43. Each paragraph of this Complaint is incorporated as if restated fully herein.

44. Defendant Village of Sunnyside, by and through its agent, Defendant Jones, wrongfully asserted control, dominion, and/or ownership of Fred's property without legal justification or authorization.

45. Fred had an absolute right in the property, and a right to immediate, absolute, and unconditional possession of the property.

46. Fred demanded possession of the property, which Defendant Village of Sunnyside, by and through its agent Defendant Jones, refused.

47. As a proximate result of Defendant Village of Sunnyside's misconduct, Fred suffered and continues to suffer inconvenience, disruption, frustration, mental anguish, and emotional pain and suffering.

7

WHEREFORE, the Plaintiff, FRED SMITH, prays for judgment against Defendants in a fair and reasonable amount, including compensatory and punitive damages, attorney's fees and costs, and for any additional relief this Court deems just and proper.

COUNT VI – STATE CLAIM
INTENTIONAL INFLICTION OF EMOTIONAL DISTRESS
DEFENDANTS VILLAGE OF SUNNYSIDE, JONES

48. Each paragraph of this Complaint is incorporated as if restated fully herein.

49. The conduct of Defendant Jones and Defendant Village of Sunnyside, by and through its agent, Defendant Jones, as set forth herein, was extreme and outrageous.

50. Defendants intended to cause or recklessly or consciously disregarded the probability of causing emotional distress, and Fred suffered severe emotional distress as a proximate result of Defendants' actions.

51. As a proximate result of Defendants' misconduct, Fred suffered severe anxiety, mental anguish, and emotional pain and suffering.

WHEREFORE, the Plaintiff, FRED SMITH, prays for judgment against Defendants in a fair and reasonable amount, including compensatory and punitive damages, attorney's fees and costs, and for any additional relief this Court deems just and proper.

COUNT VII – STATE LAW CLAIM
INDEMNIFICATION
VILLAGE OF SUNNYSIDE

52. Each paragraph of this Complaint is incorporated as if restated fully herein.

53. At all relevant times, Village of Sunnyside was the employer of Defendant Jones.

54. Defendant Jones committed the acts alleged above under color of law and in the scope of his employment as an employee of the Village of Sunnyside.

8

55. Illinois law provides that government entities are directed to pay any tort judgment for any damages for which employees are liable within the scope of their employment activities.

56. Should Defendant Jones be found liable on one or more of the claims set forth above, Plaintiff Fred Smith demands, pursuant to Illinois law, that his employer, Defendant Village of Sunnyside, be found liable for any judgment plaintiff obtains against Defendant Jones, as well as attorney's fees and costs awarded, and for any additional relief this Court deems just and proper.

WHEREFORE, the Plaintiff, FRED SMITH, prays for judgment against Defendants in a fair and reasonable amount, including compensatory and punitive damages, attorney's fees and costs, and for any additional relief this Court deems just and proper.

JURY DEMAND

The Plaintiff FRED SMITH, hereby requests a trial by jury.

DATED: May 24, 2022.

Respectfully submitted,

By: /s/ Susan Miller
           Attorney for the Plaintiff

LAW OFFICE OF SUSAN MILLER
12345 Sunnyside Drive
Sunnyside IL 61234
(312) 456-7892
susan@millerlaw.com

9

1   **LAW OFFICE OF SUSAN MILLER**
    12345 Sunnyside Drive
2   Sunnyside IL 61234
    (312) 456-7892
3   susan@millerlaw.com

4   *Counsel for Plaintiff, FRED SMITH*

5

6   **UNITED STATES DISTRICT COURT**
                        DISTRICT OF NEVADA
7

8   FRED SMITH,   CASE NO.: 2:22-cv-00987-GMN-DJA

9   Plaintiff,

10   SECOND AMENDED
    vs.   COMPLAINT
11

12 VILLAGE OF SUNNYSIDE, a
    Political Subdivision of the State of Nevada;
13 North Las Vegas Police Officer ROGER
    JONES;
14

15   Defendants.

16

17   **SECOND AMENDED COMPLAINT AT LAW**

18   NOW COMES, Plaintiff FRED SMITH, by his counsel, LAW OFFICE OF SUSAN

19 MILLER, complaining of Defendants, VILLAGE OF SUNNYSIDE, A Political Subdivision of

20 the State of Nevada, and Sunnyside Police Detective ROBERT JONES, and states the following:

21   **INTRODUCTION**

22   1.   This matter concerns the false arrest, unlawful detention, and malicious prosecution

23 of Plaintiff Fred Smith for the alleged assault of a 15-year old boy, J.S.[1]

24   2.   Fred was arrested on September 16, 2021, and charged with four felonies that could

25 have put him in prison for the rest of his life.

26

27 _____

28

    [1] Pursuant to Fed. R. Civ. P. 5.2, J.S. will be referred to herein by his initials. His father's last name
    will also be abbreviated.

    SECOND AMENDED COMPLAINT
                                           1

[If you need additional space for ANY section, please attach an additional sheet and reference that section.]

UNITED STATES DISTRICT COURT
NORTHERN DISTRICT OF ILLINOIS

_____

_____

_____

(Enter above the full name
of the plaintiff or plaintiffs in
this action)

vs.   Case No:_____
(To be supplied by the <u>Clerk of this Court</u>)

_____

_____

_____

_____

_____

(Enter above the full name of ALL
defendants in this action. <u>Do not</u>
<u>use "et al."</u>)

CHECK ONE ONLY:

_____   **COMPLAINT UNDER THE CIVIL RIGHTS ACT, TITLE 42 SECTION 1983**
U.S. Code (state, county, or municipal defendants)

_____   **COMPLAINT UNDER THE CONSTITUTION ("BIVENS" ACTION), TITLE**
28 SECTION 1331 U.S. Code (federal defendants)

_____   **OTHER** (cite statute, if known)

BEFORE FILLING OUT THIS COMPLAINT, PLEASE REFER TO "INSTRUCTIONS FOR
FILING." FOLLOW THESE INSTRUCTIONS CAREFULLY.

[If you need additional space for ANY section, please attach an additional sheet and reference that section.]

[If you need additional space for ANY section, please attach an additional sheet and reference that section.]

I.   **Plaintiff(s):**

    A.   Name: _____

    B.   List all aliases: _____

    C.   Prisoner identification number: _____

    D.   Place of present confinement: _____

    E.   Address: _____

(If there is more than one plaintiff, then each plaintiff must list his or her name, aliases, I.D. number, place of confinement, and current address according to the above format on a separate sheet of paper.)

II.   **Defendant(s):**
(In **A** below, place the full name of the first defendant in the first blank, his or her official position in the second blank, and his or her place of employment in the third blank. Space for two additional defendants is provided in **B** and **C**.)

    A.   Defendant: _____

           Title: _____

           Place of Employment: _____

    B.   Defendant: _____

           Title: _____

           Place of Employment: _____

    C.   Defendant: _____

           Title: _____

           Place of Employment: _____

(If you have more than three defendants, then all additional defendants must be listed according to the above format on a separate sheet of paper.)

2   Revised 9/2007

[If you need additional space for ANY section, please attach an additional sheet and reference that section.]

[If you need additional space for ANY section, please attach an additional sheet and reference that section.]

III.   List ALL lawsuits you (and your co-plaintiffs, if any) have filed in any state or federal
        court in the United States:

        A.   Name of case and docket number: _____
              _____

        B.   Approximate date of filing lawsuit: _____

        C.   List all plaintiffs (if you had co-plaintiffs), including any aliases: _____
              _____
              _____
              _____

        D.   List all defendants: _____
              _____
              _____
              _____

        E.   Court in which the lawsuit was filed (if federal court, name the district; if state court,
              name the county): _____

        F.   Name of judge to whom case was assigned: _____
              _____

        G.   Basic claim made:_____
              _____
              _____

        H.   Disposition of this case (for example: Was the case dismissed? Was it appealed?
              Is it still pending?): _____
              _____
              _____

        I.   Approximate date of disposition: _____

**IF YOU HAVE FILED MORE THAN ONE LAWSUIT, THEN YOU MUST DESCRIBE THE
ADDITIONAL LAWSUITS ON ANOTHER PIECE OF PAPER, USING THIS SAME
FORMAT. REGARDLESS OF HOW MANY CASES YOU HAVE PREVIOUSLY FILED,
YOU WILL NOT BE EXCUSED FROM FILLING OUT THIS SECTION COMPLETELY,
AND FAILURE TO DO SO MAY RESULT IN DISMISSAL OF YOUR CASE. CO-
PLAINTIFFS MUST ALSO LIST ALL CASES THEY HAVE FILED.**

Revised 9/2007

[If you need additional space for ANY section, please attach an additional sheet and reference that section.]

[If you need additional space for ANY section, please attach an additional sheet and reference that section.]

IV.   Statement of Claim:

State here as briefly as possible the facts of your case. Describe how each defendant is involved, including names, dates, and places. **Do not give any legal arguments or cite any cases or statutes.** If you intend to allege a number of related claims, number and set forth each claim in a separate paragraph. (Use as much space as you need. Attach extra sheets if necessary.)

_____

_____

_____

_____

_____

_____

_____

_____

_____

_____

_____

_____

_____

_____

_____

_____

4

Revised 9/2007

[If you need additional space for ANY section, please attach an additional sheet and reference that section.]

[If you need additional space for ANY section, please attach an additional sheet and reference that section.]

V.   Relief:

State briefly exactly what you want the court to do for you. Make no legal arguments. Cite no cases or statutes.

_____
_____
_____
_____
_____
_____

VI.   The plaintiff demands that the case be tried by a jury.   ☐ YES   ☐ NO

CERTIFICATION

By signing this Complaint, I certify that the facts stated in this Complaint are true to the best of my knowledge, information and belief. I understand that if this certification is not correct, I may be subject to sanctions by the Court.

Signed this _____ day of _____, 20_____

_____

(Signature of plaintiff or plaintiffs)

_____

(Print name)

_____

(I.D. Number)

_____

_____

(Address)

THE UNITED STATES DISTRICT COURT
FOR THE NORTHERN DISTRICT OF ILLINOIS
EASTERN DIVISION

FRED SMITH,

       Plaintiff,

       v.

VILLAGE OF SUNNYSIDE, Sunnyside
Police Officers Robert Jones, John Doe 1,
John Doe 2, John Doe 3, John Doe 4, John
Doe 5, and Sunnyside police officer who
pointed an assault rifle at plaintiff,

       Defendants,

No. 22-cv-3456

Jury Trial Demanded.

COMPLAINT

Plaintiff, by counsel, alleges as follows:

1. This is a civil action arising under 42 U.S.C. § 1983. The jurisdiction of this Court is conferred by 28 U.S.C. § 1343.

2. Plaintiff Fred Smith is a middle-aged, law-abiding resident of the Northern District of Illinois.

3. Defendant Village of Sunnyside is an Illinois municipal corporation.

4. Defendants Robert Jones, John Doe 1, John Doe 2, John Doe 3, John Doe 4, and John Doe 5 were at all relevant times acting under color of their authority as police officers of the Village of Sunnyside.

5. The name of defendant "Sunnyside police officer who pointed an assault rifle at plaintiff" (hereinafter "assault rifle officer") is not currently known to plaintiff.

6. The "assault rifle officer" was at all relevant times acting under color of his authority as a police officer of the City of Sunnyside.

7. On March 31, 2021, the Sunnyside police department informed its police officers that an anonymous caller had reported "a white male, approximately 5 feet tall to 6 feet tall, in a dark coat and jeans" carrying a handgun north of the beach at 501 Sheridan Square in the City of Sunnyside.

8. Defendants Jones, John Doe 1, John Doe 2, John Doe 3, John Doe 4, John Doe 5, the "assault rifle officer," and other Sunnyside police officers responded to that report.

9. Defendant Jones was the first officer to arrive at the scene.

10. Jones saw plaintiff, who is a non-white male, standing about 200 feet north of the beach at 501 Sheridan Square in the City of Sunnyside.

11. Jones did not see plaintiff violating any law or ordinance.

12. Jones unholstered his firearm, pointed it at plaintiff, and ordered him: "Put your hands up. Get on the ground."

13. Jones instructed plaintiff that he would get hurt if he disobeyed Jones' order to get on the ground.

14. Defendant John Doe 1 joined Jones, unholstered his firearm, and pointed it at plaintiff.

15. Plaintiff, who was in fear of life, obeyed the police officers and got on the ground.

16. Other Sunnyside police officers, including defendants Doe 2, Doe 3, Doe 4, Doe 5, and the Sunnyside police officer depicted in paragraph 6 above arrived at the scene, unholstered their firearms, and pointed their weapons at plaintiff. Defendants John Doe 1 and Doe 3 then handcuffed plaintiff while he remained on the ground and while defendant "assault rifle officer" pointed his assault rifle at plaintiff at point-blank range.

17. Defendants Doe 1 and Doe 3 then searched plaintiff and did not find anything that justified the stop, search, and use of deadly force.

18. Defendants Jones, Doe 2, Doe 4, Doe 5, and the Sunnyside police officer depicted in paragraph 6 failed to intervene to stop Doe 1 and Doe 3 from conducting the above-described unreasonable and unconstitutional search.

19. At all relevant times, an express policy of the Village of Sunnyside authorized its police officers to point loaded firearms, including assault rifles, at a person without reasonable suspicion that the individual was involved in criminal activity. This policy was a moving force of the unconstitutional conduct described above.

20. At all relevant times, the Village of Sunnyside has failed to instruct and train its police officers that an anonymous tip that a person is carrying a firearm does not permit a police officer to point a firearm at a person, order that person to lay on the ground, and comply with the police orders under penalty of death while the officers search that person. This failure to train was a moving force of the unconstitutional conduct described above.

21. As a result of the foregoing, plaintiff was deprived of rights secured by the

Fourth and Fourteenth Amendments and incurred physical and other injuries.

22. Plaintiff hereby demands trial by jury.

WHEREFORE plaintiff requests that the Court enter judgment for appropriate compensatory and punitive damages against the individual police officer defendants and for appropriate compensatory damages against the defendant Village of Sunnyside and that the costs of this action, including fees and costs, be taxed against all defendants.

/s/ Susan Miller

LAW OFFICE OF SUSAN MILLER
12345 Sunnyside Drive
Sunnyside IL 61234
(312) 456-7892
susan@millerlaw.com

-4-

INSTRUCTIONS FOR FILING
A COMPLAINT UNDER THE CIVIL RIGHTS ACT
42 U.S.C. § 1983 (against state, county, or municipal defendants) or
A "BIVENS" ACTION, 28 U.S.C. § 1331
(against federal defendants)

This packet includes a complaint form and one application to proceed in forma pauperis (as a poor person) with financial affidavit. Local Rule 81.1 of the Local Rules of this court requires prisoners in custody filing suit under 42 U.S.C.§1983 to use the court's form. This form is not something submitted with the complaint, it is the complaint. **All** questions on this form must be answered on the form. (You may attach additional sheets if necessary to complete your answer.) It is not permitted to answer a question "see attached" or "see attached complaint." Such complaints may be summarily dismissed without prejudice. If you should choose to draft your own complaint instead of using the court's form, you must still include the information asked for in the court's form.

To bring a lawsuit, you must submit a complaint bearing your original signature. If you do not have access to a photocopier, you may request more copies of the complaint form from the Clerk of the Court so that you may make conformed copies. You should keep a copy of the complaint for your own records. In forma pauperis status does not entitle you to free copies of court records or documents. Therefore, the Clerk of the Court must charge you if you need photocopies of your complaint or any other motion or document.

If your defendants are state, county, or municipal employees, you should file your case under 42 U.S.C. § 1983. If your defendants are employees of the United States Government, you should file your case under 28 U.S.C. § 1331. If neither statute applies, you should cite the applicable statute, if known.

Your complaint and all other documents must be legibly handwritten or typewritten on one side of letter-sized (8½" x 11") paper and signed by all plaintiffs. It is not necessary to swear to the complaint before a notary public. However, you are warned that any false statement of a material fact may subject you to dismissal of your case as well as prosecution and conviction for perjury.

All questions must be answered concisely in the proper space on the forms. If you need additional space to answer a question, you may use additional blank pages. **YOUR COMPLAINT SHOULD NOT CONTAIN LEGAL ARGUMENTS OR CITATIONS**. You are required only to state the facts. You must describe how each defendant is personally involved in the activities upon which your claim is based.

Personal Identifiers
Federal Rules of Civil Procedure 5.2 addresses privacy and security concerns over public access to electronic court files. Under this rule, papers filed with the court should not contain anyone's full social-security number or full birth date; the name of a person known to be a minor; or a complete financial-account number. A filing may include only the last four digits of a social-security number or taxpayer identification number; the year of someone's birth; a minor's initials; and the last four digits of a financial-account number. Please review the rule for a complete listing and exceptions.

Rev. 04/27/2021

Filing Fee
The filing fee is $402. In addition, the United States Marshal may require you to pay the cost of serving the complaint on each of the defendants. If you are unable to pay the filing fee of $402 and service costs for this action, you must petition the court to allow you to proceed in forma pauperis (that is, without prepaying costs and fees).

The Prison Litigation Reform Act ("PLRA") has changed the process for proceeding in forma pauperis. **Even if you are granted leave to proceed in forma pauperis, you will be responsible for paying the full amount of the $402 fee for filing a complaint or the $505 fee for filing an appeal in installment payments.** The initial installment is 20 percent of the greater of (1) the average monthly deposits (including any state pay and gifts) to your inmate trust fund account or (2) the average monthly balance in your account for the six-month period immediately preceding the filing of your complaint or notice of appeal. The court will calculate the initial installment and inform the institution having custody of you to remit this amount.

After the first installment is paid, you will be required to make monthly payments of 20 percent of the preceding month's income credited to your account. You should not send these monthly payments yourself. The institution having custody of you will forward the payments from your account to the clerk of the court each time the amount in your account exceeds $10 until the filing fees are paid in full.

If you have no assets or other means to pay the **initial** installment, you will still be allowed to bring your action or appeal. However, you will be required to pay the entire filing fee in installments as described above as money becomes available in your account.

If a court issues a judgment against you that includes the payment of costs, you will be required to pay these costs and they will be collected in the same manner as your filing fee.

***In Forma Pauperis* Application**
To file your application to proceed *in forma pauperis*, you must complete, sign, and attest as true and correct under penalty of perjury the enclosed application and financial affidavit. You must have an authorized officer at the correctional institution complete the certificate as to the amount of money and securities on deposit to your credit in any account in the institution. **You must also attach a certified copy showing all transactions in your inmate trust fund account from each institution where you resided for the six-month period immediately preceding the filing of your complaint.** If you have been in more than one institution during the past six months, you must attach trust fund accounts from each institution. If there is more than one plaintiff, then each plaintiff must complete a separate in forma pauperis application and attach a copy of his or her trust fund account.

Other PLRA Provisions
You should be aware of several other provisions of the PLRA. **(1) "Three Strike" Provision.** If you file three cases or appeals that are dismissed as frivolous, malicious, or failing to state a claim, you will be barred from filing any more cases *in forma pauperis* unless you are in imminent bodily danger. Some common examples of dismissals that will count toward the three-strike limit include, but are not limited to, failure to name a suable and non-immune defendant; failure to allege facts that would indicate a violation of a federal right; dismissal of your action in

response to a defendant's motion to dismiss for failure to state a claim upon which relief may be granted; dismissal of an appeal as frivolous or not taken in good faith. Note: If the district court dismisses your case for one of these reasons, that will count as one strike. If you appeal the dismissal and the court of appeals dismisses your appeal, that may count as a second strike. **(2) Exhaustion.** You are now required to exhaust all your available administrative remedies before bringing an action in federal court. **(3) Physical Injury.** The law now provides that a prisoner, while confined, may not file a federal claim for mental or emotional injury suffered while in custody without a prior showing of physical injury.

Exhaustion of Administrative Remedies

The Prison Litigation Reform Act requires that a prisoner take all steps required by the prison's grievance system (from filing a grievance to finalizing the appeal process) before filing a lawsuit in federal court. See 42 U.S.C. § 1997e(a). If you do not file a grievance through the prison's grievance procedure, file an appeal, and await a final decision before filing suit, you will undoubtedly experience delay in your case in federal court. This is because the court will need to determine whether or not you have completed the grievance process because the Court is not permitted to hear your claim if you have not completed those necessary steps. If the court finds that you have not completed the grievance process, you may be required to go back and do so before you can proceed in federal court or, if the failure to complete the grievance process was your fault, your case may be dismissed. You do not have to set forth in your federal court complaint that you have, have not, or could not, finish the grievance process. However, in order to avoid delay or possible dismissal of your case in federal court, it might be in your best interest to set out in your complaint the steps you have taken to complete the prison grievance process.

U.S. Marshal's Forms and Summons

USM 285 forms should be completed and submitted at the time you submit your complaint. Summons will be prepared and issued by the Clerk's office, pursuant to a court order. You must complete a separate USM 285 form for each named defendant, giving the address where the U.S. Marshal can attempt to serve that defendant. No summons will be sent to you. You must provide a completed USM 285 form for each defendant named in your complaint.

Where to File

Your complaint should be filed in this district only if one or more of the named defendants resides within this district or if the events upon which you base your complaint took place in this district. The Stateville and Sheridan Illinois Correctional Centers are located in the Northern District of Illinois Eastern Division. The Dixon and Thompson Illinois Correctional Centers are located in the Northern District of Illinois Western Division. The Federal Metropolitan Correctional Center in Chicago is located in the Northern District of Illinois Eastern Division. A complaint filed in this court against officials at other state prisons may be subject to dismissal or transfer to the proper district. When these forms are properly completed, mail them to Prisoner Correspondent, United States District Court, 219 S. Dearborn Street, 20th Floor, Chicago IL 60604. Complaints concerning claims arising at the Dixon or Thompson Correctional Center should be sent to the Clerk, United States District Court, 327 S. Court Street, Rockford, IL 61101. Always keep the court informed of your address; failure to do so may result in dismissal of your case.

[If you need additional space for ANY section, please attach an additional sheet and reference that section.]

UNITED STATES DISTRICT COURT
FOR THE NORTHERN DISTRICT OF ILLINOIS

_____)
)
_____)
)
Plaintiff(s),) Case Number: _____
)
v.)
_____)
)
_____)
)
Defendant(s).)

COMPLAINT OF EMPLOYMENT DISCRIMINATION

1. This is an action for employment discrimination.

2. The plaintiff is_____of the

county of_____in the state of_____.

3. The defendant is_____, whose

street address is_____,

(city)_____(county)_____(state)_____(ZIP)_____

(Defendant's telephone number)   (____) – _____

4. The plaintiff sought employment or was employed by the defendant at (street address)

_____(city)_____

(county)_____(state)_____(ZIP code)_____

[If you need additional space for ANY section, please attach an additional sheet and reference that section.]

Rev. 06/27/2016

5.   The plaintiff [*check one box*]

(a) ☐   was denied employment by the defendant.

(b) ☐   was hired and is still employed by the defendant.

(c) ☐   was employed but is no longer employed by the defendant.

6.   The defendant discriminated against the plaintiff on or about, or beginning on or about, (month)_____, (day)_____, (year)_____.

7.1   *(Choose paragraph 7.1 or 7.2, do not complete both.)*

(a)   The defendant is not a federal governmental agency, and the plaintiff [*check one box*] ☐*has* ☐*has not* filed a charge or charges against the defendant

asserting the acts of discrimination indicated in this complaint with any of the

following government agencies:

(i)   ☐ the United States Equal Employment Opportunity Commission, on or about

(month)_____ (day)_____ (year)_____.

(ii)   ☐ the Illinois Department of Human Rights, on or about

(month)_____ (day)_____ (year)_____.

(b)   If charges *were* filed with an agency indicated above, a copy of the charge is

attached. ☐ Yes, ☐ No, **but plaintiff will file a copy of the charge within 14 days**.

It is the policy of both the Equal Employment Opportunity Commission and the Illinois

Department of Human Rights to cross-file with the other agency all charges received. The

plaintiff has no reason to believe that this policy was not followed in this case.

7.2   The defendant is a federal governmental agency, and

(a)   the plaintiff previously filed a Complaint of Employment Discrimination with the

[If you need additional space for ANY section, please attach an additional sheet and reference that section.]

[If you need additional space for ANY section, please attach an additional sheet and reference that section.]

defendant asserting the acts of discrimination indicated in this court complaint.

       ☐ Yes (month)_____ (day)_____ (year) _____

       ☐ No, did not file Complaint of Employment Discrimination

(b)   The plaintiff received a Final Agency Decision on (month)_____

      (day) _____ (year) _____.

(c)   Attached is a copy of the

      (i) Complaint of Employment Discrimination,

          ☐ Yes   ☐ No, but a copy will be filed within 14 days.

      (ii) Final Agency Decision

          ☐ Yes   ☐ N0, but a copy will be filed within 14 days.

8.   *(Complete paragraph 8 only if defendant is not a federal governmental agency.)*

   (a) ☐   the United States Equal Employment Opportunity Commission has not

           issued a *Notice of Right to Sue.*

   (b) ☐ the United States Equal Employment Opportunity Commission has issued

           a *Notice of Right to Sue*, which was received by the plaintiff on

           (month)_____ (day)_____ (year)_____ a copy of which

           Notice is attached to this complaint.

9.   The defendant discriminated against the plaintiff because of the plaintiff's *[check only*

those that apply]:

   (a) ☐ Age (Age Discrimination Employment Act).

   (b) ☐ Color (Title VII of the Civil Rights Act of 1964 and 42 U.S.C. §1981).

[If you need additional space for ANY section, please attach an additional sheet and reference that section.]

[If you need additional space for ANY section, please attach an additional sheet and reference that section.]

    (c) ☐ Disability (Americans with Disabilities Act or Rehabilitation Act)

    (d) ☐ National Origin (Title VII of the Civil Rights Act of 1964 and 42 U.S.C. §1981).

    (e) ☐ Race (Title VII of the Civil Rights Act of 1964 and 42 U.S.C. §1981).

    (f) ☐ Religion (Title VII of the Civil Rights Act of 1964)

    (g) ☐ Sex (Title VII of the Civil Rights Act of 1964)

10.   If the defendant is a state, county, municipal (city, town or village) or other local governmental agency, plaintiff further alleges discrimination on the basis of race, color, or national origin (42 U.S.C. § 1983).

11.   Jurisdiction over the statutory violation alleged is conferred as follows: for Title VII claims by 28 U.S.C.§1331, 28 U.S.C.§1343(a)(3), and 42 U.S.C.§2000e-5(f)(3); for 42 U.S.C.§1981 and §1983 by 42 U.S.C.§1988; for the ADA by 42 U.S.C.§12117; for the Rehabilitation Act, 29 U.S.C. § 791; and for the ADEA, 29 U.S.C. § 626(c).

12.   The defendant [*check only those that apply*]

    (a) ☐ failed to hire the plaintiff.

    (b) ☐ terminated the plaintiff's employment.

    (c) ☐ failed to promote the plaintiff.

    (d) ☐ failed to reasonably accommodate the plaintiff's religion.

    (e) ☐ failed to reasonably accommodate the plaintiff's disabilities.

    (f) ☐ failed to stop harassment;

    (g) ☐ retaliated against the plaintiff because the plaintiff did something to assert rights protected by the laws identified in paragraphs 9 and 10 above;

    (h) ☐ other (specify): _____

[If you need additional space for ANY section, please attach an additional sheet and reference that section.]

[If you need additional space for ANY section, please attach an additional sheet and reference that section.]

_____

_____

_____

_____

13.   The facts supporting the plaintiff's claim of discrimination are as follows:

_____

_____

_____

_____

_____

14.   [*AGE DISCRIMINATION ONLY*] Defendant knowingly, intentionally, and willfully
       discriminated against the plaintiff.

15.   The plaintiff demands that the case be tried by a jury. ☐ Yes ☐ No

16.   THEREFORE, the plaintiff asks that the court grant the following relief to the plaintiff
       [*check only those that apply*]

       (a)   ☐ Direct the defendant to hire the plaintiff.

       (b)   ☐ Direct the defendant to re-employ the plaintiff.

       (c)   ☐ Direct the defendant to promote the plaintiff.

       (d)   ☐ Direct the defendant to reasonably accommodate the plaintiff's religion.

       (e)   ☐ Direct the defendant to reasonably accommodate the plaintiff's disabilities.

       (f)   ☐ Direct the defendant to (specify): _____

       _____

       _____

[If you need additional space for ANY section, please attach an additional sheet and reference that section.]

Rev. 06/27/2016

[If you need additional space for ANY section, please attach an additional sheet and reference that section.]

_____

_____

_____

(g)   ☐   If available, grant the plaintiff appropriate injunctive relief, lost wages, liquidated/double damages, front pay, compensatory damages, punitive damages, prejudgment interest, post-judgment interest, and costs, including reasonable attorney fees and expert witness fees.

(h)   ☐   Grant such other relief as the Court may find appropriate.

_____
(Plaintiff's signature)

_____
(Plaintiff's name)

_____
(Plaintiff's street address)

(City)_____(State)_____(ZIP)_____

(Plaintiff's telephone number) (____) – _____

                                 Date: _____

[If you need additional space for ANY section, please attach an additional sheet and reference that section.]

THE UNITED STATES DISTRICT COURT
FOR THE NORTHERN DISTRICT OF ILLINOIS
EASTERN DIVISION

FRED SMITH,

    Plaintiff,

    v.

No. 22-cv-3456

VILLAGE OF SUNNYSIDE, a Municipal
Corporation, Sunnyside Police Detective
ROBERT JONES,

    Defendants,

Jury Trial Demanded.

DEFENDANT ROBERT JONES'S ANSWERS TO
PLAINTIFF'S INTERROGATORIES

NOW COMES Defendant Robert Jones, by and through his undersigned counsel, and in response to Plaintiff's First Set of Interrogatories, states as follows:

1.   Please state your full name, educational and employment history, including specific dates of graduation and employment, as well as any degrees conferred.

ANSWER: Robert Jones; Graduated from Central High School, May 2010; Graduated from Junior College, December 2016, Associate Degree; Sunnydown Police Department, October 1, 2016 - February 2018; Sunnyside Police Department, February 13, 2018 - present.

2.   Please identify with particularity all training you have received, including names, dates and training entities, including but not limited to training on making arrests, detaining subjects, and using force on subjects and arrestees.

ANSWER: See Sunnyside Police Department personnel files. I do not have my Sunnyside Police Department personnel file. 1 received training with that department but cannot recall all of the training.

3.   Have you ever been arrested, detained, or cited by a police officer or other law enforcement official? If your answer is in the affirmative, for each arrest, detention, or citation, identify the date, the law enforcement agency or officers involved, the charge, any ultimate disposition of any charges, as well as whether you have ever been convicted of any offense.

ANSWER: Officer Jones received a traffic citation from Plainville Police in 2010 and was given three (3) month supervision.

4.   Have you, or anyone on your behalf, ever filed a civil suit, or been sued, in your personal non-law enforcement capacity, including, but not limited to, a personal injury claim, worker's compensation claim, forcible detainer action or divorce proceeding? If the answer is in the affirmative, state the court in which the suit was filed, the year filed, the title and docket number of said case, the result of the case and the nature of the matter (i.e., personal injury, divorce, etc.)

ANSWER: No.

5.   Do you suffer from any disease or ailment that impacts your ability to remember events or things? If so, identify the disease or ailment as well as the name and address of each physician/medical professional that has treated you for the disease/ailment in the last five (5) years.

ANSWER: No.

6.   State/identify all positions and/or assignments you have held with any law enforcement agency, including, but not limited to, dates of employment, dates of any promotions, the dates that you have held each position/assignment, the date(s) of separation/termination from each such position, and the reasons for each such separation/termination. This interrogatory includes a request for any specialized assignments you have held such as, for example, patrol officer, investigator, detective, juvenile officers, FTO, supervisor, or any other position/assignment. Also, this interrogatory seeks all such information, whether it relates to your employment with the Village of Sunnyside, or any other governmental entity/municipality.

ANSWER: See Sunnyside records for position/assignments held and dates.

7.   Have you had any complaints alleging misconduct filed against you and/or have you ever been disciplined in connection with your duties as a police officer? If the answer is in the affirmative, list all such charges by number, name of complainant, the disposition, and the nature of the charge. In this interrogatory, the Plaintiff specifically requests information regarding all complaints, and discipline, irrespective of whether they have been expunged and/or purged. Also, this interrogatory specifically requests information related to complaints and/or discipline lodged with the Sunnyside Police Department, as well as any other police departments.

ANSWER: Defendant received a written reprimand in January 2019 for a vehicle accident in a parking lot. This was expunged from his file a year later.

8.   Have you ever been named in any other lawsuit brought pursuant to the United States Constitution, 42 U.S.C. Sections 1981, 1983, 1985, 1986, any other federal

statute, and/or any claim arising under state law, in connection with your duties as a police officer? If your answer is in the affirmative, set forth the following:

a) The caption and case number of the lawsuit;

b) The court in which the lawsuit was filed;

c) The date the lawsuit was filed;

d) The disposition of the lawsuit, or the current status of the vase, if no final disposition has been reached; and

e) The nature of the allegations filed in each such matter.

ANSWER: No.

9.   Describe each and every action by Fred that supported your detention of him on May 3, 2022.

ANSWER: Objection calls for a narrative response which will be given at my deposition. See criminal report and court stenographer report from my testimony in the criminal case.

10.   Who have you spoken to regarding the incident in question? For each such conversation, identify the date(s) and time(s) on which each conversation took place, every person that was present for each such conversation, where the conversation(s) took place, what was said in each such conversation, and whether any documentation was created as a result of any such conversation.

ANSWER: Supervisors who were working on the day of the incident in question, officers that responded to the scene, State's Attorneys, and Village Attorneys.

11.   Did you author, contribute to, or review any report, record, or other document regarding the incident in question? If yes, for each such record, report or document, state:

a) Title;

b) Bates number;

c) Date and time you authored, contributed to, or reviewed said record, report, or document; and

d) Nature of your role/activity as it relates to the record, report, or document.

ANSWER: 05/03/2022; arresting/primary officer.

Respectfully Submitted,

VILLAGE OF SUNNYSIDE and
ROBERT JONES

By: /s/ Jeffrey C. Johnson
Their Attorney

Jeffrey C. Johnson
Johnson Law Firm, P.C.
780 South Elm Street
Sunnyside, IL 60987
Tel: (312) 663-2626
Fax: (312) 663-2627
jjohnson@johnsonlawfirm.com

THE UNITED STATES DISTRICT COURT
FOR THE NORTHERN DISTRICT OF ILLINOIS
EASTERN DIVISION

FRED SMITH,

     Plaintiff,

     v.

VILLAGE OF SUNNYSIDE, a
Municipal Corporation, Sunnyside Police
Officer ROBERT JONES,

     Defendants,

No. 22-cv-3456

Jury Trial Demanded.

NOTICE OF 30 (b)(6) VIDEO DEPOSITION

PLEASE TAKE NOTICE that pursuant to Rule 30(b)(6) of the Federal Rules of Civil Procedure, Plaintiff shall take the deposition of the **Village of Sunnyside,** by its designee Cmdr. John Doe 1, on **January 5, 2023, at 1:00 p.m.,** via Zoom, to be recorded by audio and video, before a notary public or other officer duly authorized to administer oaths, upon oral interrogatories propounded pursuant to the Federal Rules of Civil Procedure, on the following topics:

1.   Sunnyside Police Department policies and practices regarding lineup procedures.

2.   Sunnyside Police Department policies and practices regarding the retention, preservation, and destruction of audio and video footage from criminal investigations.

3.   Actions taken with respect to the unlawful detention, seizure, or mistreatment of Fred Smith.

4.   The Village's receipt of Plaintiff's counsel's May 12, 2022 preservation request letter, and all actions taken by the Village or its employees relating to that preservation request.

The designated witness is directed to bring to the depositions any and all materials he will have reviewed in preparation for the depositions.

/s/ Susan Miller

LAW OFFICE OF SUSAN MILLER
12345 Sunnyside Drive. Sunnyside IL 61234
(312) 456-7892 - susan@millerlaw.com

CERTIFICATE OF SERVICE

Susan Miller, an attorney, certifies that on December 15, 2022, she served a copy of the foregoing document by electronic mail to the following:

Jeffrey C. Johnson
Johnson Law Firm, P.C.
780 South Elm Street
Sunnyside, IL 60987
Tel: (312) 663-2626
Fax: (312) 663-2627
jjohnson@johnsonlawfirm.com

                                                  /s/ Susan Miller

THE UNITED STATES DISTRICT COURT
FOR THE NORTHERN DISTRICT OF ILLINOIS
EASTERN DIVISION

FRED SMITH,

      Plaintiff,

    v.

VILLAGE OF SUNNYSIDE, a
Municipal Corporation, Sunnyside
Police Detective ROBERT JONES,

      Defendants,

No. 22-cv-3456

Jury Trial Demanded.

NOTICE OF VIDEO DEPOSITION

PLEASE TAKE NOTICE that pursuant to Rule 30 of the Federal Rules of Civil Procedure, Plaintiff shall take the subpoenaed deposition of the following individual on the following date and time, or such other dates and times as the parties may agree, via Zoom, to be recorded by audio and video, before a licensed notary public or certified court reporter, upon oral interrogatories propounded pursuant to the Federal Rules of Civil Procedure:

Assistant State's Attorney Jane Doe　　　　**March 21, 2023**　　　**10:00 a.m.**

/s/ Susan Miller

LAW OFFICE OF SUSAN MILLER
12345 Sunnyside Drive, Sunnyside IL 61234
susan@millerlaw.com

CERTIFICATE OF SERVICE

Susan Miller, an attorney, certifies that on February 21, 2023, she served a copy of the foregoing document by electronic mail to the following:

Jeffrey C. Johnson
Johnson Law Firm, P.C.
780 South Elm Street. Sunnyside, IL 60987
jjohnson@johnsonlawfirm.com

/s/ Susan Miller

THE UNITED STATES DISTRICT COURT
FOR THE NORTHERN DISTRICT OF ILLINOIS
EASTERN DIVISION

FRED SMITH,

     Plaintiff,

v.

VILLAGE OF SUNNYSIDE, a
Municipal Corporation, Sunnyside
Police Detective ROBERT JONES,

     Defendants,

No. 22-cv-3456

Jury Trial Demanded.

DISCOVERY PLAN

Counsel for Plaintiff, LAW OFFICE OF SUSAN MILLER, and counsel for Defendants, JOHNSON LAW FIRM, P.C., having conferred on May 21, 2024, for the purpose of formulating a proposed discovery schedule for consideration by the Court, hereby submit the following agreed deadlines for the Court's consideration:

1. **Initial disclosures pursuant to Fed. R. Civ. P. 26(a)(1):** June 24, 2024.

2. **Amendment of the pleadings:** September 6, 2024.

3. **Joining additional parties:** September 6, 2024.

4. **Close of fact discovery:** February 28, 2025.

5. **Disclosure of Plaintiff's experts:** N/A.

6. **Disclosure of Plaintiff's expert reports:** N/A.

7. **Plaintiff's experts deposed by:** N/A.

8. **Disclosure of Defendant's experts:** N/A.

9. **Disclosure of Defendant's expert reports:** N/A.

10. **Defendant's experts deposed by:** N/A.

11. **Completion of all discovery:** February 28, 2025.

12. **Dispositive motions:** March 21, 2025.

Respectfully submitted,

/s/ Susan Miller   /s/ Jeffrey C. Johnson
Attorney for the Plaintiff   *Attorney for the Defendants*

LAW OFFICE OF SUSAN MILLER   **JOHNSON LAW FIRM, P.C.**
12345 Sunnyside Drive   780 South Elm Street
Sunnyside IL 61234   Sunnyside, IL 60987
(312) 456-7892   (312) 663-2626
susan@millerlaw.com   jjohnson@johnsonlawfirm.com

CERTIFICATE OF SERVICE

I certify that on May 21, 2024, I served a copy of the foregoing on all counsel of record by filing the same on the Court's ECF system.

/s/ Susan Miller

FILING A CIVIL CASE
WITHOUT AN ATTORNEY:
EMPLOYMENT DISCRIMINATION
FORMS & INSTRUCTIONS

UNITED STATES DISTRICT COURT
NORTHERN DISTRICT OF ILLINOIS

(07/13/16)

Personal Identifiers in Paper Filings

Federal Rules of Civil Procedure 5.2 addresses privacy and security concerns over public access to electronic court files. Under this rule, papers filed with the court should not contain anyone's full social-security number or full birth date; the name of a person known to be a minor; or a complete financial-account number. A filing may include only the last four digits of a social-security number or taxpayer identification number; the year of someone's birth; a minor's initials; and the last four digits of a financial-account number. Please review the rule for a complete listing and exceptions.

<u>Filing a Complaint of Employment Discrimination</u>

A blank copy of the employment discrimination complaint form has been included in the packet. Additional forms are available on the Court's <u>website</u> under On-line forms and on the Court's kiosk located on the 20th floor outside the Clerk's Office.

The remainder of this section tells you how to complete the employment discrimination complaint form. If you need additional room for your answer to any of the items on the form, you may enter the extra information on a plain piece of paper that is the same size as the employment discrimination form. If you add an extra page for one of the items in the form, write "see additional page" in the place on the form where you run out of room to write. On your additional page, write the number of the item and the word "continued" (For example, "Item 13 continued").

Identifying the Parties

At the top of the form, write your name in the lined space above "(Name of the plaintiff or plaintiffs)." On the lines above "(Name of the defendant or defendants)," write the name of the party or parties you want to sue. If you need more space to list plaintiff or defendants, use an extra sheet of paper, and indicate on the original form that the list of parties continues to another page. Identify each party as a plaintiff or defendant.

Numbered Items in the Employment Discrimination Complaint Form

1)   This item simply identifies the complaint as a legal action involving a claim of employment discrimination. You do not need to write anything here.

2)   Item 2) tells the court who you are. Complete this item by entering your name and the county and state where you live. If there are more than one plaintiffs, you need to add the counties and states where each plaintiff lives.

3)   Item 3) identifies the defendant. Complete this item by entering the name, address, and (if available) the telephone number of each defendant. Please note that, in general, the defendant named in the complaint filed in this Court must be the same person or company that was named in the EEOC proceeding.

4)   Item 4) identifies the place of business where you believe the employment discrimination happened. Complete this item by entering the address of the business.

5)   Item 5) describes your employment relationship with the defendant at the time you are filing your complaint. Complete this item by putting an "X" or a "✓ " in the box that describes your current status.

6)   Item 6) indicates when you believe the employment discrimination occurred or—if you believe the discrimination is still going on—when the discrimination started. Complete this item by entering the date. If you do not know a specific date, complete item 6 by

entering the date that is your best estimate of when the discrimination happened or started.

7)   Item 7) indicates whether you have or have not previously taken your employment discrimination complaint to either the Equal Employment Opportunity Commission (EEOC) *or* the Illinois Department of Human Rights. Record your response by entering an "X" or a "✔ " in the box labeled "has not" or the box labeled "has."

If you indicated in 7)(a) that you *have* filed your complaint with the EEOC or the Illinois Department of Human Rights, complete items 7)(a)(i) or 7)(a)(ii) to indicate which of these agencies you have been before and the date you filed your complaint with them.

In item 7)(b), enter an "X" or a "✔ " in the box labeled "Yes" or "No" to indicate whether you have attached a copy of the charge you brought before the EEOC and/or the Illinois Human Rights Commission.

8)   If the EEOC has not issued you a document called a "Notice of Right to Sue," enter an "X" or a "✔ " in box 8)(a).

If the EEOC *has* issued you a "Notice of Right to Sue," enter an "X" or a "✔ " in box 8)(b). Complete the rest of item 8)(b) by entering the date on which you received the EEOC notice. Attach a copy of your 'Notice of Right to Sue" to the complaint form.

9)   Item 9) indicates the type of discrimination covered by your complaint. Read the list of discrimination types, then enter an "X" or a "✔ " in the boxes or boxes that you believe apply to your situation.

10)   If the defendant in your complaint is a state or local government agency *and* you are claiming discrimination on the basis of race, color, or national origin, complete item 10) by entering an "X" or a "✔ " in the box labeled "YES." For all other complaints, enter an "X" or a "✔ " in the box labeled "NO."

11)   This item lists the laws that give the District Court jurisdiction over the case. You do not need to write anything here.

12)   Use item 12) to indicate what action or actions you believe the defendant took that affected your employment. Read the list of six actions, then enter an "X" or a "✔ " in the boxes or boxes that you believe apply to your situation. Note that this item 12)(f) allows additional space for you to write more if you believe that items 12)(a) through 12)(e) don't apply to your complaint. Please note that a plaintiff is generally permitted to proceed in this Court *only* on claims that have been presented to the EEOC.

13.)   Use item 13) to briefly describe the facts that lead you to believe that you have been discriminated against by the defendant.

14)   Item 14) consists of specific language that is required in employment complaints that claim discrimination on the basis of age. You do not need to write anything here.

15)   Use item 15) to indicate whether or not you want your case to be tried by a jury. If you want a trial by jury, enter an "X" or a "✔" in the box labeled "YES." If you do not want to demand a jury trial, enter an "X" or a "✔" in the box labeled "NO."

16)   Use Item 16) to tell the Court what you want to happen as a result of your employment discrimination complaint. Read the list of kinds of relief, then enter an "X" or a "✔" in the boxes or boxes that indicate the result you want. Note that item 16)(f) allows additional space for you to write more if necessary.

Signature, Date, Name, and Address

You must sign the employment discrimination complaint. Do this on the last page of the form. You must also enter your name, address, and telephone number.

Completing the Civil Cover Sheet for an Employment Discrimination Complaint

The civil cover sheet is a form that you need to complete and submit along with your complaint. The civil cover sheet records basic information about your civil case. There are instructions on the reverse side of the civil cover sheet describing how the cover sheet should be completed. However, a brief summary for employment discrimination complaints may be helpful.

- Identifying the parties. Record the names of the parties in the spaces labeled "plaintiffs" and "defendants" at the top of the civil cover sheet.

- Basis of jurisdiction. Unless you are suing the federal government, enter an "X" or a "✔" in the box labeled "federal question." If you are suing the federal government enter an "X" or a "✔" in the box labeled "U.S. Government Defendant."

- In an employment discrimination case you do not need to enter anything in the section of the civil cover sheet labeled "Citizenship of Principal Parties."

- In the section labeled "Origin," enter an "X" or a "✔" in the box labeled "Original Proceeding."

- In the part of the civil cover sheet section labeled "Nature of Suit," find the section labeled "Civil Rights." Next, enter an "X" or a "✓" in the box labeled "442 Employment."

- In the section labeled "Cause of Action," enter "complaint of employment discrimination."

- In the part of the civil cover sheet labeled "Requested in Complaint," find the section labeled "Demand $." If you are asking that the court order the defendant to pay you a specific amount of money, enter that amount next to "Demand $." If you are *not* requesting an award of money, enter "0" next to "Demand $."

  In the same section of the civil cover sheet, enter the same information about your request for a jury trial that you entered in item 15) of your employment discrimination complaint form.

- Refiling a Previously Dismissed Case. If you have previously filed a complaint involving the same claim of discrimination by the same defendant, enter the name of the judge and the case number in the space provided in this section of the civil cover sheet.

- Date and signature. Record the date and sign the civil cover sheet in the space labeled "signature of attorney of record."

Summary of Instructions for Filing a Civil Case

Document	General Information	Number of Copies Required
Complaint	• List all plaintiffs and defendants in the caption, the top left of the complaint. • State your case in your own words, using additional pages if you need them. • Your signature, address, and telephone number must appear on the last page of your complaint. • Exhibits may be attached to your complaint.	• You must provide an original, one copy for the assigned judge, and one copy for *each* defendant named in your complaint. • If you are suing the federal government or federal agency, you need to provide three extra copies.
Civil Cover Sheet (JS-44)	• This is a form used by the Court in preparing the docket for your case. • Instructions for completing this form appear on the reverse side of the form.	• Only the original is required.
Appearance Form for Pro Se Litigants	• **The appearance form, which must be filed, provides your name and address information. It is listed on the case docket. It also identifies where notices of orders and filings in your case are sent. If you have access to email, you should indicate on your appearance form that you wish to receive notices electronically rather than in paper form.** • If you do not have an attorney and will be proceeding without counsel, fill in the appearance form in accordance with the instructions found on the reverse side of the form, supplying your name and address.	• Only the original is required.
Filing fees	• There is a fee for the filing of a civil case other than a writ of habeas corpus. • If you are unable to afford the fee, see the information below about in forma pauperis application. • See the Court's current fee schedule for filing fee information.	
In Forma Pauperis Application	• This petition is used by a plaintiff who requests approval by the Court for a civil case to proceed without the prepayment of the filing fee. • Complete all appropriate sections of the application, sign and date.	• You must provide an original and one copy for the assigned judge.
Motion for Attorney Representation	• This motion is a request that the Court appoint an attorney. • Complete the motion form in accordance with the instructions attached to the form.	• You must provide an original and one copy for the assigned judge.
Summons	• Complete the original and one copy for service to each defendant. • Your own name and address should appear under the heading labeled "Plaintiff's Attorney."	• You must provide an original and one copy for *each* defendant named in your complaint. • If you are suing the federal government or federal agency, you need to provide three extra copies.

| USM-285 | • This form is designed as a control document for process served by a U.S. Marshal.
• Complete all appropriate sections of the form.
• Submit a completed copy of the form for each defendant named in your complaint. | • You must provide an original for *each* defendant named in your complaint.
• If you are suing the federal government or federal agency, you need to provide two extra copies. |

Law Office of
Susan Miller

May 5, 2022

Via Electronic Mail
Sunnyside Police Department
John Doe, FOIA Department
jdoe@vil.sunnyside.il.us

To whom it may concern:

I am writing on behalf of my client **Fred Smith** pursuant to the Illinois Freedom of Information Act to request the following:

1. Any and all documents – including but not limited to photographs, accident reports, police reports, arrest reports, supplementary reports, general offense case reports, General Progress Reports, signed and unsigned complaints, notes, memoranda, communications, correspondence, faxes, search warrants, applications for search warrant, property inventories, and e-mails regarding **Fred Smith**, who was placed in police custody on May 3, 2022.

2. Any and all video and audio footage, including but not limited to **dispatch audio, surveillance video, and body worn camera video,** related to Mr. Smith.

I am enclosing a signed release of records with this request. This is a non-commercial request. Preferred format of materials is electronic, i.e. PDF, other than audio and video footage, which should be universal format (i.e. Windows Media Player). Please contact me with any questions or if you wish to discuss this request in any detail.

Sincerely yours,

/s/ Susan Miller

Susan Miller
Attorney

UNITED STATES DISTRICT COURT
NORTHERN DISTRICT OF ILLINOIS

(full name of plaintiff or petitioner)

vs.

(full name of defendant(s) or respondent(s))

**APPLICATION TO PROCEED
WITHOUT PREPAYING FEES OR
COSTS / FINANCIAL AFFIDAVIT
(NON-PRISONER CASE)**

Case number:

Instructions: Please answer every question. Do not leave blanks.
If the answer is "0" or "none," say so.

Application: I am one of the parties in this case. I believe that I am entitled to the relief I am requesting in this case. I am providing the following information under penalty of perjury in support of my request (check all that apply):

☐ to proceed *in forma pauperis* (IFP) (without prepaying fees or costs)

☐ to request an attorney

1. *Are you employed?*

   ☐ Yes   Name and address of employer: _____

   Total amount of monthly take-home pay: _____

   ☐ No   Date(s) of last employment: _____ Last monthly take-home pay:_____

2. *If married, is your spouse employed?* ☐ Not married

   ☐ Yes   Name and address of spouse's employer: _____

   Total amount of spouse's monthly take-home pay: _____

   ☐ No   Date(s) of spouse's last employment: Spouse's last monthly take-home pay:

3. *Other sources of income / money:* For the past 12 months, list the amount of money that you and/or your spouse have received from any of the following sources:

(list the 12-month total for each)

Self-employment, business, or profession:	$ _____
Income from interest or dividends:	$ _____
Income from rent payments:	$ _____
Pensions, annuities, or life insurance:	$ _____
Disability or worker's compensation:	$ _____
Gifts (including deposits into any accounts in your name):	$ _____
Unemployment, public assistance, or welfare:	$ _____
Settlements or judgments (include any that are expected):	$ _____
Any other source of money:	$ _____

Rev. 2/2020

4. *Cash and bank accounts:* Do you and/or your spouse have any money in cash or in a checking or savings account? ☐ Yes   ☐ No   If yes, how much? _____

5. *Other assets:* Do you and/or your spouse own or have an interest in any real estate (including your home), stocks, bonds, other securities, retirement plans, automobiles, jewelry, or other valuable property (not including ordinary household furnishings and clothing)? ☐ Yes   ☐ No

   If yes, list each item of property and state its approximate value:

   _____

   _____

   _____

6. *Dependents:* Is anyone dependent on you and/or your spouse for support? ☐ Yes   ☐ No

   If yes, please list their names (for minor children, use only initials); relationship to you; and how much you and/or your spouse contribute toward their support each month:

   _____

   _____

7. *Debts and financial obligations:* List any amounts you owe to others:

   _____

   _____

   _____

8. *Provide any other information that will help explain why you cannot afford to pay court fees / hire an attorney:*

   _____

   _____

   _____

Declaration: I declare under penalty of perjury that all of the information listed above is true and correct. I understand that a false statement may result in dismissal of my claims or other sanctions.

Date: _____   _____
                                            Applicant's signature

                                          _____
                                            Printed name

Rev. 2/2020

UNITED STATES DISTRICT COURT
NORTHERN DISTRICT OF ILLINOIS

(full name of plaintiff or petitioner)

vs.

(full name of defendant(s) or respondent(s))

**APPLICATION TO PROCEED
WITHOUT PREPAYING FEES OR
COSTS / FINANCIAL AFFIDAVIT
(PRISONER CASES)**

Case number:

Instructions: Please answer every question. Do not leave blanks.
If the answer is "0" or "none," say so.

If you are in custody, you are subject to the Prison Litigation Reform Act ("PLRA"). The PLRA requires all pretrial detainees and prisoners to pay the filing fee. If you cannot pay the full filing fee at this time, you may seek leave to proceed *in forma pauperis*. A pretrial detainee or prisoner who proceeds *in forma pauperis* pays the full filing fee over time, with monthly installments taken from his or her trust fund account.

Application: I am the plaintiff / petitioner in this case. I believe that I am entitled to the relief I am requesting in this case. I am providing the following information under penalty of perjury in support of my request (check all that apply):

☐ to proceed *in forma pauperis* (IFP) (without prepaying fees or costs)

☐ to request an attorney

1. *Are you in custody?* ☐ Yes   ☐ No

    ID #_____   Name of jail or prison: _____

    Do you receive any payment from this institution? ☐ Yes   ☐ No

    If "Yes," how much per month? $_____

2. *Other sources of income / money:* For the past 12 months, list the amount of money that you have received from any of the following sources:

    (list the 12-month total for each)

    Self-employment, business, or profession: $_____
    Income from interest or dividends: $_____
    Income from rent payments: $_____
    Pensions, annuities, or life insurance: $_____
    Disability or worker's compensation: $_____
    Gifts: $_____
    Deposits by others into your jail or prison account: $_____
    Unemployment, public assistance, or welfare: $_____
    Settlements or judgments: $_____
    Any other source of money: $_____

Page 1 of 2

Rev. 2/2020

3. *Cash and bank accounts:* Do you have any money in cash or in a checking or savings account? ☐ Yes   ☐ No   If yes, how much? _____

4. *Other assets:* Do you have an interest in any real estate (including your home), stocks, bonds, other securities, retirement plans, automobiles, jewelry, or other valuable property (not including ordinary household furnishings and clothing)?   ☐ Yes   ☐ No

   If yes, list each item of property and state its approximate value:

   _____

   _____

5. *Dependents:* Is anyone dependent on you for support?   ☐ Yes   ☐ No

   If yes, please list their names (for minor children, use only initials); relationship to you; and how much you and/or your spouse contribute toward their support each month:

   _____

   _____

6. *Debts and financial obligations:* List any amounts you owe to others:

   _____

   _____

Declaration: I declare under penalty of perjury that all of the information listed above is true and correct. I understand that a false statement may result in dismissal of my claims or other sanctions.

Date: _____   _____

                             Applicant's signature

                             _____

                             Printed name

NOTICE TO PRISONERS: In addition to the Certificate below, you must attach a print-out from the institution(s) where you have been in custody during the last six months showing all receipts, expenditures and balances in your prison or jail trust fund accounts during that period. Because the law requires information as to such accounts covering a full six months before you have filed your lawsuit, you must attach a sheet covering transactions in your own account – prepared by each institution where you have been in custody during that six-month period. You must also have the Certificate below completed by an authorized officer at each institution.

CERTIFICATE (Incarcerated applicants only)
(To be completed by the institution of incarceration)

I certify that the applicant named above, _____, ID # _____, has the sum of $ _____ on account to his/her credit at _____ (name of institution). I also certify that during the past six months, the applicant's average monthly deposit was $ _____. (Add all deposits from all sources and then divide by the number of months.)

Date: _____   _____

                             Signature of authorized officer

                             _____

                             Printed name

Rev. 2/2020

THE UNITED STATES DISTRICT COURT
FOR THE NORTHERN DISTRICT OF ILLINOIS
EASTERN DIVISION

FRED SMITH,

Plaintiff,

v.

VILLAGE OF SUNNYSIDE, a Municipal
Corporation, Sunnyside Police Detective
ROBERT JONES,

Defendants,

No. 22-cv-3456

Jury Trial Demanded.

JOINT STATUS REPORT

On September 2, 2022, the parties conferred as required by Fed. R. Civ. P. 26(f). Plaintiff

participated in the conference via his counsel, Susan Miller, of the Law Office of Susan Miller, and

Defendants participated via their counsel, Jeffrey C. Johnson, of Johnson Law Firm, P.C. The

parties discussed the matters required by Rule 26(f)(2).

1. Service of process

All parties have been served and have appeared and answered.

2. Nature of the Case

A. Attorneys of record:

For Plaintiff:
Susan Miller
Law Office of Susan Miller
12345 Sunnyside Drive
Sunnyside IL 61234
(312) 456-7892
susan@millerlaw.com

1

For Defendants:
Jeffrey C. Johnson
Johnson Law Firm, P.C.
780 South Elm Street
Sunnyside, IL 60987
Tel: (312) 663-2626
Fax: (312) 663-2627
jjohnson@johnsonlawfirm.com

B. Basis for federal jurisdiction

This case arises under the Fourth and Fourteenth Amendments to the Constitution of the United States, under the laws of the United States, particularly the Civil Rights Act, Title 42 of the United States Code, Sections 1983 and 1988. This Court has jurisdiction over this action pursuant to Title 28 of the United States Code §§ 1331 and 1367, as Plaintiff asserts claims under federal law.

C. Nature of claims asserted

This case arises out of the unlawful detention of Plaintiff Fred Smith by Defendant Jones, on May 3, 2022. Fred asserts that Defendant Jones arrested and/or detained him without reasonable suspicion or probable cause to believe he had committed a crime, and that he confiscated and retained Fred's telephone without probable cause to believe it contained evidence of a crime, without a warrant, and without legal process.

Fred asserts federal claims of false arrest, unlawful detention, and illegal seizure against Defendant Jones, and state law claims of False Arrest/Wrongful Imprisonment, conversion, and intentional infliction of emotional distress against Defendants Jones and the Village of Sunnyside.

Defendants deny each and every one of Plaintiff's claims, and assert various affirmative defenses, including qualified immunity.

2

D. Major legal and factual issues in the case

1. Did Defendant Jones have probable cause or reasonable suspicion to believe Fred had committed a crime at the time Fred was detained and/or arrested on May 3, 2022?

2. Did Defendant Jones have legal justification for taking possession of Fred's phone on May 3, 2022, and retaining possession of the phone until it was returned to Fred?

3. Did Defendant Jones conduct a search of Fred's phone, and if so, did he have legal justification to do so at the time he conducted the search?

4. Is Defendant Jones entitled to qualified immunity on the federal allegations?

5. Did Defendant Jones intentionally or recklessly cause Fred to suffer severe emotional distress?

E. Relief sought

Plaintiff seeks compensatory and punitive damages, and reasonable attorney's fees and costs. Defendants deny that he is entitled to any relief.

F. Pending motions and case plan

1. There are no pending motions.

2. The parties agree that discovery may be requested on the following subjects (without waiver of any objections to such requests): Plaintiff's claims; Plaintiff's alleged damages; and Defendants' defenses. The parties agree that the format of discovery will be written discovery requests, requests to admit, subpoenas, and depositions.

3. The parties anticipate that discovery may encompass some electronically stored information ("ESI"), and will work to amicably and cooperatively resolve any ESI discovery issues if any issues arise. The parties agree to produce hard copies of all requested electronic data when available,

3

absent any privileges or objections which would preclude or protect such data from being disclosed. However, either party may request that ESI be produced in a different form if desired. The parties further agree to cooperate in good faith concerning the form in which ESI is to be produced when requested in a different format. The parties reserve the right to withhold any discovery documents/data based on a known privilege or objection. Any extraordinary costs for duplication shall be allocated to the requesting party.

4. Rule 26(a)(1) disclosures will be issued by September 9, 2022.

5. Written discovery will be propounded by September 16, 2022.

8. The parties will complete fact discovery by March 3, 2023.

9. The parties are uncertain as to whether they will be retaining expert witnesses. Any party seeking to retain an expert witness will file a motion to adjust the discovery schedule before the close of fact discovery.

10. Dispositive motions will be filed on or before April 7, 2023.

11. The parties anticipate being ready for trial on or after July 7, 2023.

12. The parties request a jury trial, and anticipate a trial lasting no longer than four days, including jury selection.

G. Magistrate Judge Referral

The parties have discussed the advantages of a Magistrate Judge referral, and at this time do not unanimously consent to proceed before a Magistrate Judge.

H. Settlement

The parties have not discussed settlement, and do not request a settlement conference at this time.

Dated: September 2, 2022.

Respectfully submitted,

/s/ **Susan Miller**

Law Office of Susan Miller
12345 Sunnyside Drive
Sunnyside IL 61234
(312) 456-7892
susan@millerlaw.com

/s/ **Jeffrey C. Johnson**

Johnson Law Firm, P.C.
780 South Elm Street
Sunnyside, IL 60987
Tel: (312) 663-2626
jjohnson@johnsonlawfirm.com

[If you need additional space for ANY section, please attach an additional sheet and reference that section.]

UNITED STATES DISTRICT COURT
NORTHERN DISTRICT OF ILLINOIS

Plaintiff(s)

v.

Defendant(s

)
)
)
)
)
)
)
)

Case Number:

Judge:

MOTION FOR ATTORNEY REPRESENTATION
(NOTE: Failure to complete all items may result in the denial of this motion.)

1.   I, _____, declare that I am the (check appropriate box)
☐ plaintiff   ☐ defendant in this case and that I am unable to afford the services of an
attorney. I hereby ask the Court for an attorney to represent me in this case.

2.   I declare that I have contacted the following attorneys/organizations seeking representation:
(NOTE: This item must be completed.)

but I have been unable to find an attorney because:

3.   I declare that (check all that apply):
(Now:)
☐   I *am not* currently represented by an attorney requested by the Court in any federal
criminal or civil case.
OR
☐   I *am* currently represented by an attorney requested by the Court in a federal criminal
or civil case. The case is described on the back of this page.

(Earlier:)
☐   I *have not* previously been represented by an attorney requested by the Court in any
federal criminal or civil case.
OR
☐   I *have* previously been represented by an attorney requested by the Court in a federal
criminal or civil case. The case is described on the back of this page.

4.   I declare that (check ·one):
☐   I have attached an original Application for Leave to Proceed *In Forma Pauperis*
detailing my financial status.

Rev. 06/23/2016

[If you need additional space for ANY section, please attach an additional sheet and reference that section.]

[If you need additional space for ANY section, please attach an additional sheet and reference that section.]

☐   I have previously filed an Application for Leave to Proceed In Forma Pauperis in this case, and it is still true and correct.

☐   I have previously filed an Application for Leave to Proceed In Forma Pauperis in this case. However, my financial status has changed and I have attached an Amended Application to Proceed In Forma Pauperis to reflect my current financial status.

5.   ☐   I declare that my highest level of education is (check one):

☐ Grammar school   ☐ Some high school   ☐ High school graduate
☐ Some college   ☐ College graduate   ☐ Post-graduate

6.   ☐   I declare that my ability to speak, write, and/or read English is limited because English is not my primary language. (Check only if applicable.)

7.   ☐   I declare that this form and/or other documents in this case were prepared with the help of an attorney from the U.S. District Court Pro Se Assistance Program. (Check only if applicable.)

8.   ☐   I declare under penalty of perjury that the foregoing is true and correct.

_____   _____
Signature of Movant   Street Address

_____   _____
Date   City, State, Zip

Other cases in which an attorney requested by this Court has represented me:

| Case Name: _____ Case No.: _____ |
| Attorney's Name: _____ This case is still pending ☐ Yes ☐ No |
| The appointment was limited to settlement assistance: ☐ Yes ☐ No |
| Case Name: _____ Case No.: _____ |
| Attorney's Name: _____ This case is still pending ☐ Yes ☐ No |
| The appointment was limited to settlement assistance: ☐ Yes ☐ No |
| Case Name: _____ Case No.: _____ |
| Attorney's Name: _____ This case is still pending ☐ Yes ☐ No |
| The appointment was limited to settlement assistance: ☐ Yes ☐ No |

Rev. 06/23/2016

[If you need additional space for ANY section, please attach an additional sheet and reference that section.]

THE UNITED STATES DISTRICT COURT
FOR THE NORTHERN DISTRICT OF ILLINOIS
EASTERN DIVISION

FRED SMITH,

    Plaintiff,

    v.

VILLAGE OF SUNNYSIDE, a
Municipal Corporation, Sunnyside
Police Detective ROBERT JONES,

    Defendants,

No. 22-cv-3456

Jury Trial Demanded.

MOTION TO COMPEL

NOW COMES Plaintiff Fred Smith, by and through his undersigned counsel, and moves this Court for an order compelling more complete answers to Plaintiff's discovery requests, and in support thereof states as follows:

INTRODUCTION

As the court is aware, this matter presents an unlawful detention claim in the Village of Sunnyside. *See Smith v. Sunnyside,* Seventh Circuit order, No. 23-3456, attached hereto as Exhibit A, at p. 1.

Plaintiff issued his first Request to Produce on May 21, 2023, and Defendants responded on June 22, 2023. (See Production Response, attached hereto as Exhibit B.)

Plaintiff sent Defense Counsel a letter pursuant to Federal Rule of Procedure 37 on May 25, suggesting deficiencies in Defendants' Production response. (Exhibit C.)

On that same day, the parties' counsel engaged in a discussion by telephone to attempt to resolve their differences. Plaintiff's counsel followed up with a letter documenting their discussion. (Exhibit D.)

On July 16, in an effort to resolve their differences, the parties participated in a discovery conference with the Honorable Magistrate Judge John Doe. Unfortunately, the conference was not successful.

STANDARD

The scope of discovery is defined by Federal Rule of Civil Procedure as follows:

> Parties may obtain discovery regarding any nonprivileged matter that is relevant to any party's claim or defense and proportional to the needs of the case, considering the importance of the issues at stake in the action, the amount in controversy, the parties' relative access to relevant information, the parties' resources, the importance of the discovery in resolving the issues, and whether the burden or expense of the proposed discovery outweighs its likely benefit. Information within this scope of discovery need not be admissible in evidence to be discoverable.

Fed. R. Civ. Proc. 26(b)(1).

The key phrase in this definition— "relevant to the subject matter involved in the pending action"— has been construed broadly to encompass any matter that bears on, or that reasonably could lead to other matter that could bear on, any issue that is or may be in the case. *Oppenheimer Fund, Inc v. Sanders*, 437 U.S. 340, 351 (1978) (*citing Hickman v. Taylor*, 329 U.S. 495, 501 (1947)). Discovery is not limited to issues raised by the pleadings, for discovery itself is designed to help define and clarify the issues. *Id.*

ARGUMENT

Plaintiff submits that each of his requests is well within the scope of discovery as defined by Rule 26 (b)(1) and the cases interpreting it. Plaintiff notes additionally that Defendant has failed to provide any evidence to establish how any of these requests would be unduly burdensome.

Issues in Dispute

The primary issues requiring resolution are as follows:[1]

---

[1] Unless otherwise noted, quoted language is From Defendants' Answer to Plaintiff's First Requests for Production, attached hereto as Exhibit B.

2

- **Timeline** (applicable to multiple requests): Plaintiff requested documents from 2010 to the present. Defendants assert that the relevant starting point is April 25, 2022, when Plaintiff was first called to the Sunnyside Police Department. Plaintiff submits that, as declared by the Seventh Circuit, this is a conditions of confinement claim, and the relevant timeline for both liability and damages is far broader than Defendants' preferred week long period when Plaintiff was physically at the police department.

- **Request No. 4 : Communications, e-mails, ESI.** Plaintiff requested communications involving one or more defendants relating to unlawful detention issues at Pontiac, using the following keywords: Any version (including but not limited to present, future, past tenses, singular and plural) of the following words: Fred, Smith, detention, extended, cell, phone, mobile, seizure, possession, Jones.

  o **Defendant's Response:** Defendant claims that the request is overly broad in scope and time, is cumulative, seeks the disclosure of information not relevant to any claims or defenses asserted in this litigation, and unduly burdensome. Defendants state further that "a search for electronically-stored information responsive to this request would involve a search of thousands of emails, phone records, mailings, etc. No such search has been conducted." Defendants claim that "the burden and expense of locating the requested documents vastly outweighs the potential benefit of such information. The documents that could potentially be responsive to this request are numerous and not relevant to any claim or defense asserted in the present litigation, and is not proportional to the needs of this case pursuant to Rule 26."
  o During the parties' Rule 37 conference, Defendants suggested a limiting factor such as pairing the requested keywords with "detained". Plaintiff suggests that this limitation is unnecessarily limiting, and notes that Defendants have failed to provide any evidence of how many hits Plaintiff's requested searches would generate, or any other evidence as to why the searches would be unduly burdensome.

- **Request No. 6: Grievances and complaints by peoples and Sunnyside employees related to infestation.** Plaintiff requested any and all grievances and complaints by peoples and/or staff involving detention and/or seizure issues at PCC, since 2010.

  o **Defendants' Response:** Defendants claim that the request "is overly broad in scope and time, is cumulative, seeks the disclosure of information not relevant to any claims or defenses asserted in this litigation, and unduly burdensome. Plaintiff's complaint was filed on June 29, 2016 and only alleges he worked in Pontiac's inmate kitchen from May 15-17, 2015. Plaintiff is requesting information regarding nonparties and Plaintiff's Motion for Class Action was denied on July 26, 2016. [d/e 7/26/2016]. Plaintiff's complaint is regarding the detention by Officer Jones, not the entire staff."

- **Request No. 7: Grievances and complaints by specific peoples (who we know have filed grievances on the issue of detention) related to detention.**[2] Plaintiff requested any and all grievances and complaints, including records relating to those grievances and/or complaints, filed by Robert Jones, John Doe 1, John Doe 2, John Doe 3, John Doe 4, John Doe 5 involving detention and/or seizure issues.

  o **Defendants' Response:** Defendants claim this request "is overly broad in scope and time, is cumulative, seeks the disclosure of information not relevant to any claims or defenses asserted in this litigation, and unduly burdensome. Plaintiff's complaint was filed on June 29, 2016 and only alleges he was detained May 3 2022. Plaintiff is requesting information regarding nonparties; however, Plaintiff's Motion for Class Action was denied on July 26, 2016. [d/e 7/26/2016]. None of the requested peoples, other than Robert Jones, are parties to the current litigation. Without waiving those objections, Defendants directs Plaintiff to Plaintiff's grievances that were previously disclosed as part of Defendants' Initial Disclosure, bates stamped as Smith v. Sunnyside, et al. (16-1241) IDOC Document No.: 000023-000023."[3]

  o Plaintiff contends that evidence of complaints by others regarding the issue of infestation is directly relevant to the question of the existence, nature, and extent of such infestation, as well as notice to defendants, and would obviously assist Plaintiff in identifying witnesses. The request has nothing to do with any possible class action.

Rule 26(b)(1) factors

The factors enunciated in Rule 26(b)(1) that are relevant to this matter all favor production of the

requested materials with minimal if any limitations.

To begin the analysis, it is necessary to take a step back and consider the first factor in Rule 26(b)(1)'s

criteria governing discovery disputes: *the importance of the issues at stake in the action.* Plaintiff's

allegations here are serious, troubling, and well-documented, with multiple signed statements by other

peoples. If true, they have profound implications for the well-being of the Sunnyside community.

---

[2] Plaintiff has provided his copies of these grievances; this request seeks any additional grievances or related documentation by the same inmates. This request seeks a subset of Request No. 6.

[3] During the parties' Rule 37 conference, Defense counsel withdrew his objection that this request is unduly burdensome.

4

In light of this factor, discovery requests aimed at exploring the existence, nature, extent and duration of the conditions alleged go to the heart of the undisputedly serious issues associated with the possibility of unlawful detention and excessive seizure.

The third issue raised by Rule 26(b)(1) is the parties' relative access to relevant information. Obviously, this is a one-way street. With few exceptions, Defendants have exclusive access to and control of the information requested. While Defendants assert objections to producing the requested materials, that does not stop them from reviewing the materials themselves (or through their counsel), creating the potential for a serious knowledge gap between the parties. The only way to mitigate Plaintiff's natural disadvantage is to compel production of the requested materials.

The fourth factor, the relative resources of the parties, obviously favors disclosure and production as well. Plaintiff is an middle aged man who is being represented on a *pro bono* basis. Defendants have access to institutional resources such as Information Technology consultants (for the ESI being sought), experts, etc.

The fifth factor is the importance of discovery in resolving the issues. To put it plainly, discovery is the only way Plaintiff will have a chance to prove his case. Plaintiff and the other peoples who would support his allegations will always start out at a drastic disadvantage in any attempt to persuade a fact-finder of the veracity of his claims. Defendants' denials, with nothing else, will have far more persuasive power by virtue of the fact that defendants are public employees and are presumably not individuals who have been detained. This is in addition to the burden of proof that any plaintiff must meet. Thus, discovery is crucial to corroborate Plaintiff's claims and give him any chance of prevailing in this matter.

The sixth factor – whether the burden or expense of the proposed discovery outweighs its likely benefit – is immaterial at this point, as Defendants have failed to provide any evidence at all to support their claim of undue burden.

For the foregoing reasons, Plaintiff Fred Smith respectfully requests that this Court enter an order compelling Defendants to comply fully and completely with Plaintiff's Production Requests by a reasonable date.

Respectfully submitted,

/s/ Susan Miller

LAW OFFICE OF SUSAN MILLER
12345 Sunnyside Drive
Sunnyside IL 61234
(312) 456-7892
susan@millerlaw.com

CERTIFICATE OF SERVICE

I, Susan Miller Marsh, an attorney, hereby certify that on December 17, 2022, I electronically filed the above document with the Court's CM/ECF system, which simultaneously sent an electronic copy of the same to all counsel of record.

/s/   Susan Miller

THE UNITED STATES DISTRICT COURT
FOR THE NORTHERN DISTRICT OF ILLINOIS
EASTERN DIVISION

FRED SMITH,

Plaintiff,

v.   No. 22-cv-3456

VILLAGE OF SUNNYSIDE, a Municipal   *Jury Trial Demanded.*
Corporation, Sunnyside police officer
ROBERT JONES,

Defendants,

PLAINTIFF FRED SMITH'S
FIRST SET OF INTERROGATORIES TO DEFENDANT JONES

Plaintiff, Fred Smith, by and through his undersigned attorney, hereby propounds the following Interrogatories pursuant to Rule 33 of the Federal Rules of Civil Procedure upon Defendant Jones, to be answered, under oath, and in writing within thirty days of service hereof.

DEFINITIONS

1.   "Plaintiff" or "Fred" shall mean Fred Smith.

2.   "Defendants" shall mean the Defendants in this matter.

3.   "Document" shall have its broadest possible meaning, and includes all writings, books, articles, publications, records, memoranda, copies, drafts, statements, correspondence, notes, e-mails, logs, records, spreadsheets, calculations, calendars, photographs, summaries, forms, reports, checklists, logs, journals, minutes, resolutions, ordinances (proposed or passed), transcripts, pleadings, announcements, press releases, policies, rules, guidelines, pamphlets, publications, brochures, financial documents, posters, computer data or any other type of data that is capable of being printed or reproduced to writing, and shall include video, photograph and all other image recordings, and any other tangible items, whether originals or copies.

1

4.   "Communication" shall have its broadest possible meaning, and includes any manner or means of disclosure, transfer, or exchange of information, whether oral or written, or whether face-to-face, by telephone, mail, e-mail, direct computer to computer transfer, or personal delivery, and includes, but is not limited to, any "document" as herein defined.

5.   "Relate to" shall have its broadest meaning possible, and shall include the terms "pertain to," "in support of," "provide evidence of," "affects," "concerns," and "involves."

6.   When asked to "identify" a person, or provide the "identity" of same, please state the (a) full name; (b) title; (c) position and business affiliation; (d) the present or last known business address; and (e) present or last known resident address, if no business address is provided.

7.   As used herein, "basis" or a request to "state the basis for" means to describe any factual or legal reason, including all references to applicable statutes, regulations, case law, guidelines, manuals, or industry standards, or evidence that provides support for the contentions described or referenced in the request.

8.   Any perceived ambiguity in the definition of any terms herein, or of any interrogatory, should be resolved by contacting Plaintiff's Counsel to obtain clarification.

9.   Unless otherwise noted, each interrogatory relates to the arrest of Fred on or around May 3, 2022.

10.   "Incident in question" shall mean the events of May 3, 2022 which forms the basis for this lawsuit.

11.   "Department" or "SPD" shall mean the Sunnyside Police Department.

RULES OF CONSTRUCTION

1.   The singular shall include the plural and the plural shall include the singular.

2.   The terms "and" and "or" as used herein shall be construed conjunctively or disjunctively as required to include within the scope of each discovery request any information that might be excluded by the opposite construction.

3.   A masculine, feminine or neutral pronoun shall not exclude the other genders.

4.   These discovery requests shall be construed as broadly as possible to include all information that may conceivably fall within their scope.

INTERROGATORIES

1.   Please state your full name, educational and employment history, including specific dates of graduation and employment, as well as any degrees conferred.

ANSWER:

2.   Please identify with particularity all training you have received, including names, dates and training entities, including but not limited to training on making arrests, detaining subjects, and using force on subjects and arrestees.

ANSWER:

3.   Have you ever been arrested, detained or cited by a police officer or other law enforcement official? If your answer is in the affirmative, for each such arrest, detention or citation, identify the date, the law enforcement agency or officers involved, the charge, any ultimate disposition of any charges, as well as whether you have ever been convicted of any offense.

ANSWER:

4.   Have you, or anyone on your behalf, ever filed a civil suit, or been sued, in your personal non-law enforcement capacity, including, but not limited to, a personal injury claim, worker's compensation claim, forcible detainer action or divorce proceeding? If the answer is in the affirmative, state the court in which the suit was filed, the year filed, the title and docket number of said case, the result of the case and the nature of the matter (i.e., personal injury, divorce, etc.).

ANSWER:

5.   Do you suffer from any disease or ailment that impacts your ability to remember events or things? If so, identify the disease or ailment as well as the name and address of each physician/medical professional who has treated you for the disease/ailment in the last five (5) years.

ANSWER:

6.   State/identify all positions and/or assignments you have held with any law enforcement agency, including, but not limited to, dates of employment, dates of any promotions, the dates that you have held each position/assignment, the date(s) of separation/termination from each such position, and the reasons for each such separation/termination. This interrogatory includes a request for any specialized assignments you have held such as, for example, patrol officer, investigator, detective, juvenile officer, FTO, supervisor, or any other position/assignment. Also,

3

this interrogatory seeks all such information, whether it relates to your employment with the City of Sunnyside, or any other governmental entity/municipality.

ANSWER:

7. Have you had any complaints alleging misconduct filed against you and/or have you ever been disciplined in connection with your duties as a police officer? If the answer is in the affirmative, list all such charges by number, name of complainant, the disposition, and the nature of the charge. In this interrogatory, the Plaintiff specifically requests information regarding all complaints, and discipline, irrespective of whether they have been expunged and/or purged. Also, this interrogatory specifically requests information related to complaints and/or discipline lodged with the Sunnyside Police Department, as well as any other police departments.

ANSWER:

8. Have you been named in any other lawsuit brought pursuant to the United States Constitution, 42 U.S.C. Sections 1981, 1983, 1985 1986, any other federal statute, and/or any claim arising under state law, in connection with your duties as a police officer? If your answer is in the affirmative, set forth the following:

    a.   The caption and case number of the lawsuit;
    b.   The court in which the lawsuit was filed;
    c.   The date the lawsuit was filed;
    d.   The disposition of the lawsuit, or the current status of the case, if no final disposition has been reached; and
    e.   The nature of the allegations filed in each such matter.

ANSWER:

9. Describe each and every action by Fred that supported your detainment on May 3, 2022.

ANSWER:

10. Who have you spoken to regarding the incident in question? For each such conversation identify the date(s) and time(s) on which each such conversation took place, every person that was present for each such conversation, where the conversation(s) took place, what was said in each such conversation, and whether any documentation was created as a result of any such conversation.

ANSWER:

11. Did you author, contribute to, or review any report, record, or other document regarding the incident in question? If the answer is Yes, for each such record, report or document, state:

    a.   Title;
    b.   Bates number;

    c.   Date and time you authored, contributed to, or reviewed said record, report, or document;

    d.   Nature of your role/activity as it relates to the record, report, or document;

ANSWER:

/s/Susan Miller

LAW OFFICE OF SUSAN MILLER
12345 Sunnyside Drive
Sunnyside IL 61234
(312) 456-7892
susan@millerlaw.com

CERTIFICATE OF SERVICE

Susan Miller, an attorney, certifies that on July 30, 2022, she served a copy of the foregoing document by electronic mail to the following:

Jeffrey C. Johnson
Johnson Law Firm, P.C.
780 South Elm Street
Sunnyside, IL 60987
Tel: (312) 663-2626
Fax: (312) 663-2627
jjohnson@johnsonlawfirm.com

/s/ Susan Miller

THE UNITED STATES DISTRICT COURT
FOR THE NORTHERN DISTRICT OF ILLINOIS
EASTERN DIVISION

FRED SMITH,

    Plaintiff,

    v.

VILLAGE OF SUNNYSIDE, a Municipal
Corporation, Sunnyside Police Detective
ROBERT JONES,

    Defendants,

No. 22-cv-3456

Jury Trial Demanded.

PLAINTIFF FRED SMITH'S RULE 26(a)(1) INITIAL DISCLOSURES

Pursuant to Rule 26(a)(1) of the Federal Rules of Civil Procedure, Plaintiff, Fred Smith, by and through his undersigned attorney, hereby provides the following disclosures:

A. The name and, if known, the address and telephone number of each individual likely to have discoverable information that the disclosing party may use to support its claims or defenses, unless solely for impeachment, identifying the subjects of the information.

The following are parties who possess information related to liability and damages. They may be contacted through their respective counsel.

Plaintiff Fred Smith ("Fred") possesses information regarding the allegations in his complaint, and the damages he has experienced as a result of the Defendants' conduct, including his loss of liberty, mental anguish, lost wages, physical and mental pain and suffering, and other damages suffered as a result of Defendants' conduct.

Defendant Robert Jones possesses information regarding the incidents and allegations in Fred's complaint.

Defendant Village of Sunnyside, which may be contacted through Defense Counsel, possesses information regarding the incidents and allegations in Fred's complaint, and related issues.

Representatives of the Sunnyside Police Department, who may be contacted through Defense Counsel, may possess information regarding the SPD's training (including Hernandez's training), Hernandez's disciplinary history, and the orders and guidelines applicable to the Defendants' conduct in this case.

The following are non-parties who may possess information relating to this matter:

Assistant State's Attorney John Doe 3 and other as yet unidentified representatives of the Cook County State's Attorney's office possess information regarding the investigation and the approval or disapproval of charges related to the investigation. Plaintiff anticipates these witnesses will be represented by counsel appointed by the Cook County State's Attorney's Office.

John Doe 4 (123) 456-7890 1111 Manning Avenue, Montgomery IL 60538, possesses information relating to discussions he had with Fred regarding the matters alleged in his complaint.

John Doe 5 (222) 444-3333, possesses information related to his interactions with Defendant Jones.

This list of witness is preliminary, and will be supplemented as Plaintiff becomes aware of additional witnesses. Investigation continues. Plaintiff reserves the right to call any witnesses called or disclosed by any other party, and incorporates their disclosures as if set forth fully herein.

B. A copy of, or a description by category and location of, all documents, data compilations, and tangible things that are in the possession, custody, or control of the party and that the disclosing party may use to support its claims or defenses, unless solely for impeachment.

See Plaintiff 1- 28, produced herewith.

C. a computation of each category of damages claimed by the disclosing party—who must also make available for inspection and copying as under Rule 34 the documents or other evidentiary material, unless privileged or protected from disclosure, on which each computation is based, including materials bearing on the nature and extent of injuries suffered.

Plaintiff seeks all damages allowed by law, including compensatory and punitive damages, emotional distress, loss of liberty, physical and mental pain and suffering, lost wages, loss of career, and attorneys' fees. Plaintiff cannot compute lost wages without discovery.

Investigation continues.

Dated: September 9, 2022

> Respectfully submitted,
> Fred Smith
>
> By: **/s/ Susan Miller**
> *Attorney for the Plaintiff*

LAW OFFICE OF SUSAN MILLER
12345 Sunnyside Drive. Sunnyside IL 61234
(312) 456-7892 - susan@millerlaw.com

CERTIFICATE OF SERVICE

Susan Miller, an attorney, certifies that on September 9, 2022, she served a copy of the foregoing Rule 26(a)(1) Disclosures by electronic mail to the following:

Jeffrey C. Johnson
Johnson Law Firm, P.C.
780 South Elm Street
Sunnyside, IL 60987
Tel: (312) 663-2626
Fax: (312) 663-2627
jjohnson@johnsonlawfirm.com

/s/ **Susan Miller**

Law Office of

Susan Miller

May 12, 2022

<u>**Via Electronic Mail**</u>
Sunnyside Police Department
John Doe, Acting Police Chief
jdoe@vil.sunnyside.il.us

Dear Chief Doe:

This office represents Mr. Fred Smith. This letter requests your immediate action to preserve information that may contain evidence important to a future legal matter. Please consider this a notification to preserve the following materials pending legal process:

Any and all data, reports, records, photographs, video, audio, communications, e-mails, correspondence, memoranda, notes, logs, statements, transcripts, searches, warrants, warrant applications, and other investigatory materials related to Mr. Smith, and/or any investigation in which Mr. Smith is or was a suspect or a person of interest. This includes Electronically Stored Information (ESI).

This office expects that any investigatory or law enforcement action relating to Mr. Smith, his property, and his accounts, and to any investigation in which Mr. Smith is or was a suspect or a person of interest, will be fully and completely documented, and that documentation will be preserved pending legal process.

If you have any questions or wish to discuss this matter further, please do not hesitate to contact me.

Sincerely yours,

/s/Susan Miller

Susan Miller
Attorney

cc: Jeffrey C. Johnson
       jjohnson@johnsonlawfirm.com

12345 SUNNYSIDE DRIVE · SUNNYSIDE IL 61234
PHONE (312) 456-7892· FAX (312) 456-7893
susan@millerlaw.com

[If you need additional space for ANY section, please attach an additional sheet and reference that section.]

U.S. District Court for the Northern District Of Illinois
Appearance Form for Pro Se Litigants

Information entered on this form is required for any person filing a case in this court as a pro se party (that is, without an attorney). **Please PRINT legibly.**

Case Title: _____   Case Number: _____

An appearance is hereby filed by the undersigned as a pro se litigant:

Name: _____

Street Address: _____

City/State/Zip: _____

Phone Number: _____

_____   _____
           Signature   Executed on (date)

REQUEST TO RECEIVE NOTICE THROUGH E-MAIL

If you check the box below and provide an e-mail address in the space provided, you will receive notice via e-mail. By checking the box and providing an e-mail address, under Federal Rule of Civil Procedure 5(b)2(E) you are waiving your right to receive a paper copy of documents filed electronically in this case. You should not provide an e-mail address if you do not check it frequently.

☐   I request to be sent notices from the court via e-mail. I understand that by making this request, I am waiving the right to receive a paper copy of any electronically filed document in this case. I understand that if my e-mail address changes I must promptly notify the Court in writing.

_____
E-Mail Address (Please PRINT legibly.)

Rev. 06/23/2016

[If you need additional space for ANY section, please attach an additional sheet and reference that section.]

**Electronic Filing
in the
U.S. District Court
Northern District of Illinois**

Quick Reference Guide

Revised July 2022

Document Format
CM/ECF will only accept documents in Portable Document Format (PDF). Documents may be printed, published or scanned to PDF format.

Document Size
Documents filed electronically are limited to 35 megabytes (MB) in size. This applies to each individual component of an electronic filing, not to the entire filing. For example, if you are filing a motion with several exhibits, the motion and each exhibit can be up to 35 MB in size. File the motion as the main document; file exhibit as attachments.

We encourage you to combine exhibits into a single attachment if the combined exhibits do not exceed 35 MB in size. Combined exhibits must be labeled, e.g., Exhibits A through D.

Filing Sealed Documents in Sealed and Unsealed Cases
- Pro se litigants must file sealed cases and/or sealed documents in paper format.
- Attorneys must file sealed cases in paper format.
    - ✓ If an entire case is sealed, the attorney must file sealed documents in paper format.
    - ✓ The attorneys are not able to seal cases but may seal pleadings.

Electronic Signatures
Electronically filed documents must include a signature block. The name of the filing user under whose login and password the document is submitted must be preceded by an /s/ and typed in the space where the signature would otherwise appear.

Example: /s/Ted Newman
              Attorneys R Us
              111 South First Street
              Anytown, Illinois 11111
              (555) 555-5555

General Order for Signatures in Electronic Case Filing
The requirements for signing a document that you are filing electronically are set out in Section IX(A) of the General Order on Electronic Case Filing provides as follows: "Electronically filed documents must include a signature block and must set forth the name, address, telephone number and the attorney's bar registration number, if applicable. In addition, the name of the e- filer under whose login and password the document is submitted must be preceded by an /s/ and typed in the space where the signature would otherwise appear."

Checklist for Electronically Filing a Document

☐ The attorney logged into CM/ECF must be same attorney whose name appears on the signature line. Your account login and password identify you as a specific attorney; therefore, you may not share your CM/ECF with another attorney.

☐ Verify that the correct event listed at the beginning of the docket text matches the type of pleading you are filing. If incorrect, click SEARCH, type the name of your pleading, click SEARCH again and redo your filing.

☐ Verify that the case number listed is correct.

☐ If filing a motion for leave to file a document, file the subject document as an attachment to the motion. Label the subject document appropriately.

☐ If filing a notice of motion be sure to link the motion to the notice at the calendar screen.

☐ Contact the Help Desk at 312-435-5699 if you believe you have made an e-filing error.

Avoid Common e-Filing Errors

Incorrect Event
The event listed at the beginning of the docket text must match the type of pleading. If incorrect, click SEARCH, type the name of your pleading, click SEARCH again and redo your filing.

Incorrect or no electronic signature
The attorney logged into CM/ECF must be same attorney whose name appears on the signature line. The electronic signature, typed at the signature line of the document, consists of the characters /s/ and the attorney's name typed out. For example, /s/Ted Newman is a properly formatted electronic signature. Staff who support multiple attorneys should verify the name of the attorney when logging in and on the final docket text screen.

No motion linked to the Notice of motion
Verify that you have linked (checked the box) the motion being noticed to the Notice of Motion.

Please contact the Help Desk at 312-435-5699 for assistance if you believe you have made an error.

How do attorneys register for a CM/ECF Account?
CM/ECF accounts are provided to attorneys who are members of the ILND bar, attorneys who are appearing pro hac vice, attorneys who has an appearance on file in a multi-district litigation case that was transferred to this district or are attorneys representing the United States in their official capacity. Click HERE if you meet one or more of these criteria.

How do pro se litigants register for a CM/ECF Account?
Pro se litigants may be granted an e-filing account provided that the pro se litigant is NOT a restricted filer in this Court; has a civil case in this Court where they are listed as a party; and successfully completes the online e-filing training program offered by the Clerk's Office; and submits an e-filing application subsequent to training. Pro se litigants are not permitted to e-file cases.

Can my firm have a single CM/ECF account, or do I have to have my own account?
Each attorney must have his or her own CM/ECF account. Your account login and password identify you as a specific attorney; therefore, you may not share your CM/ECF with another attorney.

I submitted a completed registration form, but I have not yet received my login and password. How can I check on the status of my account?
If more than five days have passed since you submitted your registration form, you can check on the status of your account by emailing ProSe_ECF_Registration_ILND@ilnd.uscourts.gov .

Can the general public view CM/ECF cases and documents in the Clerk's Office?
Yes. Terminals providing public access to case data in CM/ECF without the need to have a PACER login and password are available in the Clerk's Office, located in Chicago on the 20th floor of the Dirksen Courthouse, 219 South Dearborn. Public terminals are available in the Clerk's Office in the Rockford, Illinois courthouse located at 327 South Church Street. The Clerk's Office is open to the public Monday through Friday, 8:30 a.m. through 4:30 p.m., except for legal holidays.

Can any member of the public use CM/ECF to file documents with the court?
No. Access to the filing portion of CM/ECF is available to authorized case participants only.

How can I get training in how to file electronically?
Free self-directed online training is available. Training classes are open to everyone. Click HERE for additional information and to request online training.

4

Do I need both a PACER account and a CM/ECF account to be an e-filer?
Yes, you need both a CM/ECF account and a PACER account. The PACER account gives you
the ability to read case dockets and view electronic images of documents. Your CM/ECF account
allows you to electronically file a document with the Court. Once you have both accounts, you
must link your CM/ECF account to your PACER account.

What is the difference between a PACER account and a CM/ECF Account?
The PACER account gives you the ability to read case dockets and view electronic images of
documents. Your CM/ECF account allows you to electronically file a document with the Court.

How can I get a PACER account?
Call the PACER Service Center toll free at 1-800-676-6856 or go to the PACER Service Center's
website at https://pacer.psc.uscourts.gov/pscof/regWizard.jsf and complete the online form.

**My law firm has a single PACER account. Can I use that, or do I need my own PACER
account?**
Every attorney needs an individual PACER account.

What constitutes a page in CM/ECF for PACER billing purposes?
Billable pages are calculated in two ways in CM/ECF. PACER uses a formula to determine the
number of pages for an HTML formatted report. Any information extracted from the CM/ECF
database, such as the data used to create a docket sheet, is billed using a formula based on the
number of bytes extracted. For a PDF document, the actual number of pages determines the
number of billable pages. For report data retrieved from the CM/ECF system that is printed, the
print job will not always match the number of pages billed. The number of pages printed is
dependent on individual printer and browser settings. All users are charged equally for the same
information regardless of the browser settings or printer configurations. A transaction receipt and
the Review Billing History option are provided under Utilities for reviewing charges. Also,
Review Transaction History is available on the PACER Service Center site in Account
Information for reviewing transactions from all courts. The transactions are updated on the
PACER Web Site by the middle of each month.

**Can the general public view CM/ECF cases and the documents in those cases using the
Internet?**
The public can access case data in CM/ECF unless it has been sealed by the court. To have
access to case dockets and electronic documents using the Internet, you must have an account in
the Public Access to Court Electronic Records (PACER) system.

What are the rules and procedures regarding filing electronically?
Please refer to General Order on Electronic Case Filing.

5

I noticed that I made a mistake in the electronic filing. What do I do?
If you believe that you have made an e-filing error that needs to be corrected, contact the Help Desk at 312-435-5699.

How do I add a signature to a document I am filing electronically?
The requirements for signing a document that you are filing electronically are set out in Section IX(A) of the General Order on Electronic Case Filing provides as follows: "Electronically filed documents must include a signature block and must set forth the name, address, telephone number and the attorney's bar registration number, if applicable. In addition, the name of the e-filer under whose login and password the document is submitted must be preceded by an /s/ and typed in the space where the signature would otherwise appear."

Does a certificate of service need to be included with documents filed electronically?
Section X (E) of the General Order on Electronic Case Filing states that "Where service is made as to any party who is not an E-Filer or is represented by an E-Filer, a certificate or affidavit of service must be included with all documents filed electronically. Such certificate or affidavit shall comply with LR 5.5 Such certificate or affidavit is not required as to any party who is an E-filer or is represented by an E-filer."

How many times will I be able to view my case documents as an attorney of record?
If you are an attorney of record in a case, you will not be charged the first time you view a document. However, the next time you view the same document, you will be charged by PACER.

Can I combine a motion and a notice of motion in a single electronic filing?
No. The motion and the notice of motion must be filed separately. In addition, the motion must be filed before the notice of motion.

What kind of notification does the attorney of record receive on a case?
All registered CM/ECF e-filers will receive an email notification of all filings, which includes a hyperlink to the document. Participants who are not registered users must be mailed a copy of the filing by the attorney filing electronically.

An attorney in our office is out of town. He has asked us to file a motion for him in his absence, on behalf of his client. Can I file this document electronically?
On the motion itself, sign the document with your name, on behalf of the absent attorney, i.e., /s/ John Worker on behalf of John P. Vacationer. When you electronically file the motion in CM/ECF, you will see the following on your screen: "The following attorney/party associations do not exist for this case. Please check which associations should be created for this case: John Doe, (pty:pla) represented by John Worker (aty)". Do not check this box; doing so adds you as

an attorney on the case. The docket text will read that the document was filed by Attorney John Worker on behalf of Susie Client. Under no circumstances should this practice be used when filing an initial appearance.

Are there fees associated with e-filing?
There are no fees to file electronically. For viewing documents in cases, you get one free look at documents that are filed in cases in which you are an attorney of record. For each subsequent viewing, you will be required to log in to PACER and pay the fees established by PACER. We strongly recommend that you print or save the document during the first viewing to avoid these charges.

Can I combine separate exhibits in a single attachment?
As long as the combined exhibits do not exceed 35 MB in size, we encourage you to combine them into a single attachment. Each exhibit must be labeled, e.g., Exhibits A through D.

How do I add counsel to a case?
To add counsel in a case, that attorney needs to electronically file an attorney appearance.

Do I have to file a paper copy of a document that I have filed electronically?
Please refer to Local Rule 5.2(e), the General Order on Electronic Case Filing, and the assigned judge's webpage for specific guidance.

What electronic versions of documents (images) are available?

Civil Cases
Initiating documents, e.g., complaints, and orders filed after 3/1/2000. Motions and responsive pleadings filed after 12/01/2001. All documents, except lengthy exhibits, filed after 10/1/2002. All documents filed after 10/26/2007.

Criminal Cases
The same criteria apply to criminal cases except that documents filed in criminal cases may be viewed via the Internet only by case participants, i.e., attorney and defendants.

Is the system available 24 hours a day, 7 days a week?
Yes, CM/ECF is available 24 hours a day, 7 days a week. The system may be down temporarily on other occasions if an unplanned need for maintenance arises.

7

What hardware and software do I need to use CM/ECF?

- PC or MAC
- Acrobat Reader
- Compatible browsers include:
  o Microsoft Edge
  o Firefox/Mozilla
  o Safari version
  o Google Chrome

Why is my login failing?
The system is case sensitive. If you have the CAPS lock on, your login will fail. Be sure that you are not using your PACER login to try to access your CM/ECF account. You can also try to clear the cache of your computer.

How large can my electronic filing be?
The General Order on Electronic Case Filing provides that an electronic filing should not exceed 35 MB in size. This applies to each individual component of an electronic filing, not to the entire filing. In other words, if you are filing a motion with several exhibits, the motion itself and each exhibit can each be up to 35 MB in size.

The exhibits I need to file with my main document are too large. What can I do?
Subdivide the exhibit, and label each attachment, e.g., Exhibit A, Part 1, Exhibit A, Part 2.

When I click on the document link in my email, it prompts me for a login and password.

In **civil** cases, the first time you click on a document link in your email the system should display the document without requiring a login. For each subsequent viewing, you will be required to log into PACER and the fees established by PACER. If you do not have a PACER login and password, contact the PACER Service Center at 1-800- 676-6856 or the PACER Service Center's website at http://www.pacer.psc.uscourts.gov/register.html.

In **criminal** cases, the first time you click on a document link in your email the system requires you to enter your CM/ECF login and password. Next, you need to enter your PACER login and password. You will not be charged the first time you view a criminal document. If you do not have a PACER login and password, contact the PACER Service Center at 1-800- 676-6856 or the PACER Service Center's website at http://www.pacer.psc.uscourts.gov/register.html.

8

For **Civil Social Security** cases, the first time you click on a document link in your email, the system requires you to enter your CM/ECF login and password. Next, enter your PACER login and password. You will not be charged the first time you view a document. If you do not have a PACER login and password, contact the PACER Service Center at 1-800- 676-6856 or the PACER Service Center's website at http://www.pacer.psc.uscourts.gov/register.html.

How do I change my CM/ECF password?
Please refer to the instructions available in the User Guide.

How do I add additional email addresses so someone else in my office can receive Notices of Electronic Filing?
Please refer to the instructions available in the User Guide.

How do I know if my electronic filing was successful?
The last screen you see when you electronically file a document is a copy of the Notice of Electronic Filing (NEF). If you see the NEF, you know that your filing was successful. Another way to verify your filing is to view a copy of the case docket. If you do this, standard PACER fees will be charged.

I'm not seeing the correct menu options in CM/ECF. What should I do?
Verify that you have logged into CM/ECF from the Court's website. In most cases, users who do not see the correct menu items have logged into PACER instead of CM/ECF.

9

Law Office of

Susan Miller

October 22, 2022

Via Electronic Mail
Jeffrey C. Johnson
Johnson Law Firm, P.C.
780 South Elm Street
Sunnyside, IL 60987
Tel: (312) 663-2626
Fax: (312) 663-2627
jjohnson@johnsonlawfirm.com

Dear Jeff:

Thank you for the defendants' responses to Plaintiff's discovery requests. I would like to address some issues with the responses.

1. The Village's answers to interrogatories indicate the investigation remains open. Yet Jones requested the case be closed. (See DEF 00001.) Was Jones' request denied? I did not receive any documentation or communication about the investigation being open or Jones' request that it be closed. Is there no such documentation or communication?

2. Production Request No. 2 seeks "Any and all audio and video footage relating to the investigation." Can you tell me if any video related to this investigation was destroyed, deleted or recycled?

3. Defendants assert there are no materials related to any NVLS searches for Fred's vehicle (RFP Resp. 1), yet Jones states he "conducted multiple inquiries on both the offender and his vehicle. Multiple NVLS hits were received, all with the vehicle in transit." (DEF 00023.) Were there no records of these searches or their findings?

4. Production Request No. 3 seeks "Any and all communications and records of communications between the alleged victim and any employee of the Village of Sunnyside. This request includes communications from official Police devices as well as personal devices." The defendants' answer references the incident report, incident log, arrest report, and photo lineup. No emails, text messages or other such

communications were produced. Is it the defendants' position that no Sunnyside police officer or detective ever texted or emailed with Fred Smith, or communicated with him in writing in any other form?

5. Production Request No. 4 seeks communications with the members of the Cook County State's Attorney's office.   No emails, text messages or other such communications were produced. Is it the defendants' position that no Sunnyside police officer or detective ever texted or emailed with any member of the CCSAO, or communicated in writing in any other form?

6. Production Request No. 5 seeks any communications at all, regardless of who the communications involved. No emails, text messages or other such communications were produced. Is it the defendants' position that there are no text messages or emails *at all* regarding this investigation?

7. Production request 6 seeks "Any and all documents, materials, and communications related to any FOIA request received by the Village of Sunnyside regarding the investigation or Fred." The response references only the FOIA requests and responses provided by the plaintiff. Is it the defendants' position there is not a single email, text message, memo, or other document regarding any FOIA requests? There must have been communication. Was it all verbal? That seems unlikely.

Jeff, please let me know a good time to discuss these matters. I look forward to hearing from you soon.

Sincerely yours,

/s/Susan Miller

Susan Miller
Attorney

12345 SUNNYSIDE DRIVE · SUNNYSIDE IL 61234
PHONE (312) 456-7892 · FAX (312) 456-7893
susan@millerlaw.com

AO 88B (Rev. 02/14) Subpoena to Produce Documents, Information, or Objects or to Permit Inspection of Premises in a Civil Action

UNITED STATES DISTRICT COURT
for the

_____)
           Plaintiff   )
            v.   )   Civil Action No. _____
)
_____)
          Defendant   )

SUBPOENA TO PRODUCE DOCUMENTS, INFORMATION, OR OBJECTS OR TO PERMIT INSPECTION OF PREMISES IN A CIVIL ACTION

To: _____

(Name of person to whom this subpoena is directed)

    ❐ *Production:* **YOU ARE COMMANDED** to produce at the time, date, and place set forth below the following documents, electronically stored information, or objects, and to permit inspection, copying, testing, or sampling of the material:

Place:	Date and Time:

    ❐ *Inspection of Premises:* **YOU ARE COMMANDED** to permit entry onto the designated premises, land, or other property possessed or controlled by you at the time, date, and location set forth below, so that the requesting party may inspect, measure, survey, photograph, test, or sample the property or any designated object or operation on it.

Place:	Date and Time:

    The following provisions of Fed. R. Civ. P. 45 are attached – Rule 45(c), relating to the place of compliance; Rule 45(d), relating to your protection as a person subject to a subpoena; and Rule 45(e) and (g), relating to your duty to respond to this subpoena and the potential consequences of not doing so.

Date: _____

      CLERK OF COURT
                           OR

    _____   _____
      Signature of Clerk or Deputy Clerk   *Attorney's signature*

The name, address, e-mail address, and telephone number of the attorney representing *(name of party)* _____
_____ , who issues or requests this subpoena, are:

Notice to the person who issues or requests this subpoena
If this subpoena commands the production of documents, electronically stored information, or tangible things or the inspection of premises before trial, a notice and a copy of the subpoena must be served on each party in this case before it is served on the person to whom it is directed. Fed. R. Civ. P. 45(a)(4).

AO 88B (Rev. 02/14) Subpoena to Produce Documents, Information, or Objects or to Permit Inspection of Premises in a Civil Action (Page 2)

Civil Action No.

PROOF OF SERVICE
(This section should not be filed with the court unless required by Fed. R. Civ. P. 45.)

I received this subpoena for *(name of individual and title, if any)* _____

on *(date)* _____ .

❑ I served the subpoena by delivering a copy to the named person as follows: _____

_____ on *(date)* _____ ; or

❑ I returned the subpoena unexecuted because: _____

_____ .

Unless the subpoena was issued on behalf of the United States, or one of its officers or agents, I have also
tendered to the witness the fees for one day's attendance, and the mileage allowed by law, in the amount of

$ _____ .

My fees are $ _____ for travel and $ _____ for services, for a total of $ 0.00   .

I declare under penalty of perjury that this information is true.

Date: _____

_____
Server's signature

_____
Printed name and title

_____
Server's address

Additional information regarding attempted service, etc.:

AO 88B (Rev. 02/14) Subpoena to Produce Documents, Information, or Objects or to Permit Inspection of Premises in a Civil Action(Page 3)

Federal Rule of Civil Procedure 45 (c), (d), (e), and (g) (Effective 12/1/13)

(c) Place of Compliance.

(1) *For a Trial, Hearing, or Deposition.* A subpoena may command a person to attend a trial, hearing, or deposition only as follows:
  (A) within 100 miles of where the person resides, is employed, or regularly transacts business in person; or
  (B) within the state where the person resides, is employed, or regularly transacts business in person, if the person
    (i) is a party or a party's officer; or
    (ii) is commanded to attend a trial and would not incur substantial expense.

(2) *For Other Discovery.* A subpoena may command:
  (A) production of documents, electronically stored information, or tangible things at a place within 100 miles of where the person resides, is employed, or regularly transacts business in person; and
  (B) inspection of premises at the premises to be inspected.

(d) Protecting a Person Subject to a Subpoena; Enforcement.

(1) *Avoiding Undue Burden or Expense; Sanctions.* A party or attorney responsible for issuing and serving a subpoena must take reasonable steps to avoid imposing undue burden or expense on a person subject to the subpoena. The court for the district where compliance is required must enforce this duty and impose an appropriate sanction—which may include lost earnings and reasonable attorney's fees—on a party or attorney who fails to comply.

(2) *Command to Produce Materials or Permit Inspection.*
  (A) *Appearance Not Required.* A person commanded to produce documents, electronically stored information, or tangible things, or to permit the inspection of premises, need not appear in person at the place of production or inspection unless also commanded to appear for a deposition, hearing, or trial.
  (B) *Objections.* A person commanded to produce documents or tangible things or to permit inspection may serve on the party or attorney designated in the subpoena a written objection to inspecting, copying, testing, or sampling any or all of the materials or to inspecting the premises—or to producing electronically stored information in the form or forms requested. The objection must be served before the earlier of the time specified for compliance or 14 days after the subpoena is served. If an objection is made, the following rules apply:
    (i) At any time, on notice to the commanded person, the serving party may move the court for the district where compliance is required for an order compelling production or inspection.
    (ii) These acts may be required only as directed in the order, and the order must protect a person who is neither a party nor a party's officer from significant expense resulting from compliance.

(3) *Quashing or Modifying a Subpoena.*
  (A) *When Required.* On timely motion, the court for the district where compliance is required must quash or modify a subpoena that:
    (i) fails to allow a reasonable time to comply;
    (ii) requires a person to comply beyond the geographical limits specified in Rule 45(c);
    (iii) requires disclosure of privileged or other protected matter, if no exception or waiver applies; or
    (iv) subjects a person to undue burden.
  (B) *When Permitted.* To protect a person subject to or affected by a subpoena, the court for the district where compliance is required may, on motion, quash or modify the subpoena if it requires:
    (i) disclosing a trade secret or other confidential research, development, or commercial information; or

(ii) disclosing an unretained expert's opinion or information that does not describe specific occurrences in dispute and results from the expert's study that was not requested by a party.
  (C) *Specifying Conditions as an Alternative.* In the circumstances described in Rule 45(d)(3)(B), the court may, instead of quashing or modifying a subpoena, order appearance or production under specified conditions if the serving party:
    (i) shows a substantial need for the testimony or material that cannot be otherwise met without undue hardship; and
    (ii) ensures that the subpoenaed person will be reasonably compensated.

(e) Duties in Responding to a Subpoena.

(1) *Producing Documents or Electronically Stored Information.* These procedures apply to producing documents or electronically stored information:
  (A) *Documents.* A person responding to a subpoena to produce documents must produce them as they are kept in the ordinary course of business or must organize and label them to correspond to the categories in the demand.
  (B) *Form for Producing Electronically Stored Information Not Specified.* If a subpoena does not specify a form for producing electronically stored information, the person responding must produce it in a form or forms in which it is ordinarily maintained or in a reasonably usable form or forms.
  (C) *Electronically Stored Information Produced in Only One Form.* The person responding need not produce the same electronically stored information in more than one form.
  (D) *Inaccessible Electronically Stored Information.* The person responding need not provide discovery of electronically stored information from sources that the person identifies as not reasonably accessible because of undue burden or cost. On motion to compel discovery or for a protective order, the person responding must show that the information is not reasonably accessible because of undue burden or cost. If that showing is made, the court may nonetheless order discovery from such sources if the requesting party shows good cause, considering the limitations of Rule 26(b)(2)(C). The court may specify conditions for the discovery.

(2) *Claiming Privilege or Protection.*
  (A) *Information Withheld.* A person withholding subpoenaed information under a claim that it is privileged or subject to protection as trial-preparation material must:
    (i) expressly make the claim; and
    (ii) describe the nature of the withheld documents, communications, or tangible things in a manner that, without revealing information itself privileged or protected, will enable the parties to assess the claim.
  (B) *Information Produced.* If information produced in response to a subpoena is subject to a claim of privilege or of protection as trial-preparation material, the person making the claim may notify any party that received the information of the claim and the basis for it. After being notified, a party must promptly return, sequester, or destroy the specified information and any copies it has; must not use or disclose the information until the claim is resolved; must take reasonable steps to retrieve the information if the party disclosed it before being notified; and may promptly present the information under seal to the court for the district where compliance is required for a determination of the claim. The person who produced the information must preserve the information until the claim is resolved.

(g) Contempt.
The court for the district where compliance is required—and also, after a motion is transferred, the issuing court—may hold in contempt a person who, having been served, fails without adequate excuse to obey the subpoena or an order related to it.

For access to subpoena materials, see Fed. R. Civ. P. 45(a) Committee Note (2013).

AO 88A (Rev. 12/20) Subpoena to Testify at a Deposition in a Civil Action

UNITED STATES DISTRICT COURT
for the

_____)	
Plaintiff)	
v.)	Civil Action No.
)	
_____)	
Defendant)	

SUBPOENA TO TESTIFY AT A DEPOSITION IN A CIVIL ACTION

To:

_____
(Name of person to whom this subpoena is directed)

❏ Testimony: YOU ARE COMMANDED to appear at the time, date, and place set forth below to testify at a deposition to be taken in this civil action. If you are an organization, you must promptly confer in good faith with the party serving this subpoena about the following matters, or those set forth in an attachment, and you must designate one or more officers, directors, or managing agents, or designate other persons who consent to testify on your behalf about these matters:

Place:	Date and Time:

The deposition will be recorded by this method: _____

❏ *Production:* You, or your representatives, must also bring with you to the deposition the following documents, electronically stored information, or objects, and must permit inspection, copying, testing, or sampling of the material:

The following provisions of Fed. R. Civ. P. 45 are attached – Rule 45(c), relating to the place of compliance; Rule 45(d), relating to your protection as a person subject to a subpoena; and Rule 45(e) and (g), relating to your duty to respond to this subpoena and the potential consequences of not doing so.

Date: _____

CLERK OF COURT	
	OR
_____	_____
Signature of Clerk or Deputy Clerk	*Attorney's signature*

The name, address, e-mail address, and telephone number of the attorney representing *(name of party)* _____
_____ , who issues or requests this subpoena, are:

Notice to the person who issues or requests this subpoena
If this subpoena commands the production of documents, electronically stored information, or tangible things before trial, a notice and a copy of the subpoena must be served on each party in this case before it is served on the person to whom it is directed. Fed. R. Civ. P. 45(a)(4).

AO 88A (Rev. 12/20) Subpoena to Testify at a Deposition in a Civil Action (Page 2)

Civil Action No.

PROOF OF SERVICE

(This section should not be filed with the court unless required by Fed. R. Civ. P. 45.)

I received this subpoena for *(name of individual and title, if any)* _____

on *(date)* _____ .

☐ I served the subpoena by delivering a copy to the named individual as follows: _____

_____   on *(date)* _____ ; or

☐ I returned the subpoena unexecuted because: _____

_____ .

Unless the subpoena was issued on behalf of the United States, or one of its officers or agents, I have also
tendered to the witness the fees for one day's attendance, and the mileage allowed by law, in the amount of

$ _____ .

My fees are $ _____ for travel and $ _____ for services, for a total of $ ___0.00___ .

I declare under penalty of perjury that this information is true.

Date: _____   _____
Server's signature

_____
Printed name and title

_____
Server's address

Additional information regarding attempted service, etc.:

Federal Rule of Civil Procedure 45 (c), (d), (e), and (g) (Effective 12/1/13)

(c) Place of Compliance.

(1) For a Trial, Hearing, or Deposition. A subpoena may command a person to attend a trial, hearing, or deposition only as follows:
   (A) within 100 miles of where the person resides, is employed, or regularly transacts business in person; or
   (B) within the state where the person resides, is employed, or regularly transacts business in person, if the person
      (i) is a party or a party's officer; or
      (ii) is commanded to attend a trial and would not incur substantial expense.

(2) For Other Discovery. A subpoena may command:
   (A) production of documents, electronically stored information, or tangible things at a place within 100 miles of where the person resides, is employed, or regularly transacts business in person; and
   (B) inspection of premises at the premises to be inspected.

(d) Protecting a Person Subject to a Subpoena; Enforcement.

(1) Avoiding Undue Burden or Expense; Sanctions. A party or attorney responsible for issuing and serving a subpoena must take reasonable steps to avoid imposing undue burden or expense on a person subject to the subpoena. The court for the district where compliance is required must enforce this duty and impose an appropriate sanction—which may include lost earnings and reasonable attorney's fees—on a party or attorney who fails to comply.

(2) Command to Produce Materials or Permit Inspection.
   (A) Appearance Not Required. A person commanded to produce documents, electronically stored information, or tangible things, or to permit the inspection of premises, need not appear in person at the place of production or inspection unless also commanded to appear for a deposition, hearing, or trial.
   (B) Objections. A person commanded to produce documents or tangible things or to permit inspection may serve on the party or attorney designated in the subpoena a written objection to inspecting, copying, testing, or sampling any or all of the materials or to inspecting the premises—or to producing electronically stored information in the form or forms requested. The objection must be served before the earlier of the time specified for compliance or 14 days after the subpoena is served. If an objection is made, the following rules apply:
      (i) At any time, on notice to the commanded person, the serving party may move the court for the district where compliance is required for an order compelling production or inspection.
      (ii) These acts may be required only as directed in the order, and the order must protect a person who is neither a party nor a party's officer from significant expense resulting from compliance.

(3) Quashing or Modifying a Subpoena.

   (A) When Required. On timely motion, the court for the district where compliance is required must quash or modify a subpoena that:
      (i) fails to allow a reasonable time to comply;
      (ii) requires a person to comply beyond the geographical limits specified in Rule 45(c);
      (iii) requires disclosure of privileged or other protected matter, if no exception or waiver applies; or
      (iv) subjects a person to undue burden.
   (B) When Permitted. To protect a person subject to or affected by a subpoena, the court for the district where compliance is required may, on motion, quash or modify the subpoena if it requires:

      (i) disclosing a trade secret or other confidential research, development, or commercial information; or
      (ii) disclosing an unretained expert's opinion or information that does not describe specific occurrences in dispute and results from the expert's study that was not requested by a party.
   (C) Specifying Conditions as an Alternative. In the circumstances described in Rule 45(d)(3)(B), the court may, instead of quashing or modifying a subpoena, order appearance or production under specified conditions if the serving party:
      (i) shows a substantial need for the testimony or material that cannot be otherwise met without undue hardship; and
      (ii) ensures that the subpoenaed person will be reasonably compensated.

(e) Duties in Responding to a Subpoena.

(1) Producing Documents or Electronically Stored Information. These procedures apply to producing documents or electronically stored information:
   (A) Documents. A person responding to a subpoena to produce documents must produce them as they are kept in the ordinary course of business or must organize and label them to correspond to the categories in the demand.
   (B) Form for Producing Electronically Stored Information Not Specified. If a subpoena does not specify a form for producing electronically stored information, the person responding must produce it in a form or forms in which it is ordinarily maintained or in a reasonably usable form or forms.
   (C) Electronically Stored Information Produced in Only One Form. The person responding need not produce the same electronically stored information in more than one form.
   (D) Inaccessible Electronically Stored Information. The person responding need not provide discovery of electronically stored information from sources that the person identifies as not reasonably accessible because of undue burden or cost. On motion to compel discovery or for a protective order, the person responding must show that the information is not reasonably accessible because of undue burden or cost. If that showing is made, the court may nonetheless order discovery from such sources if the requesting party shows good cause, considering the limitations of Rule 26(b)(2)(C). The court may specify conditions for the discovery.

(2) Claiming Privilege or Protection.
   (A) Information Withheld. A person withholding subpoenaed information under a claim that it is privileged or subject to protection as trial-preparation material must:
      (i) expressly make the claim; and
      (ii) describe the nature of the withheld documents, communications, or tangible things in a manner that, without revealing information itself privileged or protected, will enable the parties to assess the claim.
   (B) Information Produced. If information produced in response to a subpoena is subject to a claim of privilege or of protection as trial-preparation material, the person making the claim may notify any party that received the information of the claim and the basis for it. After being notified, a party must promptly return, sequester, or destroy the specified information and any copies it has; must not use or disclose the information until the claim is resolved; must take reasonable steps to retrieve the information if the party disclosed it before being notified; and may promptly present the information under seal to the court for the district where compliance is required for a determination of the claim. The person who produced the information must preserve the information until the claim is resolved.

(g) Contempt.
The court for the district where compliance is required—and also, after a motion is transferred, the issuing court—may hold in contempt a person who, having been served, fails without adequate excuse to obey the subpoena or an order related to it.

For access to subpoena materials, see Fed. R. Civ. P. 45(a) Committee Note (2013).

AO 88 (Rev. 02/14) Subpoena to Appear and Testify at a Hearing or Trial in a Civil Action

UNITED STATES DISTRICT COURT
for the

	)	
_____ *Plaintiff*	))	
v.	)	Civil Action No. _____
_____ *Defendant*	))	

SUBPOENA TO APPEAR AND TESTIFY
AT A HEARING OR TRIAL IN A CIVIL ACTION

To: _____

(Name of person to whom this subpoena is directed)

YOU ARE COMMANDED to appear in the United States district court at the time, date, and place set forth below to testify at a hearing or trial in this civil action. When you arrive, you must remain at the court until the judge or a court officer allows you to leave.

Place:	Courtroom No.:
	Date and Time:

You must also bring with you the following documents, electronically stored information, or objects *(leave blank if not applicable)*:

The following provisions of Fed. R. Civ. P. 45 are attached – Rule 45(c), relating to the place of compliance; Rule 45(d), relating to your protection as a person subject to a subpoena; and Rule 45(e) and (g), relating to your duty to respond to this subpoena and the potential consequences of not doing so.

Date: _____

CLERK OF COURT

OR

_____   _____
Signature of Clerk or Deputy Clerk   *Attorney's signature*

The name, address, e-mail address, and telephone number of the attorney representing *(name of party)* _____
_____ , who issues or requests this subpoena, are:

Notice to the person who issues or requests this subpoena
If this subpoena commands the production of documents, electronically stored information, or tangible things before trial, a notice and a copy of the subpoena must be served on each party in this case before it is served on the person to whom it is directed. Fed. R. Civ. P. 45(a)(4).

AO 88 (Rev. 02/14) Subpoena to Appear and Testify at a Hearing or Trial in a Civil Action (page 2)

Civil Action No. _____

PROOF OF SERVICE
(This section should not be filed with the court unless required by Fed. R. Civ. P. 45.)

    I received this subpoena for *(name of individual and title, if any)* _____

on *(date)* _____ .

    ❏ I served the subpoena by delivering a copy to the named person as follows: _____

_____ on *(date)* _____ ; or

    ❏ I returned the subpoena unexecuted because: _____

_____ .

    Unless the subpoena was issued on behalf of the United States, or one of its officers or agents, I have also tendered to the witness the fees for one day's attendance, and the mileage allowed by law, in the amount of

    $ _____ .

My fees are $ _____ for travel and $ _____ for services, for a total of $ 0.00   .

    I declare under penalty of perjury that this information is true.

Date: _____   _____
                                                   Server's signature

                         _____
                                                Printed name and title

                         _____
                                                Server's address

Additional information regarding attempted service, etc.:

AO 88 (Rev. 02/14) Subpoena to Appear and Testify at a Hearing or Trial in a Civil Action (page 3)

Federal Rule of Civil Procedure 45 (c), (d), (e), and (g) (Effective 12/1/13)

(c) Place of Compliance.

(1) *For a Trial, Hearing, or Deposition.* A subpoena may command a person to attend a trial, hearing, or deposition only as follows:
  (A) within 100 miles of where the person resides, is employed, or regularly transacts business in person; or
  (B) within the state where the person resides, is employed, or regularly transacts business in person, if the person
    (i) is a party or a party's officer; or
    (ii) is commanded to attend a trial and would not incur substantial expense.

(2) *For Other Discovery.* A subpoena may command:
  (A) production of documents, electronically stored information, or tangible things at a place within 100 miles of where the person resides, is employed, or regularly transacts business in person; and
  (B) inspection of premises at the premises to be inspected.

(d) Protecting a Person Subject to a Subpoena; Enforcement.

(1) *Avoiding Undue Burden or Expense; Sanctions.* A party or attorney responsible for issuing and serving a subpoena must take reasonable steps to avoid imposing undue burden or expense on a person subject to the subpoena. The court for the district where compliance is required must enforce this duty and impose an appropriate sanction—which may include lost earnings and reasonable attorney's fees—on a party or attorney who fails to comply.

(2) *Command to Produce Materials or Permit Inspection.*
  (A) *Appearance Not Required.* A person commanded to produce documents, electronically stored information, or tangible things, or to permit the inspection of premises, need not appear in person at the place of production or inspection unless also commanded to appear for a deposition, hearing, or trial.
  (B) *Objections.* A person commanded to produce documents or tangible things or to permit inspection may serve on the party or attorney designated in the subpoena a written objection to inspecting, copying, testing, or sampling any or all of the materials or to inspecting the premises—or to producing electronically stored information in the form or forms requested. The objection must be served before the earlier of the time specified for compliance or 14 days after the subpoena is served. If an objection is made, the following rules apply:
    (i) At any time, on notice to the commanded person, the serving party may move the court for the district where compliance is required for an order compelling production or inspection.
    (ii) These acts may be required only as directed in the order, and the order must protect a person who is neither a party nor a party's officer from significant expense resulting from compliance.

(3) *Quashing or Modifying a Subpoena.*
  (A) *When Required.* On timely motion, the court for the district where compliance is required must quash or modify a subpoena that:
    (i) fails to allow a reasonable time to comply;
    (ii) requires a person to comply beyond the geographical limits specified in Rule 45(c);
    (iii) requires disclosure of privileged or other protected matter, if no exception or waiver applies; or
    (iv) subjects a person to undue burden.
  (B) *When Permitted.* To protect a person subject to or affected by a subpoena, the court for the district where compliance is required may, on motion, quash or modify the subpoena if it requires:
    (i) disclosing a trade secret or other confidential research, development, or commercial information; or

(ii) disclosing an unretained expert's opinion or information that does not describe specific occurrences in dispute and results from the expert's study that was not requested by a party.
  (C) *Specifying Conditions as an Alternative.* In the circumstances described in Rule 45(d)(3)(B), the court may, instead of quashing or modifying a subpoena, order appearance or production under specified conditions if the serving party:
    (i) shows a substantial need for the testimony or material that cannot be otherwise met without undue hardship; and
    (ii) ensures that the subpoenaed person will be reasonably compensated.

(e) Duties in Responding to a Subpoena.

(1) *Producing Documents or Electronically Stored Information.* These procedures apply to producing documents or electronically stored information:
  (A) *Documents.* A person responding to a subpoena to produce documents must produce them as they are kept in the ordinary course of business or must organize and label them to correspond to the categories in the demand.
  (B) *Form for Producing Electronically Stored Information Not Specified.* If a subpoena does not specify a form for producing electronically stored information, the person responding must produce it in a form or forms in which it is ordinarily maintained or in a reasonably usable form or forms.
  (C) *Electronically Stored Information Produced in Only One Form.* The person responding need not produce the same electronically stored information in more than one form.
  (D) *Inaccessible Electronically Stored Information.* The person responding need not provide discovery of electronically stored information from sources that the person identifies as not reasonably accessible because of undue burden or cost. On motion to compel discovery or for a protective order, the person responding must show that the information is not reasonably accessible because of undue burden or cost. If that showing is made, the court may nonetheless order discovery from such sources if the requesting party shows good cause, considering the limitations of Rule 26(b)(2)(C). The court may specify conditions for the discovery.

(2) *Claiming Privilege or Protection.*
  (A) *Information Withheld.* A person withholding subpoenaed information under a claim that it is privileged or subject to protection as trial-preparation material must:
    (i) expressly make the claim; and
    (ii) describe the nature of the withheld documents, communications, or tangible things in a manner that, without revealing information itself privileged or protected, will enable the parties to assess the claim.
  (B) *Information Produced.* If information produced in response to a subpoena is subject to a claim of privilege or of protection as trial-preparation material, the person making the claim may notify any party that received the information of the claim and the basis for it. After being notified, a party must promptly return, sequester, or destroy the specified information and any copies it has; must not use or disclose the information until the claim is resolved; must take reasonable steps to retrieve the information if the party disclosed it before being notified; and may promptly present the information under seal to the court for the district where compliance is required for a determination of the claim. The person who produced the information must preserve the information until the claim is resolved.

(g) Contempt.
The court for the district where compliance is required—and also, after a motion is transferred—the issuing court—may hold in contempt a person who, having been served, fails without adequate excuse to obey the subpoena or an order related to it.

For access to subpoena materials, see Fed. R. Civ. P. 45(a) Committee Note (2013).

AO 440 (Rev. 06/12) Summons in a Civil Action

UNITED STATES DISTRICT COURT

for the

Northern District of Illinois

	)	
	)	
	)	
	)	
_____	)	
Plaintiff(s)	)	
v.	)	Civil Action No.
	)	
	)	
	)	
	)	
_____	)	
Defendant(s)	)	

SUMMONS IN A CIVIL ACTION

To: *(Defendant's name and address)*

A lawsuit has been filed against you.

Within 21 days after service of this summons on you (not counting the day you received it) — or 60 days if you are the United States or a United States agency, or an officer or employee of the United States described in Fed. R. Civ. P. 12 (a)(2) or (3) — you must serve on the plaintiff an answer to the attached complaint or a motion under Rule 12 of the Federal Rules of Civil Procedure. The answer or motion must be served on the plaintiff or plaintiff's attorney, whose name and address are:

If you fail to respond, judgment by default will be entered against you for the relief demanded in the complaint. You also must file your answer or motion with the court.

CLERK OF COURT

Date: _____   _____
                                            Signature of Clerk or Deputy Clerk

AO 440 (Rev. 06/12) Summons in a Civil Action (Page 2)

Civil Action No.

PROOF OF SERVICE
(This section should not be filed with the court unless required by Fed. R. Civ. P. 4 (l))

This summons for *(name of individual and title, if any)* _____

was received by me on *(date)* _____ .

❏ I personally served the summons on the individual at *(place)* _____

_____ on *(date)* _____ ; or

❏ I left the summons at the individual's residence or usual place of abode with *(name)* _____

_____ , a person of suitable age and discretion who resides there,

on *(date)* _____ , and mailed a copy to the individual's last known address; or

❏ I served the summons on *(name of individual)* _____ , who is

designated by law to accept service of process on behalf of *(name of organization)* _____

_____ on *(date)* _____ ; or

❏ I returned the summons unexecuted because _____ ; or

❏ Other *(specify)*:

My fees are $ _____ for travel and $ _____ for services, for a total of $ 0.00   .

I declare under penalty of perjury that this information is true.

Date: _____   _____
                                         Server's signature

                                 _____
                                         Printed name and title

                                 _____
                                         Server's address

Additional information regarding attempted service, etc:

AO 398 (Rev. 01/09) Notice of a Lawsuit and Request to Waive Service of a Summons

UNITED STATES DISTRICT COURT
for the
Northern District of Illinois

_____	)	
Plaintiff	)	
v.	)	Civil Action No.
_____	)	
Defendant	)	

NOTICE OF A LAWSUIT AND REQUEST TO WAIVE SERVICE OF A SUMMONS

To: _____

    (Name of the defendant or - if the defendant is a corporation, partnership, or association - an officer or agent authorized to receive service)

Why are you getting this?

    A lawsuit has been filed against you, or the entity you represent, in this court under the number shown above. A copy of the complaint is attached.

    This is not a summons, or an official notice from the court. It is a request that, to avoid expenses, you waive formal service of a summons by signing and returning the enclosed waiver. To avoid these expenses, you must return the signed waiver within _____ days *(give at least 30 days, or at least 60 days if the defendant is outside any judicial district of the United States)* from the date shown below, which is the date this notice was sent. Two copies of the waiver form are enclosed, along with a stamped, self-addressed envelope or other prepaid means for returning one copy. You may keep the other copy.

What happens next?

    If you return the signed waiver, I will file it with the court. The action will then proceed as if you had been served on the date the waiver is filed, but no summons will be served on you and you will have 60 days from the date this notice is sent (see the date below) to answer the complaint (or 90 days if this notice is sent to you outside any judicial district of the United States).

    If you do not return the signed waiver within the time indicated, I will arrange to have the summons and complaint served on you. And I will ask the court to require you, or the entity you represent, to pay the expenses of making service.

    Please read the enclosed statement about the duty to avoid unnecessary expenses.

    I certify that this request is being sent to you on the date below.

Date: _____

                                   _____
                                           Signature of the attorney or unrepresented party

                                   _____
                                               Printed name

                                   _____
                                               Address

                                   _____
                                             E-mail address

                                   _____
                                             Telephone number

AO 399 (01/09) Waiver of the Service of Summons

UNITED STATES DISTRICT COURT
for the
Northern District of Illinois

_____	)	
Plaintiff	)	
v.	)	Civil Action No.
_____	)	
Defendant	)	

WAIVER OF THE SERVICE OF SUMMONS

To: _____
    (Name of the plaintiff's attorney or unrepresented plaintiff)

    I have received your request to waive service of a summons in this action along with a copy of the complaint, two copies of this waiver form, and a prepaid means of returning one signed copy of the form to you.

    I, or the entity I represent, agree to save the expense of serving a summons and complaint in this case.

    I understand that I, or the entity I represent, will keep all defenses or objections to the lawsuit, the court's jurisdiction, and the venue of the action, but that I waive any objections to the absence of a summons or of service.

    I also understand that I, or the entity I represent, must file and serve an answer or a motion under Rule 12 within 60 days from _____, the date when this request was sent (or 90 days if it was sent outside the United States). If I fail to do so, a default judgment will be entered against me or the entity I represent.

Date: _____   _____
                                 Signature of the attorney or unrepresented party

_____   _____
Printed name of party waiving service of summons   *Printed name*

                                 _____
                                 Address

                                 _____
                                 E-mail address

                                 _____
                                 Telephone number

Duty to Avoid Unnecessary Expenses of Serving a Summons

    Rule 4 of the Federal Rules of Civil Procedure requires certain defendants to cooperate in saving unnecessary expenses of serving a summons and complaint. A defendant who is located in the United States and who fails to return a signed waiver of service requested by a plaintiff located in the United States will be required to pay the expenses of service, unless the defendant shows good cause for the failure.

    "Good cause" does *not* include a belief that the lawsuit is groundless, or that it has been brought in an improper venue, or that the court has no jurisdiction over this matter or over the defendant or the defendant's property.

    If the waiver is signed and returned, you can still make these and all other defenses and objections, but you cannot object to the absence of a summons or of service.

    If you waive service, then you must, within the time specified on the waiver form, serve an answer or a motion under Rule 12 on the plaintiff and file a copy with the court. By signing and returning the waiver form, you are allowed more time to respond than if a summons had been served.

Index

Acknowledgements

While I have no one to blame but myself if this book stinks, I have many to thank if it doesn't. (And I think it doesn't.) My family acted as a constant inspiration to keep the bad jokes to a minimum, so my readers don't hurt their shoulders with exaggerated thumbs-down gestures, as my kids like to do. To the extent working on this book kept me away from my kids and subjected their mom to even more solo parenting time than she is normally exposed to, I am forever grateful and somewhat regretful. You all give me a reason – the only one I need – to do the things I've been able to do, and to always try to do better. I love you.

Working with Amanda Kern at Emerald Creative Content has been one of the best business decisions I have made. Her editing prowess has been to this book what her content creation has been to my firm's success in establishing a digital presence in this crazy social media landscape. I also owe her a debt of gratitude for introducing me to Jessie Shea at 2Shea Creative LLC. Jessie nailed the cover graphics on her first try, and achieved the aesthetic sense I was looking for almost immediately. She made the book look like a book – and a well-designed book at that.

Of course, I would not have been able to spend the time on this project (and could not run my firm) without the increased capacity afforded by the Law Office of Jordan Marsh team: Jormary Griego and Nelson Morales, who keep things running smoothly at the office, increasing my ability to handle cases and write at the same time. They also contributed to the content and marketing of this book. Shout out to Get Staffed Up, the virtual staffing firm that brought me Jormary and Nelson. They do a great job.

Thanks to all the folks at Lawyerist, who created a community for solos and small-firm people like me to thrive and get better, and particularly to my coach, Sara Muender, who regularly and tirelessly holds me accountable and pushes me to achieve my goals. Thanks to Stephanie Everett, Brett Trembly, Brian Thomas, Chad Hammond, and Stacey Ballis, who provided invaluable advice based on their experience as successful authors. Thanks also to Cherie Smurthwaite and Courtney Arthur for their assistance with this book. Thanks also to my law school classmate Rafi Arbel at Market JD, who remains a constant source of advice and encouragement as I navigate my way through the jungle of business ownership. A real mensch.

Thanks to my friends and former colleagues (some of whom I now oppose in court) at the City of Chicago Law Department, where I learned how to be a trial lawyer, and where I discovered my calling.

Thanks to my fellow plaintiffs' lawyers (many of whom I once opposed in court), who provide amazing and selfless support to each other, and do the hard and crucial work of holding power accountable and fighting for the vulnerable and voiceless. These are very good, very smart people.

Last but not least, thanks to all of my clients over the years. You're the reason we do what we do, and you place an inordinate amount of trust in us. I've learned so much from each one of you.

That's a lot more people than I thought I'd be thanking when I set out to write this acknowledgement. It's amazing how many people you have to be grateful for when you stop to think (and write) about it.

Thank you all.

About the Author

Jordan Marsh is the founder and principal of the Law Office of Jordan Marsh LLC, which he founded in 2016. He began his career as a legislative intern before moving on to the City of Chicago Law Department, where he represented the city and its employees in personal injury, civil rights, and other matters. Jordan litigated countless cases in state and federal courts, ranging from soft-tissue cases to catastrophic injury and wrongful death cases. He was named one of the 40 Illinois Attorneys Under 40 to Watch by the Chicago Daily Law Bulletin, which hailed him as "one of the city's most energetic and resourceful trial attorneys."

Since 2016, Jordan has been representing citizens against law enforcement and other government actors, obtaining millions of dollars in settlements and verdicts for his clients. Jordan has taught and coached trial advocacy, judged trial advocacy competitions, and served as a faculty member with the Kirkland Institute for Trial Advocacy. He has tried more than 70 jury trials and obtained millions of dollars in settlements and verdicts for his clients. Jordan lives in the Chicago area with his family and a dog named Paulie.

Try Your Own Case
Resources

Be sure to sign up for periodic updates about new resources we plan to offer the pro se community in the months and years to come.

To download editable forms and documents, go to tryyourowncase.com/resources, or scan this code.

To be part of the TYOC community, go to tryyourowncase.com, or scan this code.